Practical Teaching
A Guide to PTLLS & CTLLS

Practical Teaching
A Guide to PTLLS & CTLLS

Linda Wilson

DELMAR
CENGAGE Learning

Australia • Brazil • Japan • Korea • Mexico • Singapore • Spain • United Kingdom • United States

DELMAR
CENGAGE Learning™

Practical Teaching: A Guide to PTLLS & CTLLS
Linda Wilson

Publishing Director: Linden Harris

Publisher: Melody Dawes

Development Editor: Matthew Lane

Content Project Editor: Leonora Dawson-Bowling

Head of Manufacturing: Jane Glendening

Senior Production Controller: Paul Herbert

Marketing Manager: Jason Bennett

Typesetter: ICC Macmillan Inc.

Cover design: Adam Renvoize

Text design: Design Deluxe, Bath, UK

For product information and technology assistance, contact **emea.info@cengage.com**.

For permission to use material from this text or product, and for permission queries, email **clsuk.permissions@cengage.com**.

British Library Cataloguing-in-Publication Data
A catalogue record for this book is available from the British Library.

ISBN: 978-1-84480-744-4

Cengage Learning EMEA
Cheriton House, North Way, Andover, Hampshire, SP10 5BE, United Kingdom

Cengage Learning products are represented in Canada by Nelson Education Ltd.

For your lifelong learning solutions, visit **www.cengage.co.uk**

Purchase your next print book, e-book or e-chapter at **www.CengageBrain.com**

Printed by Seng Lee Press, Singapore
2 3 4 5 6 7 8 9 10 – 12 11 10

Brief contents

Contents

Part Three Principles and practice of assessment (PPA)

About this book

The book is intended for and written in a style to help those who are embarking on a career in teaching or newly appointed to their first teaching position. It is meant to be informative and user-friendly and concentrates on the practical aspects of the job, rather than the reasons why (the theory). Many of the examples used are from things I have seen or recommendations I have made to student teachers.

Remember that teaching can be an art or a science: what works in one situation may not work in others. So try things out, go with what feels right and be confident to accept that not every lesson will be brilliant. The important factor must always be the learner's experience.

The book is split into three main parts, each relating to a core unit in the Certificate award: Preparing to Teach (PTLLS), Planning and Enabling Learning (PEL) and Principles and Practice of Assessment (PPA). Each part of the book is divided into chapters which relate to the main learning outcomes of each unit: these are then subdivided into sections concerned with the assessment outcomes. In addition to the main parts, the Appendices contain items relating to information, guidance and support to help your achievement.

The text and activities contained in this publication are to support your studies, but it is intended that attendance of a relevant programme of study is the primary tool to learn your craft.

Terms of reference

Learners refers to the student, trainee, candidate, delegate, apprentice, pupil.

Teacher refers to the lecturer, tutor, trainer, instructor, coach, assessor.

Session refers to the lesson, training activity, class, lecture, tutorial, seminar.

Environment refers to the classroom, workshop, lecture theatre, workplace, shop floor.

Introduction

I came into education in 1984 as a variable hours lecturer, trying to balance a career with being a mum of two toddlers. My previous career as a caterer meant that long and unsociable hours made things like childcare and a social life difficult.

At first, I taught on a Friday afternoon. In those days, full-time staff were not around on a Friday afternoon and following my induction – you're in room P55 with the chefs, I learnt quickly to think on my feet and that the only information that I would receive would be that which I acquired for myself.

Anyway, I survived, and despite the endless hours of preparation (nobody told me about that!) I realised that I actually liked teaching. A few more hours appeared and by the end of that first year, I was teaching 12 hours per week. The groups weren't the easiest; I'm sure they were the ones nobody wanted, but that was how it was then.

I did my teaching qualifications over the next few years: This was also a culture shock. I'd done nothing since my own full-time education and so I found studying challenging, sometimes confusing and generally time-consuming. I had never had to do anything that academic before, but fortunately the group I studied with were helpful and together we got through. I've since had to do further Master's level qualifications which I found hard, but looking back now they really helped me to develop myself.

Changes in staff and the way FE was delivered enabled me to secure a full-time position. I still loved the job and was eager to get more responsibility and a better personal profile. Catering was one of the first subjects to go down the NVQ route. This meant that I started getting involved with employers because they needed to become workplace assessors. I'd done a Train the Trainer course when I had a 'real' job, so naturally took up this initiative. From there my role changed to training employers and staff as this new strategy started running through other vocational qualifications, combined with a cross-college middle management role getting involved in teacher training. I became utterly absorbed in teaching.

I am now Director of Human Resources, with responsibility for continuing professional development. That means I don't hire or fire, but I am involved in all aspects of staffing, from induction through to development and monitoring to appraisal and counselling.

I still love the teaching, although I don't do as much now and it is mainly with staff. Teaching is difficult, frustrating, funny, bureaucratic and rewarding. I hope that this book will help new teachers to cope with the skills required for the job, find a user-friendly route through their teaching qualifications and develop into fine professionals.

Linda Wilson

Acknowledgements

This book is dedicated to all of the Teacher Training students I have tutored. I know I have been hard, and sometimes told you things you didn't really want to hear, but you got there and I am privileged to have been part of that process.

To all the people I have observed as part of my job, you have given me some wonderful ideas and made me a better teacher. I've seen some things I wouldn't do, but . . .

To the staff at Cengage Learning, and the reviewers and City and Guilds for their feedback in what has been an extremely steep learning curve.

And finally, to my partner John, for his endless proofreading and commentary – and for borrowing the office!

In memory of Teresa (1967–2007)

Walk-through tour

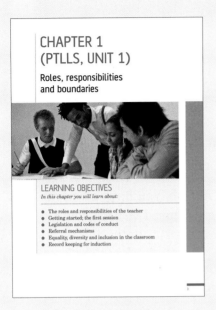

Learning objectives Featured at the beginning of each chapter, you can check at a glance what you are about to learn

Example Practical, real-world examples illustrate key points and learning objectives in the text

Activity Put your knowledge into action with these practical activities

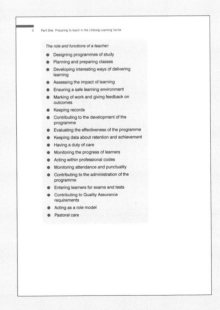

Note box Key information is drawn out in eye-catching boxes

unforeseen factors, but see them as challenges and face them confidently knowing that your scheme is fluid enough to cope with them, rather than a tablet of stone which cannot be moved.

7.3 Devising lesson plans to meet learner needs

By the end of this section, you will be able to recall the importance and key components of a lesson plan and state how plans are written to meet individual need.

REVISION

In Part One (PTLLS), we looked at lesson plans and how important it is to specify the fine points of your proposed teaching and learning strategies. We looked at why the planning and preparation of the content of the lesson is essential and considered what needed to be included in this aide-memoire. A lesson plan includes details about the group – how many, date of lesson, etc. It states the aims and outcomes of the lesson and gives a detailed breakdown of the topics to be covered, how they will be delivered and an indication of how you will know whether the learners have learned the topic. For a complete review, refer to Section 3.1.

In your lesson plan you will identify the session outcomes, content, resources and assessment methods. You may also annotate it to justify choices made, for example stating methods against visual, auditory and kinaesthetic (VAK) learning styles, or teaching/learning styles (e.g. active (learner-centred) /passive (teacher-centred), listening, note-taking, speaking etc). When you are teaching you are using differentiated strategies, but sometimes these just happen, they are not planned. By matching what you know about your learners to the topics being learned, you will be able to improve your teaching and thus the effectiveness of the learning experience.

Revision Revision boxes in parts 2 and 3 of the text help you recap on things learned in PTLLS

part of the job, paperwork is similarly important to the efficiency of the organisation.

Glossary of terms

Academic relating to education, school or scholarships
Achievement meeting learning goals
Awarding bodies the people who devise the qualifications and award the certificates
Curriculum a programme of study
Differentiation catering for the needs of all learners to reduce barriers to learning
Diversity valuing and celebrating the differences in people
Equality the state of being equal or the same
Ice-breaker an activity used to introduce learners to each other
ILP individual learning plan
Inclusion finding opportunities to integrate all learners
Learning to gain knowledge or a skill; what the learners do during a session
Learning goals what a learner sets out to do
Learning needs things which will help a learner to achieve their goal
Learning styles analysis of how learners learn
Plagiarism to pass off somebody else's work as your own
Policy course of action by an organisation
Qualification a skill that makes someone suitable for a job
Recreational learning a skill for pleasure
Sanction a penalty for disobeying rules
Teaching to impart knowledge or a skill; what the teacher does during a session
VAK visual, auditory and kinaesthetic learners – different ways learners like to learn
Vocational skills related to employment

Glossary of terms Glossary of terms highlighted in the text are listed at the end of each chapter with definitions

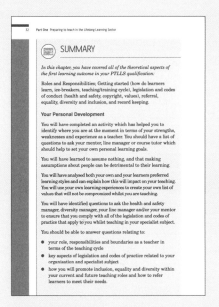

SUMMARY

In this chapter, you have covered all of the theoretical aspects of the first learning outcome in your PTLLS qualification:

Roles and Responsibilities; Getting started (how do learners learn, ice-breakers, teaching/training cycle), legislation and codes of conduct (health and safety, copyright, values), referral, equality, diversity and inclusion, and record keeping.

Your Personal Development

You will have completed an activity which has helped you to identify where you are at the moment in terms of your strengths, weaknesses and experience as a teacher. You should have a list of questions to ask your mentor, line manager or course tutor which should help to set your own personal learning goals.

You will have learned to assume nothing, and that making assumptions about people can be detrimental to their learning.

You will have analysed both your own and your learners preferred learning styles and can explain how this will impact on your teaching. You will use your own learning experiences to create your own list of values that will not be compromised whilst you are teaching.

You will have identified questions to ask the health and safety manager, diversity manager, your line manager and/or your mentor to ensure that you comply with all of the legislation and codes of practice that apply to you whilst teaching in your specialist subject.

You should be able to answer questions relating to:

- your role, responsibilities and boundaries as a teacher in terms of the teaching cycle
- key aspects of legislation and codes of practice related to your organisation and specialist subject
- how you will promote inclusion, equality and diversity within your current and future teaching roles and how to refer learners to meet their needs.

Summary Featured at the end of each chapter, summary boxes help you to consolidate what you have learned

- Explanations
- Discussing outcomes and support.

Diagnostic The final method of checking ability is usually either a routine strategy of induction or a response if you suspect that there may be inadequacies in functional skills. There are a range of tests, both paper-based and online, to ascertain the level of ability. Some learners with poor functional skills benefit from computer-aided resources. It is highly likely that learners will have what is called a 'spiky profile'. This means that they are good at some aspects and weaker in others, causing them to be at different levels on the NQF.

Useful online resources

http://www.basic-skills.co.uk/resourcecentre
http://www.learndirect-advice.co.uk/helpwithyourcareer/jobprofiles/
http://www.move-on.org.uk

8.6 Adapting resources

By the end of this section, you will be able to suggest ways of modifying resources to meet individual needs of learners and to suit curriculum requirements whilst maintaining an inclusive learning environment.

REVISION

In Part One, Section 2.5, you reviewed a range of resources and were able to identify how to use them in the context of your own teaching subject.

Useful resources Further reading feature offers suggestions for print and online reading material

Part One

Preparing to teach in the Lifelong Learning Sector

(PTLLS)

This is the first unit in your Certificate in Teaching in the Lifelong Learning Sector (CTLLS) qualification

1 Roles, responsibilities and boundaries (PTLLS unit 1)
2 Approaches to teaching and learning (PTLLS unit 2)
3 Session planning skills (PTLLS unit 3)
4 Motivation and inclusion (PTLLS unit 4)
5 Assessment and record keeping (PTLLS unit 5)

CHAPTER 1
(PTLLS, UNIT 1)

Roles, responsibilities and boundaries

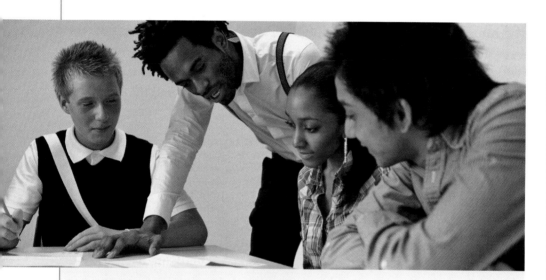

LEARNING OBJECTIVES

In this chapter you will learn about:

- The roles and responsibilities of the teacher
- Getting started; the first session
- Legislation and codes of conduct
- Referral mechanisms
- Equality, diversity and inclusion in the classroom
- Record keeping for induction

1.1 Roles and responsibilities

By the end of this section, you will be able to describe your role and responsibility as a teacher within the context of your specialist subject.

The role and responsibility of the teacher is a complex one. We are charged with ensuring our learners gain their qualifications in a manner which is favourable to their own learning needs and those of the **awarding bodies**. We have to offer value for money. We have to consider the needs and interests of their parents and employers, as well as the learning institution. Not all learners come into learning to achieve a **qualification**; some want to gain new skills to help with their employment or simply to cope with the changing world.

The role of the Lifelong Learning Sector is quite broad. It covers further education, higher education, work-based training, training for employment, adult and community learning, the voluntary sector, the armed forces and prisons. Learners in the sector may be funded by government bodies, by their employers, by funding councils or by their own finances. Some may be supported by student loans, bursaries or scholarships. In a nutshell, lifelong learning covers everything that is not compulsory education. Learners can be aged from 14 upwards and learning can occur in any suitable environment.

The student population is ever-changing due to:

- Changes in society
- The need for equality and diversity
- Changes in funding priorities
- Expectations of learners, employers and parents
- Behaviour trends
- Technological developments

Think, for example, about the typical learners in a Further Education college.

- 14-year-old pupils trying to gain vocational qualifications as an alternative to **academic** qualifications
- 16-year-olds embarking upon training and qualifications to meet potential employment needs
- 19-year-olds developing skills or perhaps catching up on missed opportunities
- The mature student, returning to learning, maybe thinking about a change in career
- The unemployed, trying to re-enter the world of work
- The adult, gaining skills relevant to their work
- The young mum, returning to a career after a period of time and finding that the workplace has moved on
- The pensioner, trying to gain skills so that they can communicate in today's electronic era
- The social learner, learning a skill to provide pleasure and enjoyment.

The teacher will come across many of these examples, each of which describes **learning goals**, in a typical working week. The skills involved will be discussed in detail later in the book, but suffice to say if the learners are all different, so the skills required to teach them will vary. Most people come into teaching because they believe they can make a difference. The amount of energy that a teacher will expend in realising that value will astound the inexperienced teacher. A teacher needs to accept that they will face many challenges in teaching, including risks, but if something goes wrong, it should be seen as more of an opportunity than a threat.

The impact of all of these influences affects the teacher, whose role is far more than just being someone who stands at the front of the class telling people things.

The role and functions of a teacher:

- Designing programmes of study
- Planning and preparing classes
- Developing interesting ways of delivering learning
- Assessing the impact of learning
- Ensuring a safe learning environment
- Marking of work and giving feedback on outcomes
- Keeping records
- Contributing to the development of the programme
- Evaluating the effectiveness of the programme
- Keeping data about retention and achievement
- Having a duty of care
- Monitoring the progress of learners
- Acting within professional codes
- Monitoring attendance and punctuality
- Contributing to the administration of the programme
- Entering learners for exams and tests
- Contributing to Quality Assurance requirements
- Acting as a role model
- Pastoral care

ACTIVITY 1

Let us consider the extent of that responsibility:

Look at each of the headings below and write down what you need to consider. It is probably best to focus on your particular subject. You should consider how you might tackle it, who will help you and how you will know if you have got it right.

You will find all the answers within this book, but try not to look yet. Use your existing knowledge and common sense! This will also be a good way of finding out about your own strengths and development needs at this early stage.

Roles and responsibilities	Thoughts and considerations
What will I teach?	
When will I teach it?	
How will I prepare for a lesson?	
How will I make it interesting?	
What will I do when things go wrong?	
Who else will be involved?	
How will I know when somebody has learnt something?	
Am I getting my topic across?	
What paperwork will I need to complete?	
How will I appear professional?	
Do I know enough to teach my topic?	

You probably now have lots of questions. Using this book and the guidance of your tutor, you can now embark on your own learning journey.

1.2 Getting started

By the end of this section, you will be able to describe strategies which help you to identify how learners learn, how to introduce learners to you and their chosen programme of study, and how learning will progress through a **teaching** cycle.

Teaching is not limited to imparting your knowledge, you will also have a responsibility for helping someone to learn. One of the first rules of teaching is:

ASSUME NOTHING

Do not assume that your learners know the most effective way of learning. They will come to you with a variety of experiences, a lot of needs and maybe some misconceptions. If you imagine that learners 'already know this', 'can do that' and 'expect this', you are in for a massive learning experience yourself! One of the most influential factors on someone's ability to learn is the teacher.

Creating a first impression

You only have one opportunity to do this. In the first few minutes of meeting someone, we all make a decision about them. Whether this is an accurate impression or not remains subjective; it is human nature! As learners walk in to the classroom, they survey their surroundings, look at the teacher and look at each other. This can be managed so that it has a positive effect by:

- Being on time
- Smiling
- Welcoming learners
- Looking clean and presentable
- Being prepared
- Looking calm and organised
- Being confident
- Making sure the room is prepared for the learners
- Friendly introductions.

Think about how you would feel if, when you arrived, there was no-one in the room, it was untidy, and then the teacher arrived mumbling about being busy and the photocopier not working: then the lesson started and you had no idea of the teacher's name or even the name of the person sitting next to you. Are you even in the right room? Would you feel valued? Would you have confidence in the teacher? Would you expect the course to be any good? Would you come back next week?

It seems obvious when presented like this, but because the first impression counts for so much, you should be particularly aware of it during the first session. When learners don't attend the second session, the teacher should always consider the impact they made during the first session.

How do learners learn?

When starting to teach and plan lessons, a teacher should consider the individuals in the class. We have already established that learners will arrive with a variety of learning goals. They will also have had differing experiences of teaching and learning in the past.

ACTIVITY 2

Think about a good learning experience. Write down what you liked about it that made it a good experience:

Now think about a bad experience. Again, write down things that made you feel uncomfortable or unhappy with that experience:

Conclude this by listing all of the positive actions that you are going to include in your own teaching sessions. These are your values or principles; things that are so important to you that you will not accept second best.

Hopefully, one of these values will be to ensure that all of your learners receive a positive learning experience and achieve their goals. One way that this can be accomplished is by analysing how learners learn: this is one of the most fundamental tasks of the teacher. A teacher who understands what helps a learner to learn will be a better teacher because they recognise differences and are prepared to alter their teaching to suit those differences. This is called **differentiation**.

There are many theories associated with identifying how learners learn. The main ones that you may come across are:

Honey and Mumford (1982, 1992) based their analysis of how people learn on Kolb's (1984), (see Chapter 11) learning cycle. They advocate that people learn best by either doing something (activist), by thinking back on something (reflector), by investigating ideas and concepts (theorist) or by finding relevance or association (pragmatist).

EXAMPLE

Think about learning to play golf

- A theorist will buy all the books they can find and read up on the best way to do everything, before even going to the practice range.

- An activist will buy all the gear, go down to the first tee and hit balls until they've got round to the 18th.

- A reflector will probably go down to the driving range, hit a few balls and then go to the clubhouse to analyse where and why it went wrong.

- The pragmatist will buy golf lessons, having carefully considered the commitment, and then experiment and analyse his or her way around the course.

Another is Gardner's Multiple Intelligence (1983, 1993). He states that understanding intelligence and categorising it will develop learning. The categories are:

- Linguistic – the use of language. Writers and poets are deemed to have a high linguistic intelligence.
- Logical/mathematical – patterns and reasoning. The ability to detect patterns, highly sought in science subjects.
- Musical – appreciation of musical pattern, for example learning the alphabet to song.

- Bodily/kinaesthetic – using body movements, using mental abilities to co-ordinate bodily movements
- Spatial – using space patterns
- Interpersonal – working with others. It requires people to understand the intentions, motivations and desires of other people. Teachers need to use this type of intelligence
- Intrapersonal – understanding oneself; to appreciate one's feelings, fears and motivations in a bid to develop.

Last, and probably the most simple to understand is the **VAK** *analysis*. This is the suggestion that people learn either through visual senses (sight), auditory senses (hearing) or through kinaesthetic (doing) senses; hence VAK. The Chinese proverb reinforces that learning is about senses:

> ## I hear, I forget
> ## I see, I remember
> ## I do, I understand

Cooper (1996) analysed people's learning preferences, following the assumption that most learning occurs through the left side of the brain (noted for logic and order), yet by using the right side of the brain (noted for creativity), learning could be enhanced. The ideal, therefore, is to create a mixture of visual, auditory and kinaesthetic experiences, both to meet individual needs and to stimulate deeper learning. It follows that the teacher will exploit these differences by including teaching methods to meet all sensory needs. This is called teaching using differentiated strategies.

It is quite common for new teachers to limit their teaching style to that of their own preferred learning style. This will have an impact on the effectiveness of that teaching, in that it does not cater for those with different learning styles. Sometimes when you finish a class, you think, 'That really went well; I enjoyed that!' The reflective (and effective) teacher will think 'I wonder if everyone enjoyed that as much as I; did all my learners learn?'

Ice-breakers

During the first meeting with your learners it is important to find out what they want from the course. Usually entrants to **vocational** courses will be interviewed to assess their suitability, but in some instances, learners just enrol and the first time the teacher has an opportunity to check suitability is the first session. Whichever route, when you meet learners for the first time, you should find out about your learners, their needs, their **learning styles**, their concerns and apprehensions, and gradually introduce them to the rest of the group and their new environment. This type of activity is generally seen as an induction and will usually include an ice-breaking activity.

I	Introduce yourself
C	Create a comfortable setting
E	Encourage communication
B	Break down barriers
R	Reveal concerns
E	Encourage team spirit
A	Ascertain needs
K	Know your learners
E	Establish rules
R	Re-visit previous learning

Different ice-breakers will be used for different things, but the key to a successful **ice-breaker** is to make it fun, useful and not intimidating for learners. You should remember that learners do not usually like to draw attention to themselves at the first meeting. If you are sensitive to this, then the ice-breaker will do what it says it will do, i.e. break the ice. If you, the teacher, start the activity, maybe by introducing yourself and answering the ice-breaker questions, that will help to relax the learners and make an activity that is interesting and rewarding.

Some ideas:

1 In pairs, interview each other to find out names, an interesting fact about each other and maybe a favourite film or book. Then each person introduces their fellow learner.

   What this does. The teacher can write down the names of the group as a table plan, so that immediately the teacher can recall names: learners like to be recognised by name. The teacher can start to create a rapport. For example, next week you can ask how the children are, or if they enjoyed a particular leisure activity. This type of information creates a positive relationship because learners know that you care and are interested in them. Knowing about learners' favourite things reveals the type of things that interest them. This can tell you a little about them. For example, are they thoughtful, active, extrovert or introvert? If you have a confident group, you might also try the, 'If you were an animal, what kind would you be, and why?' type of question. That question can usually be quite enlightening as well as very funny.

2 Devise a little questionnaire, probably written to find out what learners already know about the subject. You can then invite learners to discuss what they've written and what is concerning them.

   What this does. In a quiet group, this type of activity will help to settle the learners. Be careful to include some questions that are quite easy in order to reassure the learner. The difficult questions can be off-putting, so remember to assure learners that they will be able to do these things soon. On a **recreational** course it will tell you about your learners. It introduces the course and can be revisited regularly so that learners can track their progress. It will help you to design a programme of study that meets the group's needs.

3 Split the group into smaller groups of about 4 or 5 people and ask them to build something. (I ask my groups to build a freestanding bridge using newspaper, using only a set amount of string and sticky tape.)

   What this does. It develops a team spirit. By getting feedback after the activity it initiates discussion and the teacher can identify the roles learners take when working within groups – leaders, followers, doers, thinkers, artistic tendencies, etc. We use this to lead into a VAK questionnaire, because it has already established that everyone is different.

Can you see the connections between ice-breakers and the concepts of first impression and learning styles? There are balances to be made – are your first impressions still the same after the ice-breaker? Do the answers to the ice-breaker bear any resemblance to their learning style analysis? These first activities are pieces of a jigsaw that will gradually fit together to make a picture, but remember that some of the pieces you put in might have to be moved if they are not quite right!

The teaching cycle

Teaching and learning should be a structured process. Teaching (and learning) will follow a cycle and the teacher makes use of this to ensure achievement. The teaching cycle is a continuous process, which can be joined at any point, but needs to be followed through to be effective. The process follows the strategy of moving from the known to the unknown.

Figure 1A   The teaching cycle

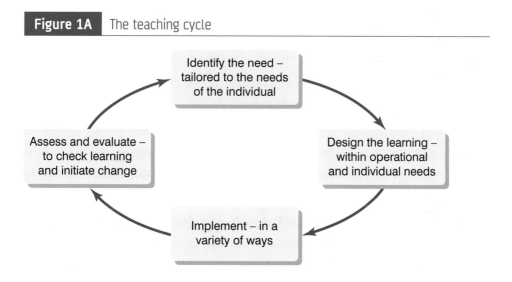

Think of our earlier examples of learners, from both the learner's and the teacher's viewpoint. Let us put them into the teaching cycle using the following case studies:

Sophie is a 16-year-old. She has had her careers interview and wants to be a hairdresser.

Stage 1	Sophie has discovered that she doesn't need high grade GCSEs, which is good because she doesn't think she'll get very many. She is artistic in her style and loves chatting to people. She has held a Saturday job in a local hairdressing salon and enjoyed it. She thinks she would like to own her own salon one day. *This is the evaluation stage.*
Stage 2	Sophie wants to go to college, but she also needs to earn some money. She finds out about the courses offered at two local colleges and a large hairdressing chain. *This is the identify need stage.*
Stage 3	She discovers that she has two main choices. She either goes to college full-time and continues with her Saturday job or she can join an apprenticeship programme where she works each day but is released to go to college one day per week. *This is the design stage.*
Stage 4	She decides on the apprenticeship, because she can earn the money she needs and practice skills learnt in college on her clients. *This is the implement stage.*
Stage 5	As she is working she finds that although she is learning skills in college, her employer will only let her do the junior's job. She wants to watch and learn from the stylists. *Sophie is now re-entering the evaluation stage, and so it goes on...*

Julie is the department head in a college. It is her job to design the hairdressing **curriculum** to meet local needs.

Stage 1	Julie knows that she needs to meet the needs of full-time and part-time learners. She also needs to offer various levels of the qualification and offer some professional updating courses. *This is the identify need stage.*
Stage 2	She looks at her staff, the size of the training salon and the number of classrooms she has available. She creates a timetable for her full-time students, which can also be dipped into by the part-time students. She decides that the professional updating would have to be done in the evenings when salons are closed and hairdressing professionals can attend. *This is the design stage.*
Stage 3	Julie creates the timetable and allocates it to her staff, playing to their strengths. They then deliver teaching and learning strategies to the groups attending the course. *This the implementation stage.*
Stage 4	Throughout the year, Julie organises quality activities to ensure that the team are delivering an effective curriculum. The awarding body visits to ensure that the standard matches national provision and teams from within the college audit several parts of the delivery. Feedback from learners also identifies development areas. These result in actions to develop the course and the staff. *This is the assess and evaluate stage.*
Stage 5	Julie uses these development points to create an action plan for future provision. *This re-starts the training cycle.*

1.3 Legislation and codes of conduct

By the end of this section, you will be able to identify the relevant laws and statutes that affect the teaching profession.

As with any area of work, teachers must work within the boundaries of the law and professional values. There are a vast number of laws, directives and professional ethics; they are constantly changing or being updated. Every organisation will have its own policies and procedures relating to these legal aspects and there are some differences in requirements, depending upon the age of learners and the environment.

Whilst this book will endeavour to cover the main aspects, every teacher remains accountable for their own familiarisation with how to remain compliant. Every opportunity should be taken to ensure that you are up to date. Go back to that first rule of teaching – ASSUME NOTHING!

 ACTIVITY 3

This may be one of your first development points:

To identify all legislation and codes of practice in relation to teaching [your subject], by:

- Attending your organisation's induction event
- Finding out who the health and safety manager or representative is
- Checking out where the policies and procedures are. They may be stored in paper or electronic formats
- Asking your line manager about particular rules relating to your subject
- Enquiring about the names of key staff to help you
- Finding out if you need a Criminal Records Board (CRB) disclosure, and how will you get it

The main acts and rules

Health and Safety at Work Act (1974)

Everyone has a responsibility for the safety of themselves and others. Therefore, rules must be followed and safe practices adhered to, you should demonstrate a model of best practice, lead by example. There are additional rules relating to taking learners on educational visits following a series of tragic accidents. Do not consider taking learners on visits without seeking advice.

The Management of Health and Safety at Work Regulations (1999)

The legislation seeks to prevent unsafe practices and minimise risk. For example, fire and emergency procedures, first aid at work, safe handling practices, visual display unit codes, risk assessment.

Risk assessment

All activities have an element of risk, some more so than others. It is the teacher's responsibility to assess the level of the risk, establish practices to minimise risk and record such activities.

Child Protection Guidelines

Recent high-profile cases have brought about the necessity to introduce legislation and guidance on protecting children and vulnerable adults against inappropriate behaviour. Each organisation should exercise their functions with a view to safeguarding and promoting the welfare of children (Protection of Children Act, 1999). Mandatory Criminal Records Bureau (CRB) checks are required of teachers working with children and vulnerable adults. The Government holds lists of those deemed unsuitable to work with these groups and organisations should check these before appointing staff. You may also find that groups of learners, for example child care students, are checked before embarking on their course of study. This is 'due diligence' on behalf of the organisation, who may send these learners into work placement in nurseries and the like.

▶

Disability Discrimination Act (1995 and onwards)
This Act gives disabled people the right to employment, education and other services. Part 3 (2004) legislated that businesses must take reasonable steps to modify physical features that may cause barriers. Part 4 (2005) extended this to include educational establishments.

Copyright guidelines
Copyright guidance protects the originators of material against **plagiarism** and compromising intellectual ownership. Materials includes books, newspapers, journals, material downloaded from the Internet, broadcasts – in fact anything which is not your own original material. It is against the Copyright, Designs and Patents Act 1998, and the subsequent amendment of 2003, to reproduce material in any way without acknowledging the originator. During research this means using a system like Harvard referencing to cite the sources. In order to devise a fair system of paying royalties to originators, the Copyright Licensing Agency (CLA) offers licences to educational establishments so that teachers can photocopy information for their learners. Usually, close to every photocopier there is a charter explaining how much can be reproduced. Your reprographics department will advise on this. Exercise caution when copying anything, as the CLA can carry out spot checks and could go through filing cabinets to check that information is not being illegally copied. Always state the originator's name, even if it is a handout devised by a colleague.

Data Protection
The Data Protection Act (1998) requires any organisation that holds any data on individuals, electronic or otherwise, for more than two months, to register as data users. It restricts the sharing of data. Caution should be taken when holding records associated with learners, staff, or partner companies. It is common sense that you should never reveal personal information about anyone to another person, however convincing the request!

Duty of care
Common, civil, statute and criminal law all apply to teachers. If you are proven to be negligent, then you may have to compensate the injured

party. This applies to individuals as well as a corporate responsibility. Teachers are, in principle, *in loco parentis* to their younger learners. This means they need to offer a safe environment, whilst balancing the need to experiment and develop independence. If you and the organisation have taken all reasonable steps to ensure safety, yet a learner is injured as a result of not following the rules, it is unlikely to be proven that you are in breach of the duty of care. So, if you are using equipment in a workshop, or scissors in a classroom, or taking a group on a visit, you should assess the risk, warn of the safety implications and use protective equipment. Failure to do so is negligence.

Equal opportunity legislation

A series of laws have been passed to ensure that no one is discriminated against, irrespective of gender, marital status, sexual orientation, disability, race, nationality, ethnic origin, age, religion or belief, domestic circumstances, trade union membership, social or employment status.

For the teacher this means ensuring language, handouts and other learning materials are free from bias, and that inappropriate comments are challenged and excluded from the classroom. When advertising courses and delivering learning, a teacher should not stereotype or in anyway disadvantage groups of learners. The environment and all support structures should enable access and include facilities to meet all learners' needs.

Disciplinary policies and sanctions

Keeping order in the classroom will in itself provide a safer learning environment. Corporal punishment is illegal and hitting (teachers hitting learners or learners hitting teachers) is criminal assault. Restraint is a difficult one because it relies on evidence of training and reasonableness. Each organisation will have its own policies on discipline and related issues and what to do if things go wrong, which will include **sanctions**, use of force, disciplinary hearings and exclusion. Managing behaviour and problems in the classroom and how to deal with them are further discussed in Chapter 4.

Dress codes

There are some vocational areas that require learners to wear particular things in order to meet professional standards, for example trainee

▶

chefs wearing 'kitchen whites', motor vehicle learners wearing personal protective clothing and equipment. Dress codes should, wherever practicable, respect safety issues and respect religious beliefs. Guidance on the wearing of uniform, jewellery and other such rules should be shared and advocated throughout the organisation. You should familiarise yourself with the organisation's rules. In terms of the dress code for teachers, one should remember professional values; there is rarely a uniform, but smart, comfortable and practical should prevail.

Terms and conditions of employment
Every teacher will receive a contract of employment which not only details pay and working hours, but defines the rules of the organisation and what would happen if the rules are breached. You should always read everything in your contract and question things that you are unsure about.

Whilst some of these aspects need only an awareness of context, many will impact from your first teaching experience and therefore require a detailed knowledge. You will need to talk this through with your line manager, your mentor or your union representative. The importance of this cannot be over-emphasised.

Useful online resources

Useful references for further reading about legislation are Cohen, Manion and Morrison (2004: 85–96)
http://www.hse.gov.uk/services/education/index.htm
http://www.teachers.org.uk/resources/pdf/law-and-you.pdf
http://www.natfhe.org.uk/
http://www.ucu.org.uk/index.cfm?articleid=1738
http://www.rospa.com/safetyeducation/atschool/index.htm
http://www.dfes.gov.uk/

1.4 Referral

By the end of this section, you will be able to identify the scope of your own responsibilities and recognise when to refer an issue or incident to a specialist.

Knowing the boundaries of the teacher's role is essential to an effective learning environment. It is also important for the teacher to realise that there are some aspects of the learners' expectations that are beyond the role of the teacher. You may also find that experience plays an important part here; you may not know all the answers because you are new to the role and/or the organisation. The teacher should always consider the interests of the learners as paramount. We might like to help, but are we really the most effective person for the learner to consult? Understanding and respecting professional boundaries is essential.

The boundary between the role the teacher has in respect of teaching, tutoring and caring for learners is rarely clear. Each aspect is important and it is equally important for the teacher to learn when their role or help is dealt with more effectively by another trained professional.

Q: *Where does the teacher's role end and the specialist's begin?*

A: If only this were a clear line! The answer really is going to alter given the particular issue the teacher is faced with. The teacher is generally tasked with the front line delivery of learning. Each individual or group of learners will usually be allocated a tutor whose role it is to support learning and academic/vocational achievement. They may also be involved in a certain amount of personal connection, which means learners may confide in them. However, whether or not the tutor has sufficient time or knowledge to problem solve on behalf of their learners is down to position and experience. You should always remember the implications of legislation and duty of care (Section 1.3): thus, if an issue discussed is beyond your knowledge, experience, accountability or responsibility you should refer to your mentor, manager or student support service department.

There are some rules here:

● Back to the first rule of teaching: assume nothing…
● Remember the first rule of customer service: if you promise to do something – do it.
● And finally, the rule of trust and tutoring – integrity and confidentiality.

Q: *Who are the specialists and how do my learners access them?*

A: If you look in the Student Charter, which is usually given to all learners either at enrolment or induction, it will inform them of the support available within the organisation (see Internal support services below). In addition to this, there are various external voluntary bodies who will offer information, advice and guidance for all members of the community (see External support services below).

Internal support services

Whilst this list is not comprehensive, it will give an idea of the mechanisms usually available within an organisation:

- Student Services Office
- Crèche
- Counselling
- Tutoring
- Financial support
- Remission of fees for recipients of means-tested benefits
- Learner support for physical and/or educational support needs
- Dyslexia/dyscalculia (words/numbers) support.

External support services

These are the professionals. Offices and telephone lines are staffed by trained personnel, are usually open 24/7 with phone lines normally free or making modest charges to cover costs. Again, this is not comprehensive, but the main ones are listed.

Samaritans	Confidential emotional support
Drugs line	Information about drugs and solvents for those who use them, or are affected by them
Citizens Advice Bureau	Local community help agency, legal advice and general information on a range of issues
Shelterline	Legal and housing advice line offering independent information and advice
Childline	Helpline for children and young people up to 18 years old in danger, distress or with a problem
Help the Aged – senior line	Welfare benefits advice for older people

▶

Parent line	Support and information for parents and those in a parenting role
National Debtline	Help for anyone in debt or concerned about falling into debt
Lesbian and gay switchboard	Support and information for lesbians and gay men
Victim Support	Emotional and practical support for anyone affected by crime
National Domestic Violence Helpline	Safe accommodation for those experiencing domestic violence
NHS Direct	Confidential health advice
Crimestoppers	Community service which helps to prevent and solve crimes

Use your local telephone directory for contact information.

It is important when working with learners that you respect their wishes and their confidentiality. You might use statements like 'if I were you...', but they are not you and you should remember that. Advice means that you give someone the benefit of your worldly experience; the nature of advice means that nobody has to accept it.

Issues relating to someone claiming they are being abused or supplied drugs should always be referred – even if only to someone more senior; it is your duty of care.

1.5 Equality, diversity and inclusion

By the end of this section, you will be able to describe and review how the learner must be at the centre of the learning experience.

Whilst **equality** generally means everyone is treated equally and fairly, it is linked directly to legislation and guidelines, which together drive the initiative. **Diversity** goes one step further by valuing the differences between individuals, and by ensuring they are participating, you are including everyone (**inclusion**).

Equality, whilst driven by legislation, should develop the culture and ethic of wanting to meet the needs of all learners. Equality, diversity and inclusion are words associated with implementing the various pieces of legislation into a specialist context. For us that means education, teaching and training.

Each of your learners is an individual who should be treated as an equal and with respect, irrespective of gender, marital status, sexual orientation, disability, race, nationality, ethnic origin, age, religion or belief, domestic circumstances, trade union membership, social or employment status. This means that you should not have favourites, nor should you allow your learners to treat each other with disrespect.

Some of the key documents relating to equal opportunities are:

● Equal Pay Act (1970)
● Rehabilitation of Offenders Act (1974)
● Sex Discrimination Act (1975)
● Race Relations Act (1976, 2000)
● Disability Discrimination Act (1995 and subsequent regulations)
● Human Rights Act (1998)
● Employment Equality (Sexual Orientation) Regulations (2003)
● Employment Equality (Religion or Belief) Regulations (2003)
● Employment Equality (Age) Regulations (2006)

For the organisation, it means setting up a **policy** and codes of practice which ensure staff are aware of the law and are familiar with how to implement it in their job roles. The table below explains how the laws relating to equal opportunities are developed into an inclusive strategy.

Equal opportunities	Diversity and inclusion
Concentrates on removing discrimination	Maximises learner potential
Can be an issue for disadvantaged groups	Is relevant to all learners
Relies on positive action by managers and the organisation as a whole	Relies on implementing policies and practices in context

Adapted from Kandola and Fullerton (1994: 49)

For the teacher this means ensuring language, handouts and other learning materials are free from bias, and that inappropriate comments are challenged and excluded from the classroom. When advertising courses and delivering **learning**, a teacher should not stereotype or in anyway disadvantage groups of learners. The environment and all support structures should enable access and include facilities to meet all learners' needs. 'Political correctness' is a commonly used term at the moment, and is used to ensure that expressions do not cause offence to any particular group of people.

Let us look at some examples:

Material	Watch points
Handouts	Never use 'he' or 'she'. Try to use 'they' or 'their'. Be prepared to photocopy large print versions if necessary
Language	Never use words like 'manpower', 'blackboard', 'craftsman'. Relate learning to experiences to aid understanding (anecdotes, analogy). The expression 'thought-shower' is preferred to 'brainstorm'
Advertising/ course leaflets	Do not stereotype. All courses should be accessible and open to all

Written and spoken text	Use clear language, without jargon, explain technical terms. Use dictionaries and vocabulary books to aid understanding of terms
Visual aids	Consider colours and their effectiveness. Write clearly in a legible style of writing. Use expressions such as wipeboard and chalkboard rather than whiteboard and blackboard
Learning aids	Offer alternative formats, i.e. electronic, paper, large print, Braille, whenever possible
Space	Ensure coats, bags, etc. are not left around the room, ensure there is sufficient space for moving around the classroom
Support	Ensure that learners needs are addressed, which may involve using a specialist team of physical and educational support workers

1.6 Record keeping

By the end of this section, you will be able to list the types of records kept by the teacher required to audit and demonstrate that learners are at the centre of the organisation's values.

It will not take you long to recognise that part of the teacher's role is that of keeping records. They may be kept electronically or in paper formats. The documents are required for several reasons:

- Auditing purposes
- Information gathering
- Quality assurance systems
- Health and safety management
- Financial accountability.

Some of the documents used at this introductory stage are:

Types of form	Use
Enrolment forms	Gathers personal details and information about declared **learning needs**, marketing information and declarations
Qualification/registration Forms	Used to register a candidate with an awarding body, thus notifying them of the intent to certificate following a period of study
Learner needs analyses	Collecting details about preferred learning styles, used by the teacher to devise appropriate classroom activities
Registers	An auditable document recording attendance and punctuality
Individual Learning Plans (ILP)	Personal targets to aid the monitoring and development of learning, used to track progress and support study
Induction records	Used to record what has been explained during induction, training on use of equipment and which documents have been issued
Training and assessment plans	Used instead of, or in support of an **ILP** to plan and track progress through a particular qualification

There are different requirements for recording progress and **achievement**, which are dealt with later.

However time-consuming the paperwork is, it must be completed regularly and accurately. Other departments in the organisation will be relying on you to do this in a timely manner. They will also use these records to inform their workloads, claim funding, ensure examination entries are made at the correct time and allocate appropriate support for learners. Record keeping is part of the contract of employment, and whilst teaching is the more enjoyable part of the job, paperwork is similarly important to the efficiency of the organisation.

Glossary of terms

Academic relating to education, school or scholarships

Achievement meeting learning goals

Awarding bodies the people who devise the qualifications and award the certificates

Curriculum a programme of study

Differentiation catering for the needs of all learners to reduce barriers to learning

Diversity valuing and celebrating the differences in people

Equality the state of being equal or the same

Ice-breaker an activity used to introduce learners to each other

ILP individual learning plan

Inclusion finding opportunities to integrate all learners

Learning to gain knowledge or a skill; what the learners do during a session

Learning goals what a learner sets out to do

Learning needs things which will help a learner to achieve their goal

Learning styles analysis of how learners learn

Plagiarism to pass off somebody else's work as your own

Policy course of action by an organisation

Qualification a skill that makes someone suitable for a job

Recreational learning a skill for pleasure

Sanction a penalty for disobeying rules

Teaching to impart knowledge or a skill; what the teacher does during a session

VAK visual, auditory and kinaesthetic learners – different ways learners like to learn

Vocational skills related to employment

SUMMARY

In this chapter, you have covered all of the theoretical aspects of the first learning outcome in your PTLLS qualification:

Roles and Responsibilities; Getting started (how do learners learn, ice-breakers, teaching/training cycle), legislation and codes of conduct (health and safety, copyright, values), referral, equality, diversity and inclusion, and record keeping.

Your Personal Development

You will have completed an activity which has helped you to identify where you are at the moment in terms of your strengths, weaknesses and experience as a teacher. You should have a list of questions to ask your mentor, line manager or course tutor which should help to set your own personal learning goals.

You will have learned to assume nothing, and that making assumptions about people can be detrimental to their learning.

You will have analysed both your own and your learners preferred learning styles and can explain how this will impact on your teaching. You will use your own learning experiences to create your own list of values that will not be compromised whilst you are teaching.

You will have identified questions to ask the health and safety manager, diversity manager, your line manager and/or your mentor to ensure that you comply with all of the legislation and codes of practice that apply to you whilst teaching in your specialist subject.

You should be able to answer questions relating to:

- your role, responsibilities and boundaries as a teacher in terms of the teaching cycle
- key aspects of legislation and codes of practice related to your organisation and specialist subject
- how you will promote inclusion, equality and diversity within your current and future teaching roles and how to refer learners to meet their needs.

CHAPTER 2 (PTLLS, UNIT 2)

Approaches to teaching and learning

EDUCATION PHOTOS / ALAMY

LEARNING OBJECTIVES

In this chapter you will learn about:

- Selecting appropriate teaching and learning strategies
- How to help your learners acquire functional skills
- Identifying the challenges and barriers to learning
- The importance of a good learning environment
- Effective use of resources

2.1 Approaches to teaching and learning

By the end of this section, you will be able to select teaching and learning strategies appropriate to your specialist area.

Teaching and learning strategies will vary according to what you want to get out of the session, what the learners are able to achieve within the time allowed, what materials and resources are available to you, the subject matter you are delivering, the needs of the learners and your personal style.

The choice of method will depend on whether you wish to deliver a formal teaching session in which all learners are working on the same topic at the same time, a learner-centred session, where learners are working on the same broad topic but using different methods and resources, or finally a self-study style where learners are working on different aspects of a topic or even different topics, using their own style of learning (Petty 2004: 430).

Factors that influence teaching:

- How learners learn and their preferred learning style
- What the teacher wants to achieve
- The subject matter
- What the learners are capable of achieving
- Time constraints
- Resource implications
- What the learners want to get out of the session
- Where you will teach
- How dependent your learners are

First of all, you should separate teaching from learning in order to understand these influences. In short, teaching is what we do; learning is what your learners will do. Each activity in the classroom will consist of teaching and learning activities. These should be balanced to meet the different needs of your learners (see Section 1.2) and to develop motivation (see Section 4.2). Modern technology allows for a **blended learning** style which incorporates traditional and computer-based methods. This is often referred to as Information learning technology (**ILT**) or Information communication technology (**ICT**). The use of computer-based technology to enhance teaching methods and resources or develop learner **autonomy** is widely promoted.

The table considers some of the most frequently used approaches and compares them in the context of teaching and learning activities.

Activity	Value to teacher	Value to learner
Lecture (verbal exposition)	High focus on teacher activity Excellent knowledge base required Uses verbal exposition to impart a lot of information in a short time Clarity and tone of voice needs to be clear, interesting and unambiguous Can be used to deliver to large groups easily Is enhanced by visual aids	Requires good listening and note-taking skills Passive learning Limited opportunities to clarify understanding Appeals to auditory learners
Demonstration	Needs to be well organised before session Explains difficult parts of the task when verbal exposition is not suitable Teacher-centred Links theory and practice	Opportunities to see, hear and smell Allows a task to be broken down into smaller chunks Limited hands-on experiences Appeals to visual learners (ensure everyone can see!)

▶

Activity	Value to teacher	Value to learner
Group work	Less teacher-focused Teacher needs to monitor progress to keep on task Takes a long time to extract key points Several different ways of working: **buzz, snowball (pyramid), jigsaw group activities**	Suits kinaesthetic learners Weak and strong learners work collectively
Discussion and debates	Free exchange of ideas on a given topic Needs careful management to ensure range of ideas and to keep on task Can be used to support other teaching methods Develops deeper understanding	Allows ideas to be shared and is an opportunity to value other learners' opinions Suits auditory learners Balanced teacher/learner input
Questioning (Q&A)	Different styles of technique: can be call-out or nominated in style Collects ideas which can be recorded on board Need to ensure everyone participates Good way of introducing or summarising a topic Assesses understanding of topic	Call-out style is not intimidating Challenges learners to think Can develop note-taking skills and increase accuracy of learners' notes Nominated style will ensure everyone is included in activity Instant feedback on response Appeals to kinaesthetic and auditory learners
Experiential	Teacher does not control the learning, thus developing autonomy Teacher is a facilitator	Learners develop their own methods of gaining information Highly learner-centred

Activity	Value to teacher	Value to learner
	Can develop personal skills in communication, number and IT May allow loss of focus	Can stimulate higher ability learners and motivate less able learners Ideal for kinaesthetic learners Ideal for **autonomous learners**
Presentations and seminars	Similar to lectures with added dimension of learner activity Key information presented, then deeper understanding acquired through gathering of further information Highly motivational	Able to gather key information and build upon it through their own research Learners investigate their topics and present back to their peers Develops individual styles Balance of teacher and learner activities Suits all learning styles
Simulation, role-play and practical work	Simulation used for expensive or dangerous activities Builds on previously demonstrated skills Mirrors work place practice Can be costly and time-consuming to organise; needs sufficient resources for all Needs to be carefully managed to ensure skill is practiced accurately Some learners may feel self-conscious Will promote and develop safe and healthy practice	Opportunity to practice skills Ideal for kinaesthetic and visual learners Can experience emotions, feel, taste and smell Reinforces previous learning Can learn from teachers, support workers or peers

▶

Activity	Value to teacher	Value to learner
Games/quizzes	Develops competitive spirit Can be used to open or close a topic Useful to keep as a contingency plan 'if time allows' or 'if you work well'	Fun activity Suits kinaesthetic learners
Research-style activities	Teacher is a **facilitator** or resource rather than leader of learning Promotes independence in learners	Suits visual and kinaesthetic learners
Case study	Develops higher levels of understanding on a topic Develops problem-solving capabilities Develops critical thinking	Enables learners to develop opinions and ideas from a given set of facts 'Safe' analysis which may impact on later application

Your second rule of teaching should be VARIETY

Variety in **teaching** and **learning** will ensure that your sessions are meeting individuals' needs and are addressing different spans of attention, as well as being interesting for you and your learners. By using a balance of teacher- and learner-centred activities you spread the responsibility of learning. Too many new teachers believe that they should 'perform' for the entire lesson; all they do is exhaust themselves to a usually passive (and possibly bored) group of learners. In the same way that you would integrate theory and practice whenever possible, intersperse passive and active learning activities – so that everyone benefits from a rest during the session!

The basic strategy for every session should be a beginning, middle and an end. This will form the structure, and will also help when you come to plan and prepare for your sessions. By following this structure you will be demonstrating an organised approach to teaching and learning. This should be the basis of role modelling for your learners; indirectly it will organise them and this will also help in managing the classroom atmosphere.

Simple structures			
Beginning	The introduction. Explain what is going to happen in the session. Setting the scene.	For example: Verbal exposition (VE) Questioning – to check previous knowledge	Teacher-centred intro. Aims on board and spoken (Auditory/visual) Collect any homework. Prompt and organised start, set any rules now
Middle	The content. Move from the known to the unknown. Give clear instruction on how the activity will progress/time allowed.	For example: Scenario 1 Demo + practical Scenario 2 VE + discuss + game	Balance of teacher/ learner activity. Visual/kinaesthetic Learner-dominated. Auditory, visual and kinaesthetic
End	Assessment of what has been learned. Conclusions and summary. Future development.	For example: Scenario 1 Discussion/ evaluation Scenario 2 Quiz or Q&A Ending in VE – prep for next session.	Learner-centred. Opportunity to complete notes Learner-centred. Corrected script provides future notes Teacher-centred. Issue homework now

In order to ensure that you are meeting individuals' needs by using visual, auditory and kinaesthetic teaching and learning strategies, look at the lists below for some ideas for your teaching sessions, remembering to include a variety of techniques:

Visual learning techniques

- Use cards, posters and prompt sheets
- Display session tasks on board
- Write key words on board
- Collate ideas from group activities on board or flip chart
- Supplement verbal exposition with pictures and diagrams
- Ask questions which exploit visual imagination: 'What would it look like?'
- Encourage learners to 'see' words/concepts in their mind
- Use highlighter pens to annotate work
- Use a glossary of terms in a vocabulary book or poster
- Vary colour, font style/size in visual aids in learners' handouts
- Use mnemonics
- Number sentences or bullet points

Auditory learning techniques

- Listen to learners (teacher and peers)
- Talk through ideas on posters, boards, handouts
- Ask questions which exploit auditory skills: 'What does it sound like?'
- Introduce new words through language games
- Give thinking time in group activities
- Use musical connections to words (sing alphabet, use rhyme)

Kinaesthetic learning techniques

- Use breaks/pauses to get learners moving, even within the room
- Locate different activities in different parts of the room
- Use role play or practical activities
- Put words on cards to be sorted into types
- Write letters on cards to make words
- Use Post-it notes to record questions in lectures or demonstrations
- Ask questions which exploit kinaesthetic skills: 'What did it feel like?'
- Provide opportunities for learners to do things

2.2 Functional skills

By the end of this section, you will be able to describe the meaning of functional skills and identify opportunities to collect evidence to support your learners' acquisition of those skills.

Functional skills are a development initiative to standardise qualifications for English, maths and ICT. In the past they have been known by several different names:

- Core skills
- Common skills
- Basic skills
- Key skills
- Minimum core.

Irrespective of the name, functional skills refer to the mastery of English/literacy, maths/numeracy and ICT/information technology. These are the skills that underpin all learning and without them learners will struggle to meet the demands of their qualification, the world of work and life skills. Each of the names listed relates to a style or level of qualification, you will still hear them referred to as such in the staff room. Do not be confused – everyone is talking about the same broad topic; it is usually the method of assessment that determines the small differences. For example:

- *Common/core skills* were attached to academic qualifications, such as General National Vocational Qualifications (GNVQs).
- *Basic skills* are an initiative introduced by government, to raise the standards of literacy and numeracy in the post compulsory sector, usually assessed by a test.
- *Key skills* are basic skills applied to or in the context of a vocational qualification, usually demonstrated by preparing a portfolio of evidence.
- *Minimum core* is what you are addressing, probably at Level 3, in your teacher training qualification. It covers language, literacy, numeracy and ICT. Included within will be the assessment of personal skills and the ability to deliver functional skills to your learners. See also Chapter 10.

Functional Skills Qualifications are not planned to be fully launched until at least 2010. In the interim, existing qualifications will remain and pilot programmes will gradually introduce the new revised qualifications.

Whatever the current name, and there will be others, it is bestowed upon the teacher to develop these skills in their learners at every opportunity. As we noted in the first rule it cannot be assumed (assume nothing) that learners leaving full-time compulsory education (school) have sufficient skills in English, maths and IT to achieve their qualification. The Government sets the target that a learner leaving school should have, amongst others, English and maths at Level 2 (GCSE), and school performance tables reflect their ability to meet these targets. Most post-compulsory providers undertake diagnostic tests with their learners during induction to confirm the level of competence of its new entrants.

The Qualifications and Curriculum Authority (QCA) publish the National Qualifications Framework (NQF). Using this table, all qualifications are aimed at a specific level.

National Qualifications Framework (NQF)		Framework for Higher Education Qualifications (FHEQ)
Previous Level (e.g.)	*Current Level (e.g.)*	*Level (e.g.)*
LEVEL 5 NVQ Diploma	LEVEL 8 Specialist Award	D Doctorates
	LEVEL 7 Diploma	M Masters Degrees, Postgraduate certificates and diplomas
LEVEL 4 National Diploma Higher National Diploma L4 Certificate	LEVEL 6 L6 National Diploma	H Honours – Bachelors, graduate certificates
	LEVEL 5 Higher National Diploma	I Intermediate – Diplomas of HE/FE, Foundation Degrees, HNDs
	LEVEL 4 Certificate	C Certificate of HE
LEVEL 3 Certificate NVQ A levels		
LEVEL 2 NVQ GCSEs Grades A*–C Basic/Key Skills L2 National Curriculum Key Stage 6		
LEVEL 1 NVQ GCSEs Grades D-G Basic/Key Skills L1 National Curriculum Key Stage 4/5		
ENTRY LEVEL Entry Level Certificates Adult Skills for Life Entry 1, 2, 3		

The structure of the NQF, adapted from www.qca.org.uk

This table shows how qualifications are currently structured and will give teachers an idea of the level of functional skills a learner should possess to be able to achieve their main qualification. For example, someone on a Level 2 NVQ in Motor Vehicle Studies should study functional skills at Level 2 – GCSE Grade A* – C or equivalent. A learner on a Level 3 Certificate in Small Animal Care should be working on Level 3 Key Skills in communication, application of number and information technology. There will be variants to this to match curriculum specifications, for example, learners on Computer Programming courses may do ICT qualifications at a higher level, or hairdressers may do communication skills and number skills to an equivalent level of their main qualification and ICT to one level lower. These variants will often be recommendations from the awarding body or may be designed by whoever writes the course programme. It will be informed by the functional skills required to meet the job role and the results of **diagnostic assessment**.

Literacy standards include reading, writing, speaking and listening. Numeracy standards include interpreting information, calculations, interpreting and presenting results. ICT standards include finding and selecting information, entering and developing information and developing presentations. Each level from entry 1 through to Level 3 and above, has progressively more complex tasks and details required to show competence. There are several sources of information on the worldwide web:

Useful online resources

Advice about progress of functional skills qualifications:
http://www.qca.org.uk

Resources and teaching information:
http://www.basic-skills.co.uk
http://www.bbc.co.uk/skillswise

Standards and qualifications:
http://www.city-and-guilds.co.uk
http://www.ocr.org.uk
http://www.edexcel.org.uk

Embedding functional skills into teaching and learning activities

Embedding skills means that functional skills (things like literacy, numeracy and information technology) are taught within the main subject topic in a seamless way. *Integrating* functional skills into your teaching means that you will set activities which meet the literacy or numeracy standards; they may or may not be in context. By incorporating functional skills into every activity they will become embedded. **Embedded** skills are always in context.

Every activity that occurs in a teaching and learning session has the potential to gather information which demonstrates a learner's ability against functional skills – the level of the functional skill will be determined by the complexity of the information. The following table demonstrates some examples of embedded functional skills.

A learner who is *listening to the teacher* at the beginning of a class is listening for and identifying relevant information

In a *question and answer session* the learner will be both listening and speaking, or if it is a written question sheet they will be reading and writing

By *designing a poster* for display in the classroom, in addition to the subject matter the learner will have to:

- calculate the overall size of the poster
- estimate the size of the smaller parts to be attached to the poster
- decide on the ratio and proportion of text, picture and white space
- present information in a visual format
- gather data from a variety of sources – the Internet, books, magazines, or people, etc.
- write text (handwritten or word processed)
- read data sources
- interpret and summarise information
- display images or pictures

A catering learner *baking a cake* will have to:

- read the recipe
- interpret the information into a time plan of work
- calculate the time the task will take

- estimate the size and number of bowls required
- measure the ingredients
- talk to the teacher or support worker for advice and listen to their reply
- talk to other learners, hopefully about the cake!
- solve problems relating to the planned activity

In *reading this* book, you are:

- understanding explanatory text
- inferring meaning
- using reading strategies – skimming, scanning or detailed reading
- summarising information

A *visit to a supermarket* will require the learners to:

- write a shopping list
- calculate the cost of two or more items
- compare the price/weight of similar items
- talk to shop assistants/cashiers
- follow basic instructions
- listen to total cost of shopping and give money
- calculate the amount of change needed

A group of learners, *investigating a topic* and *presenting their findings* to the group will:

- respond to extended questions on a range of topics
- speak clearly and confidently using informal and formal language
- design a presentation using IT software
- present information grammatically correct, in a logical order and proofread the work
- present information in graphical format
- contribute within the group, engage in discussion about findings, arguments and opinions
- summarise information from a number of sources

Functional skills are essential; they will help your learners to achieve and succeed in life. By embedding the functional skills into the curriculum both you and your learners can overcome the fear of English and maths, which may have been a barrier to earlier success in the subject. Sometimes giving something a different label, whilst confusing to the teacher, may sidetrack the learner into success.

ACTIVITY 1

Personal Development

Stage One
Take an idea or lesson plan to your organisation's Skills for Life Advisor, Teaching and Learning Mentor or your ITT tutor.
Sit with them to map the functional skills that emerge from the activity.
Ask questions like 'why' and 'how' and don't forget to ask 'how can I develop the activity to include . . .'
Deliver the session and note any unplanned functional skills that occurred.

Stage Two
Use a copy of or download the relevant functional skills standards from an awarding body and repeat the task in Stage One above on your own.
Take the completed mapping exercise to your Skills for Life Advisor, Teaching and Learning Mentor or ITT Tutor and discuss it.
Make any amendments and deliver the session.
Note any unplanned functional skills that occurred.

2.3 Challenges and barriers to learning

By the end of this section, you will be able to identify challenges, barriers and attitudes to learning which will impact upon your teaching and learning sessions.

Challenges, barriers and attitudes to learning are general expressions, which mean 'things that hold back' learning. Challenges, in this context, usually mean 'making learning difficult'; barriers mean 'things that prevent learning'. Attitudes are feelings and emotions brought into the classroom by learners. As a teacher we want our learners to work to the best of their ability, yet we empathise with factors which from time to time restrict that ability. Some learners may present themselves in our classes with more long-term barriers, challenges and attitudes.

Challenges, barriers and attitudes are often the reason (or occasionally the excuse!) for not learning. 'I can't do this' or 'I've never been any good at...' or 'I hate tests' and any number of similar expressions can be heard in classrooms up and down the country. For teachers, this is our learners 'cry for help'. When learners say things like this they are demonstrating their lack of motivation or poor self-esteem. We should think, 'how can I make this easier to understand?', 'how can I prepare learners for their future test?', 'is there something else behind that behaviour?' Whatever the cry, whatever the remedy, few people have a phobia of learning (sophophobia); many have challenges, barriers and attitudes which inhibit their learning and so their success.

Remembering some of the challenges, barriers or attitudes to learning can be made easier by using 'DELTA' to classify them:

Disability, Emotional, Language, Technology, Ability

Disability	Emotional	Language	Technology	Ability
Mobility	Finance	Foreign	Computer	Short illness
Visual	Child care	language	skills	Absence
Hearing	Dependents	Terminology	Car	Punctuality
Long illness	Concentration	Accent	breakdown	Motivation
Dyslexia	Confidence	Pace	Transport	Resources
Dyscalculia	Behaviour	Communication	Heating	Support
Mental health	Discipline	Rapport	Lighting	Study support
Dexterity	Personal	Basic skill needs	Temperature	Inaccurate
Chronic pain	problems	Cultural	Fear of	advice
	Commitments	differences	technology	Teaching
	Previous			styles
	experience			Large classes
	Fear of unknown			Personal skills
	Peer pressure			
	Parental pressure			
	Employer			
	pressure			
	Stress/worry			
	Hormones			
	New			
	surroundings			
	Returning to			
	education			
	Poverty			

Learning to recognise the symptoms of these barriers is essential in attempting to resolve the issues. As many of the barriers arise from emotions, it is difficult to predict how different learners will react, but just recognising that something in the character of your learner is different to their usual behaviour is usually enough. It returns to the idea that we should know our learners. Also, don't forget that people are human before they are teachers or learners and respect, praise and enjoyment are excellent motivators. NB It is usually a good indicator that you have lost the interest of your learners if you look up and they have gone!

Before it gets that far, here are some things to look out for:

- Limited short-term memory
- Carelessness in work
- Lack of eye contact
- Glazed looks
- Repeated and persistent errors
- Time-management difficulties
- Reactions and side-effects to prescribed drugs
- Poor concentration
- Lack of participation or reluctance to participate
- Constantly demanding attention
- Panic or anxiety
- Tiredness or weight variance
- Poor behaviour
- Hyperactivity
- Poor attention span
- Lateness
- Attempts to sidetrack topic or activity
- Excessive calling out and interruptions
- Loud or demanding behaviour
- Sighing
- Fidgeting
- Putting coats on, or taking layers off.

Before embarking on a one person mission to cure all of your learners' symptoms, you might want to consider using referral agencies such as those discussed in Section 1.4. What you can do something about are your teaching and learning strategies to ensure an inclusive learning environment. See also Section 1.5 for some ideas. Recommendations include:

- Recognise changes in your learner's behaviour and make time to listen to their concerns
- Include lots of smaller activities to build and develop the topic and praise at each stage of achievement
- Offer one-to-one support during group activities
- Use nominated questions, aimed at differentiating to meet learners' individual levels of ability, to increase self-esteem
- Vary your teaching techniques to ensure a variety of auditory, visual and kinaesthetic activities
- Know your learners
- Use signers, note-takers and support workers to aid those with visual and hearing impairments or learning disabilities
- Allow use of tape recorders; it is difficult to lip read and make notes
- Offer comfort breaks within longer sessions
- Provide additional or extended work for less able or quick learners
- Always start from things that are known before moving to the unknown
- Experiment with different colours of paper for handouts; yellow is good and makes the words easier to read
- Encourage study skills. Stress key words and when to make notes
- Use Post-it notes for learners to record issues, areas of difficulty, questions, etc., collect them in, read them and act upon the content
- Ensure writing size on boards is legible: stand at the back of the room before the class and check it out!
- Include images and pictures in handouts, overhead transparency (**OHT**) or PowerPoint presentations
- Provide moments in the class when learners can ask questions and seek clarification
- Offer rewards for good behaviour or good progress.

2.4 The learning environment

By the end of this section, you will be able to state the importance of the learning environment in relation to the delivery of teaching sessions.

The learning environment is any area in which teaching and learning takes place. This may be a classroom, a workshop, a lecture theatre or the workplace. The learning environment is not just limited to a space and equipment; it includes the atmosphere that creates a suitable learning setting. Teachers and learners will have experienced a variety of previous situations; those that are traditional in nature, full of teacher-led activities and learners taught in rows. The opposite, and more favourable route, is that of an engaging environment, i.e. that which is less formal, modern and interactive. The table compares these two environments.

Comparison of traditional and engaging learning environments	
Traditional learning environment	*Engaging learning environment*
Passive learners	Active learners
Learners absorb information	Learners interact with information
Insular learning style	Collaborative learning style
Same ability groups	Mixed ability groups
Teacher-centred	Learner-centred
Isolated themes	Integrated themes
Routine and predictable teaching	Innovative and exciting teaching
Discrete provision	Differentiated provision

The learning environment is within the power of the teacher to control. By choosing teaching and learning activities that empower learners to learn, a teacher will motivate learners and as a result they will achieve. Some of these factors are forced upon us due to funding and economic reasons, for example, the need to keep labour costs low results in different ability levels within the class groups, hence the need to meet individual needs in a group. Some factors arise from changes in thinking and technological developments. A teacher needs to accept these challenges and not create their own barriers to teaching (and learning).

The learning environment should meet the needs of individuals and of the chosen teaching strategies. Before the class starts the teacher should consider how they are going to teach during the session and arrange the furniture in an appropriate manner. Some of the options available for a 'taught' session are:

Desks or tables in rows

 A very traditional arrangement. Suitable for lecture-style presentations, when learners need to focus on the front of the room. Not suited to any session where interaction between learners is needed. When learners enter the room, they usually head for the back row, which may cause problems when delivering a session.

Desks or tables in a U shape

A modern arrangement. Suitable when learners need to see the front but also need to engage in discussion with others. The teacher can easily reach learners to support activities although the tables may still form a barrier. The teacher should be mindful that learners sitting towards the open ends of the 'u' may be in peripheral vision and therefore may be forgotten! See also Chapter 4, Activity 1.

Desks or tables in a central block (boardroom style)

 Ideal for group work, or when learners need space to arrange large pieces of work or games. Learners become the focus because the teacher is outside of the group, unless they sit down at the same table and become part of the group.

Desks or tables in small clusters (conference style)

Ideal for small group activities, such as discussion or jigsaw sessions, or as a way of arranging different activities within a single room space.

Chairs in a U shape

 Ideal for group discussions. Suits very informal sessions, such as those in counselling-type discussions. The teacher either forms part of the group or sits outside of the group as an observer. The teacher can refocus the group by using equipment at the front of the room and the absence of tables removes barriers.

Chairs in rows (theatre style)

Very formal in style. Ideal for presentations and lectures where note-taking and discussion is not required. If questions from the floor are allowed, the teacher will have to repeat questions or use a microphone to ensure everyone can hear.

Chairs around the edge of the room (open style)

Ideal when space is required for role play or active learning strategies. Small groups can perform in front of peers.

In all of the room arrangements, the teacher should remember the health and safety of themselves and others. Tables can be heavy to shift around without the help of others, and there is always the matter of what to do with spare furniture when rearranging a room. You should always put the furniture back to its original position at the end of the session, so some teaching time will be lost in the lesson. Also, the teacher should consider where learners are to put their coats and bags, how learners will move safely around the room and how those with mobility problems will cope. You should also remember that those with visual impairment may have learnt the room layout and changes will disorientate them. Whilst changing a layout has advantages and health and safety issues can be overcome, always prepare learners for a change. You can either tell them that the room will look differently next week because … or get them involved in the change, explaining why it is necessary. Do not underestimate the feelings of learners.

The size and shape of the room will impact on how the room can be arranged and the types of learning activity that can be undertaken. Rooms are usually allocated by others in your organisation, but if your learner numbers increase beyond what is acceptable, or the room is not suitable for the teaching activities or resources you need, it is worth asking to change rooms, even if only on a temporary basis.

EXAMPLE

For many weeks the learners have been attending their session in a particular room, and they will probably have claimed their seat. It will be next to their friend and certainly in a comfortable position. They will always sit there. It is their space!

Move the room around before they arrive and just watch the panic in their faces! They are uncomfortable and do not like it. They will be suspicious and reluctant to participate. If it is an examination period, they will immediately lose any self-confidence they had.

I do this to my groups of trainee teachers – by experiencing their own fears they quickly understand the impact their actions will have on their group.

Maybe not the true meaning of experiential learning – but it works!

A learning environment should be suitable for learning. Learning will only occur in a relaxed, familiar surrounding. The teacher must also consider factors such as temperature and light. In a hot room, learners will become sluggish and tire easily. In a cold room, they will be concentrating on trying to get warm. Find out where the thermostat is, or where the remote control for the air conditioning is, or how the windows open. The amount of light needed will vary according to activity. A beauty salon may need muted light, but the artist needs plenty of natural light. You might need to dim the lights to make visual aids more visible or add light to write notes. Where is the light switch?

Carefully chosen teaching strategies with good resources in a comfortable environment are the key ingredients to a successful and effective teaching and learning session.

2.5 Resources

By the end of this section, you will be able to identify and select relevant resources appropriate to your specialist area.

Resources are the equipment and aids that a teacher or learner will use to promote learning. They can be classified in the same way that learner styles are classified and therefore a teacher will be able to choose resources to meet individual needs (differentiated). The more senses a resource affects, the more useful it will be. By linking suitable teaching strategies with professional resources, effectiveness and efficiency of learning will be increased. For example: if doing a verbal exposition, by listing key points on a handout and recording discussion points on a board, or preferably by learners in their handout, most learners' learning needs will be met.

Resources will vary according to the subject, the learners, the accommodation and the skills of the teacher, but they should always be accurate in terms of content, spelling and grammar.

Some examples of resources and their link to the senses

Auditory (using the sense of hearing)

- Tape recordings
- Video, DVD – hearing + sight

Visual (using the sense of sight)

- Boards – chalk, wipe, chart or electronic
- Printed – handouts, overhead projector (**OHP**), posters
- PowerPoint presentation with note style handout (auditory + visual + kinaesthetic)

Kinaesthetic (using the sense of touch)

- Models
- Games

The age of technology has increased the types of resources available and developed existing resources to the advantage of both teacher and learner. A computer attached to a projector enables anything created using a software programme to be displayed and modified in front of the learners; the internet will become 'live' in the classroom;

resources stored on intranet or on virtual learning environments (VLE) (e.g. Moodle, Blackboard, Learnwise) are constantly accessible. These are ILTs. Information Communication Technology (ICT) is also being increasingly used, for example, email to transmit/submit work, mobile phones to send text messages to learners. Text writing is also being used to quicken learners' note-taking skills, but be careful that learners don't prepare their formal work in the same style!

Purpose of using resources

- Increase understanding
- Reinforce key facts
- Create deeper learning
- Motivate
- Variety
- Effective use of time
- Simplify ideas (Reece and Walker 2006: 157–8)

Boards

Includes chalk boards, white or wipe boards, flipcharts and stands, electronic boards. Chalk boards are a little outdated now due to the dust they create, but may still be found in some teaching venues. More commonly, you will see the dust-free wipe boards or flip charts and stands. On a safety note, beware of the fumes that are given off by some permanent pens. More and more often you will see electronic or interactive boards in rooms.

Every type of board uses the principle that words and drawings are displayed in front of the learners, using chalk, dry-wipe, permanent or electronic pens to write with. The electronic board has the additional facility that anything written on it can be saved for future use or printed to provide permanent copies. Flip chart paper can be peeled off the stand and displayed in the room to provide a reference point in classes. Unfortunately, chalk and wipe boards have to be regularly cleaned to provide sufficient space, so make sure learners have taken information into their notebooks before erasing board-work. It is essential that words and drawings on the board are clear, accurate and written in a way to encourage note-taking and of course, visible and legible. The way you use the board is generally the same way that learners will create their own notes, so 'meck shure u cheque yor spellin' and learners understand your handwriting and the presentation style.

Using boards	
Advantages	*Disadvantages*
Cheap (except electronic)	Not permanent (except electronic)
Accessible	Teacher has back to room
Easy to use	Can be messy
Can be pre-prepared	Usually fixed position
Always in view	

Hint:

If you accidentally use a permanent pen to write on a wipe board, overwrite it with a dry-wipe pen and it will come off easily.

Ensure that boards are visible to all of your learners. Remember that visibility may be reduced for those sitting at the back of the room – the most popular seats – and things like colour blindness may limit visual impact for some learners.

Projectors

Overhead projectors (OHPs) are used to display overhead transparencies (OHTs). They are common in most areas and there are portable varieties for those working in community based venues. The skill in the use of the OHP is in the creation of professional OHTs. The modern equivalent is the laptop computer and a portable or ceiling-mounted projector. Both are displayed onto a suitable pale coloured surface. A pen or pencil point makes a convenient pointer to identify a word or phrase.

Single sheet transparencies, which are sometimes called view foils or slides, are useful to display text or diagrams. It is easy to incorporate colour and they are relatively easy to make. They can be handwritten or printed using photocopiers and computer printers, although each type uses different qualities of transparency slides. A transparency suitable for handwriting will melt if used in a photocopier, and printers need slides which absorb the ink, so be careful. Transparencies can be stored for future use in envelopes or clear plastic wallets.

Using overhead transparencies (1)

Reveal technique

A sheet of paper can be used to slowly display facts or information on transparencies, which is a good way of focusing on a fact or pacing the session.

Overlay technique

A series of two or more transparencies placed on top of each other in sequence to build up a picture.

Liquid crystal display (LCD) projectors are used with electronic/ interactive boards, computers or video/DVD machines to display information to learners. They are either portable or ceiling mounted and offer a high quality method of display. They are, however, expensive and not available in all teaching rooms. In order to use them efficiently and connect them correctly, a teacher needs to be trained in how to use the software and associated equipment and cables.

As projectors rely on an electricity supply and electronic components to operate them you should always check that they are working before the start of the session. You are advised to have a back-up plan just in case the equipment is faulty. Your organisation should also check that they are safe to use (portable appliance testing – PAT), and may insist that personal equipment has been safety checked.

Using overhead transparencies (2)	
Advantages	*Disadvantages*
Colourful	Prone to breakdown
Interactive	Slightly noisy to use
Can pace learning	Needs window blinds or dimmed
Versatile	lights to be clearly visible
Easy to use (OHP)	Light from projector can shine in
Professional	teacher's eyes

Hints:

- Use sentence case when preparing slides
- Stand to one side and face learners
- Do not overcrowd slides
- Read from projector not viewing board
- Use legible font style and size

Note: Creating PowerPoint presentations uses similar skills to making OHTs, although it is a more modern and professional style; they can also include animations which add interest. Beware of 'death by PowerPoint'

Handouts

The most commonly used resource due to availability of photocopying and printing facilities. Their versatility makes them useful in the classroom as information sheets, records of key words, *aides-memoire,* question sheets or notes pages. When creating a handout, the teacher should always consider the purpose of the resource:

- Is it to be used to support the session or as additional information?
- Are learners expected to write on it?
- Does it need hole-punching to put into files?
- Would it be better with pictures?
- Does it comply with copyright guidance?
- Is it user-friendly and does it respect **equality of opportunity**?
- Is the writing legible?
- Will learners read it or just file it?
- Would coloured paper or coloured font make it clearer to read?

- Would it be better enlarged onto A3-sized paper?
- Would it be enhanced by borders, bullet points etc.?

There are several different types of handout, the main ones being:

Information sheets. Usually text based, but there is a danger that they will be distributed and filed before being read and understood, thus rendering them useless in terms of learning. If a handout is used in that way it is a waste of paper! It would be better to write key words, maybe using a bullet format and have plenty of white space on the sheet for learners to annotate with meaning, paraphrasing or similar explanations. Or ask learners to highlight key words as you are discussing the topic. Hole punch handouts before issuing to learners – it saves time whilst waiting for the hole punch to follow the distribution and/or saves them falling out of their files on the way home!

Gapped handouts are ideal as a means of differentiating information according to ability. They can be used to aid learning by getting learners to complete them during discussions or as a test to check that a topic is understood. For example:

Text	Level	Strategy
'Resources are the equipment and aids that a teacher or learner will use to promote learning. They can be classified in the same way that learner styles are classified and therefore a teacher will be able to choose resources to meet individual needs (differentiated). The more senses a resource affects, the more useful it will be' (see p. 56).	Difficult	Omit words. 'Resources are … and … that a…. Or learner use to … learning. The more … a resource affects, the more … it will be.'
	Average	Omit words – leave correct number of dashes to replace letters. 'The more ------ a resource affects, the more ------ it will be.'
	Easy	Omit words – leave first letter and dashes to replace words. 'The more s----- a resource affects, the more u----- it will be.'
	Very simple	As above but list the missing words at bottom of sheet. 'The more s----- a resource affects, the more u----- it will be.' useful, senses

Help sheets are a means of developing learning by interacting with the learners. By leaving white space on the page, learners can be encouraged to add their own notes. The printing of PowerPoint slides as 'handouts – three per page' is a very professional style of presentation. Add label tags to diagrams so that learners can complete them as you say the words or copy them from the board as you complete them. Just the simple strategy of leaving lines under a question for the learners to answer, helps them to understand how much to write in their response.

Posters and display materials are useful tools to consolidate learning. They can be created by learners, who will, hopefully, be quite proud to display their work, or created by the teacher. A poster displayed in the room will be looked at during the class as eyes and concentration wanders; the content is then subconsciously noted. It is a good way of using colour to stimulate learning and is seen as a fun exercise rather than hard work.

Teachers can laminate key handouts to ensure that they are kept in pristine condition, small activities used with learners will also keep longer if preserved by laminating them.

Models and games

These offer visual and kinaesthetic learners the opportunity to see or feel an item, albeit a model. A model is three-dimensional and can be a tactile way of looking at something. Games provide fun activities to experience or practice topics. Think about how different spelling tests would become using word games rather than a pen and paper. However, games and models tend to be expensive and the use of a particularly costly item has to be supervised. There are also problems associated with obtaining and storing such things.

Audiovisual resources

For example, DVD, video, slide shows. These are frequently used resources and offer good ways of visualising an activity or initiating discussion. They are usually of a high standard. If recording items from the television or radio, you should ensure that you have the necessary permissions for use. The teacher should prepare well – it is not usually just popping the thing into the recorder or projector. A good lesson around a video or DVD will have a list of prepared discussion points or questions. This focuses the learner on things to look for during the screening and a basis for a later discussion or question activity. The necessary equipment must be available: this might mean hiring equipment or moving to a room with equipment already in it. In most cases there will be a key involved – who's got it? Where is it? What will I do if it doesn't work?

Again, as with teaching and learning activities, the success of resources will be *variety*: variety in terms of resources used and the way in which the teacher uses them, but also in terms of meeting needs of learners.

ACTIVITY 2

Personal Development

Ask (your mentor) where you can borrow specialist equipment. For example a portable overhead projector?

Practice preparing some handouts/overhead transparencies. Try different types, e.g. a handwritten type, a printed type, and then make them useful for two different ability levels.

Check your spelling and grammar skills by asking a colleague to proofread for you.

Do an assessment to identify your IT skills.

Glossary of terms

Autonomy independence in the ability to learn

Autonomous learner one who requires minimal guidance from the teacher

Blended learning a mixture of traditional and computer learning technologies

Buzz group activities small groups interact with the teacher to gather answers

Diagnostic assessment assessment used to identify capability or skill level

Dyscalculia associated with difficulties in making sense of numbers and calculations

Dyslexia associated with a difficulty in reading or interpreting words and symbols

Embedded fixed firmly in the vocational context

Equality of opportunity legislation and focus on gender, age, culture etc.

Facilitator one who supports or stimulates learning

ICT Information communication technology

ILT Information learning technology

IT Information technology

Jigsaw group activities small groups discuss different themes within a topic, which are collated by the teacher at the end of the activity

Learning to gain knowledge or a skill; what the learners do during the session

OHP overhead projector

OHT overhead transparency

Snowball (pyramid) group activities pairs discuss then form gradually larger groups to gain a consensus of opinion on a topic or subject

Teaching to impart knowledge or a skill; what the teacher does in the session

SUMMARY

In this chapter, you have covered all of the theoretical aspects of the second learning outcome in your PTLLS qualification:

Approaches to teaching and learning; functional skills; challenges and barriers to learning; the learning environment; resources.

Your Personal Development

You will have had the opportunity to compare many different types of teaching and learning methods and resources and consider how they will be used in your learning sessions.

You will have understood the need for variety to minimise boredom, increase motivation and meet the different needs of your learners and how your teaching, the environment and your resource choices influence this.

You have learned about functional skills and the many ways they are referred to in the staff room and carried out an activity to embed them into your sessions and map them to qualifications.

You can now use DELTA to categorise barriers and challenges to learning and devise ways to use teaching and learning methods, resources and personal skills to minimise them, resulting in learners who are eager to learn.

Finally, you have looked around you to check if the area in which you work is suitable to learning and provides an engaging and stimulating environment.

You should be able to answer questions relating to:

- Explaining ways to embed elements of functional skills in your specialist area
- Explaining why you have made choices of teaching and learning approaches and use of resources, justifying your strategies, and
- demonstrate a selection of teaching and learning approaches to engage and motivate learners in your teaching sessions.

CHAPTER 3
(PTLLS, UNIT 3)

Session planning skills

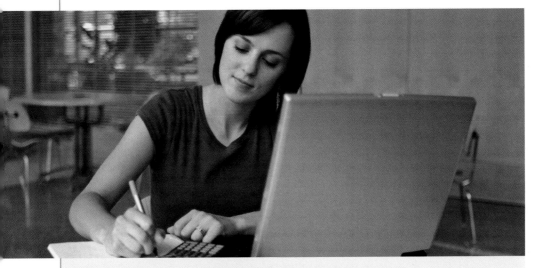

LEARNING OBJECTIVES

In this chapter you will learn about:

- Schemes of work
- Preparing and structuring session plans
- How to meet the individual needs of your learners
- Different types of learner groups
- The Educational Maintenance Allowance

3.1 Planning sessions

By the end of this section, you will be able to describe the key features and purpose of schemes of work, session **(lesson) plans**, how to structure them and state the difference between aims and outcomes and write meaningful statements.

First of all the basics: a scheme of work is the overall programme of study. It may last for example, one week, ten weeks or two years. It is merely a breakdown of the whole programme into smaller chunks based on the frequency of your meetings with learners. A lesson or **session** plan is a detailed description of one of those chunks in terms of how you will deliver the topic to your learners and what learning development will occur.

Neither the Scheme of Work nor the Lesson Plan is fixed. They should be considered as 'work in progress' and will alter in response to organisational and learner needs.

Scheme of work

This may be called a **scheme of work** (SoW), 'a learning programme', or 'a **programme of study**'. When you start teaching you will probably be asked to take X group in Y room and teach them Z. The first thing you must establish is what 'Z' is. If you are teaching any type of subject that is qualification based, someone, usually the organisation that issues the certificates, will already have determined what has to be taught. This is usually broken down into smaller components and you will have been employed to deliver one of those components, i.e. Z.

This may be described to you as a unit, module, subject or even its title. You should always ask to see the official content of the subject. It is usually called the **syllabus**. Once you have seen the syllabus, then, as a specialist in that subject, you will be able to break it down into smaller chunks. You will include sessions relating to what *must* be known, what *should* be known and what *could* be known (if time allows), thus creating the Scheme of Work or Programme of Study. Do not be surprised if this brings on your first panic. New teachers often doubt their knowledge in their specialist area. It is only panic. Just relax and ask yourself 'What is the first thing a new learner must understand before moving to the next?'

Remember, always move from the *known* to the *unknown* (Section 2.1).

For example, when you learnt to drive, what did you do first? Did you go backwards? No! Did you go forwards? Yes – but I bet you learnt about the controls first!

So on this simple scheme of work the first session would include some information about the pedals, switches and steering wheel. Then you would build on that and start moving off and stopping, then gears and turning etc.

This would be underpinned by the theory – importance of mirrors, what makes the vehicle go and so on, and learning the Highway Code. Can you see how this is starting to build into a 'programme of study?'

However, you may not be working to a subject which is part of a qualification. You may be delivering a recreational programme or addressing a company's training need. In this case, the strategy is the same as above but the goals (the end result) will either be determined by the learners or by the company's training manager. In this case, it is not a syllabus but specified learning outcomes. The same principles will follow. You must breakdown the **learning outcomes** (or end result) into small chunks of learning. If you are delivering a one-off training session you would not be expected to complete a scheme of work, they only really apply to multiple sessions.

You will usually be asked to write your scheme of work and present it to your line manager. It is also a good idea to present it to your learners. They are also interested in how they will progress their learning.

Why do a scheme of work?

- To identify the smaller stages of learning
- To prepare for planning of sessions
- To give structure to the learning
- To evenly distribute learning
- To identify resource needs
- To ensure variety
- To monitor progress
- To inform learners of the stages of learning
- To record proposals for learning
- To inform line managers of strategy
- To help colleagues if cover necessary
- To assist quality processes

A scheme of work should include:

1 General Information:
   - Who the group is, usually described as a qualification and/or subject. For example: First Year National Diploma, Unit 8; Intro to Watercolours, Washes; Key Skills L1 Communication; Management Information Group, Intro to Software.
   - Location and Duration of meetings. A record of how often, where and how long sessions are. For example: Monday 9.30 to 11.30 (30 weeks – Room LG004); or Wednesday 7.00 to 9.00 Autumn Term – Apple Centre; or 9.00 till 13.00 in the MIS room.

2 Aims and outcomes of the programme. Detail about what the end result of the programme will be, written from both the teacher's and the learners viewpoints.

3 Content and structure:
   - Brief detail about the content of each session
   - Details about the teaching and learning methods to be used

- Links to functional skills
- Information about assessment of learning.

4 Additional information:

- Examination or assessment practice
- Revision periods
- Assessment planning sessions
- Progress or tutorial sessions
- Assignment or catch-up workshops
- Study skills

AN EXAMPLE OF A SCHEME OF WORK PROFORMA					
Programme title:					
Programme area:			Module/unit:		
Tutor:			Duration:		
Aims and outcomes of programme:					
Assessment and qualification:					
Wk	Topic	Method	Resource	Functional skills	Assessment method
1					
2					
3					
4					
etc					

The way you break down the syllabus into smaller chunks will depend on how many sessions you have allocated to the topic, the level of the learners, the complexity of the topic and the needs of the learners. The detail is usually recorded on the session/lesson plan.

The lesson plan

To fail to plan is to plan to fail

(Petty 2004: 422)

The lesson plan, usually abbreviated to LP, is the detail that relates to each session/week on your scheme of work. It states the specific expectations (outcomes) of the lesson, and provides a guide or order of work describing how the teacher will achieve those outcomes. It is the teacher's *aide-memoire*. It will help to provide structure – a beginning, middle and end, remind you of the order you have planned to do things, how you thought to do it and what you have planned and prepared to support you in the session. It will be there in case you forget where you've got to, it will remind you of what is left to do – and provide you with the opportunity to reflect on which bits worked and which bits did not. By timing the activities it will help you to ensure that you have the correct amount of work for the time allowed. This is usually a second period of panic. Have I got enough stuff? Have I got too much? Again, this is perfectly normal – and with practice comes more accuracy in pacing your lesson. If you want a comfort zone then plan an activity that goes in to the lesson if time allows or can come out if you run out of time, i.e. give yourself a contingency plan.

Things to consider when writing a lesson plan

1 What is the purpose of the session?

2 What do you (the teacher) want out of the session (aim)?

3 What do you want/need your learners to get out of the session (outcome)?

4 Who are your learners?

5 How will you differentiate your teaching?

6 What order will you need to teach things in?

7 How will you keep learners interested?

8 What will be the ratio of teacher- and learner-centred activities?

9 How long is the session?

10 How far into the course/programme is this session?

11 What has happened before?

12 How long will each activity last?

13 What accommodation and resources will you want to use?

14 How will you know that learning has occurred?

15 What contingency plan do you have?

Let's think about putting all of those answers into your lesson plan. Here is a typical format, but you will probably find that your organisation has already got a form that is in regular use.

LESSON PLAN

Teacher	Date
Course/level/year of group	

Subject	Time
Number	Age *14–16 16–18 19+*

Previous knowledge

Write here what the learners already know, for example: key words and similar skills/knowledge. Always remember to move from the known to the unknown so this section is your starting point

Aim of session

Should be written from the teacher's perspective, for example – understand about..., be aware of... know about...

Outcomes of session

Should be written from the learners perspective, for example:

By the end of this session, the learner will be able to ...
Describe, write, explain, state etc i.e. measurable statements/verbs
Alternative expression is 'objectives' which means the same thing

Outcomes assessed by

How you will know that learning has occurred in this session?

Content	Method
Firstly – Share lesson outcomes with learners	List here the teaching and learning methods you plan to use. Remember variety.
Secondly – Introduction (x minutes) Then – Development (x minutes) Next – Conclusion (x minutes) Finally – Summary (x minutes)	

Resources	Planned differentiation
List the resources you need to deliver the session	How are you going to meet the needs of individuals in your session?

> Lesson evaluation
>
> This section would be completed soon after the session, and the teacher would talk about what worked and what didn't work. Was there too much, not enough? Which bit was understood well and which bit might have to be revisited? What would be done differently next time? Were the learning outcomes met?

Aims, objectives and outcomes

In the sections about schemes of work and lesson plans, the expression 'aims and outcomes' has been used repeatedly.

The word **aim** is used as a general statement of intent, usually written from the teacher's perspective. For example 'to raise awareness of the use of filing systems'. As you can see this is really describing the topic: it does not say to what extent a learner should be aware, or the types of filing systems to be included. It is a very broad topic. Other words you may use when writing aims are 'to know about', 'to understand', or 'to appreciate'. These are very general words and can be used to indicate the type of topic or subject that is about to be taught. As it is almost impossible to measure someone's knowledge, understanding or how much they value or appreciate something, these words cannot be used as outcomes.

The word **objective** is a smaller chunk or more specific statement relating to how the aims will be delivered, they are written as a measurable statement, usually expressed as an outcome. An outcome would use words – verbs – to describe what the learner will be able to do. For example 'to list the main types of storage systems used in a legal office'. The statement is an outcome because the word 'list' is measurable. You would be able to do an activity to find out (measure) whether or not the students can 'list' or not. Other words that can be used when writing outcomes are:

Analyse, bake, compare, demonstrate, explain, fill in, gather, highlight, identify, justify, knit, list, make, note, outline, plan, question, research,

ACTIVITY 1

Which of these statements are aims and which are outcomes?

1 To know about exhausts

2 To list the names of six organisations…

3 To gain knowledge of the digestive system

4 To label a two-dimensional diagram

5 To save and print a document

6 To understand the development of a child

7 To explain the Theory of Relativity

8 To prepare a trial balance

9 To investigate the role of the Royal Marines

10 To state four types of root vegetable*

*Answers: 1, 3 and 6 are aims, the rest are outcomes

state, translate, use, visit, write, extract, y, z (you can do the last two for yourself!) See also the command words section in Appendix C: Study Skills (p. 376).

3.2 Planning to meet individual needs

By the end of this section, you will be able to explain your choice of appropriate strategies to meet the needs of individuals in your sessions.

The way you choose to teach your sessions will depend on a number of factors, but the primary factor should be influenced by your learners. As teachers we need to ensure that as well as us 'doing our stuff' in the classroom, the learners must be 'learning our stuff' too! This is done by meeting their needs. In the previous two sections we have considered how we select teaching and learning methods, resources and how previous experiences of learning influence learners and what we need to do to overcome this. In future sections (Section 7.4) we will investigate some useful theories to support the need to meet learner's needs. Strategies are varied according to how learners like to learn and the simplest way of ensuring variety is to remember that learners learn using their senses and will respond to things that they can see (visual learners), hear (auditory learners), or do (kinaesthetic learners). In any class you teach, there will be a mixture of these preferred styles and therefore to meet the needs of all of your learners you must mix and match your teaching and resource selections.

Things that appeal to visual learners are:

- Videos/DVDs
- Handouts
- Demonstrations.

Things that appeal to auditory learners are:

- Teacher talk (verbal exposition)
- Lectures
- Tape recordings
- Oral questioning.

Things that appeal to kinaesthetic learners are:

- Work sheets
- Discussion
- Workshop (practical) activities.

When planning a lesson, you need to think about your learners and what you are going to do to meet their needs. Here are some examples of things you may need to plan when preparing your lessons.

Things to write when planning for differentiated strategies on your lesson plan:

- Abigail and Sunita need to complete assignment task three
- Use nominated questioning to challenge learners
- Support learners struggling with activity by doing 1:1 support
- Prepare handouts for William on A3 paper
- Extension exercises in case Peter and Sarah finish quickly
- Give feedback to Iain, Jessica and Faisal on how to improve their assignment grade
- Two learners require large font task sheet

- B needs to have handouts copied onto pale yellow paper
- Arrange learners into ability groups for task 2
- Level 3 learners to work with Level 2 learners in salon
- George, Joseph to library to continue research, Petra away last week needs intro to task, rest continue with task sheet
- Use screenshot handout for Level 1 learners

As you can see, this will only work if you really know your learners and are methodical about recording their progress. However, it is also important to remember that good teachers have been working in this way for many years and it is only recently that there has been a name for this style of teaching. So, continue 'patrolling' your classroom or workshop, pausing to advise or correct learners and, working with mixed levels of ability within the same classroom. Nothing new in this respect, but now you can record it on your lesson plan as differentiation.

3.3 The learning context

By the end of this section, you will be able to describe the many types of learning **domains** within the post-compulsory sector.

Teaching 14–16 year olds

Further Education (FE) colleges are working with schools to offer a **vocational** programme of study as an alternative option to academic study; this is called 'The Increased Flexibility Programme'. Teachers in FE may teach younger learners within their institution or they may be required to teach in partnership with schools. The strategies of teaching are the same, but younger learners have different needs and the teacher should bear these in mind when preparing their sessions.

Some of the differences that a younger learner will see are:

- Classes are longer in FE timetables
- FE is less teacher-dominated
- Learners are treated as adults – although their immaturity sometimes restricts the development of independence
- Children are still developing emotionally and may act before thinking
- Instances of vocational programme being seen as second to academic routes
- Shift of teaching from teacher-dependent models to learner-centred independent strategies
- Older learners in classrooms
- Unsupervised periods (breaks, lunch, etc.).

Which may result in:

- Fear
- Lack of confidence
- Noisy outbursts
- Disruptive behaviour
- Transitional problems concerned with moving from school to FE environments.

So the teacher should:

- Increase the importance of analysis of individual learning styles and creating individual learning plans (ILPs) to chart progress
- Deliver an induction to introduce the differences between school and FE
- Create and maintain classroom rules
- Devise small chunks of activity to maintain interest, promote motivation and increase self-esteem

- Offer plenty of variety in classes
- Initiate relevant support mechanisms
- Follow recommendations to promote the care of younger learners, Protection of Children Act (1999), Every Child Matters and *in loco parentis* – duty of care.
- Prepare learners for the world of work
- Use rewards and sanctions to control behaviour
- Be patient; be in control (firm but fair)
- Praise and encourage at every opportunity
- Use strategies to develop rapport and mutual respect.

Teaching 16–19 year olds

Programmes for this age group are generally either vocationally based or **academic** subjects. Learners usually come into their programme of study from school and the main provider is the further education sector. Courses tend to be full-time and are funded by the Learning and Skills Council (LSC). Priority areas are based on national and local skills needs and funding is allocated accordingly. This leads to colleges having to plan their curriculum offer according to trends. Provision that is not a funding priority is offered on a self-financing basis. Academic subjects, for example A levels, are usually, but not exclusively, delivered within sixth form colleges or schools.

The needs of the age group are often very similar to those of the 14–16 groups. As they are usually entering directly from school, there has to be a period of personal development towards adulthood, and of course hormones play a big part in influencing behaviour at this age!

There is an assumption (remember that first rule!) that learners entering at 16 are following their chosen career path and are eager to learn skills which will prepare them for employment. Teachers involved with this age group, especially if on a vocational programme, are usually practitioners in the subject and have moved into teaching; this brings a wealth of technical knowledge into the classroom.

Teaching adults

The term given to teaching adults is **andragogy** (how adults learn) as distinct from how children learn. Adult teaching tends to be more learner-centred. Adults may come into the environment on work-related training sessions or in recreational evening sessions. The teacher should remember that adults come into education with a range of life skills and previous educational experiences. They are generally independent and usually have clear goals for their learning – although there will be some variations (see Section 2.3, Challenges and barriers to learning).

Adults expect:

- To be treated as adults
- Their teaching sessions to be relevant to their learning goals
- To be taught in a way that motivates them and meets their needs.

There are different beliefs in expectations when it comes to the teachers role; some adults expect the teacher to teach them, via loads of handouts and teacher-led sessions – maybe similar to their own learning background. Others are independent and just need the teacher to facilitate their learning (learner-centred). Your role as the teacher is to identify this and reflect it in your choice of teaching strategies and promote a shared responsibility to learning.

Adult and community learning

Recreational or social learning used to be within the funding responsibility of Local Education Authorities. Then in 1998 the Adult and Community Learning Fund was established with the aim of widening and increasing the participation in learning and improving the standards of basic skills. The fund set out to support those who would not normally participate in education or training and took learning out into the community, rather than expecting the community to come to learning establishments. There were clear links between learning and social regeneration. The Fund ceased in

2004 when it was taken over by the Learning and Skills Council, with broadly the same mandate. However, in 2006 came a different funding methodology with priorities given to younger learners, with the result that less funding was available to adult community learning. Now, any provision offered is usually based on a self-financing strategy, which in some areas has resulted in a significant decrease in courses offered for recreational or personal interest outcomes.

Work-based learning

Work-based learning (**WBL**) is the term used to identify those learners who are on government-sponsored training programmes, as opposed to work-based training (WBT), which refers to in-service training and development. There are initiatives to support young people to train for employment as well as schemes to support those who are unemployed or inactive and equip them with the skills they need to re-enter the world of work. There are/have been Youth Training Schemes (YTS), New Deal, Apprenticeships and Train to Gain as well as work-related foundation degrees. Whilst work-based learning schemes are usually associated with 16– to 24–year-olds, they are not limited solely to that age group.

Generally the programmes are a method of gaining employability skills through a combination of work-based practice and training, which is usually day-release type at the premises of a training provider. Training providers may be private training companies, small or large organisations or FE colleges; the link is the commitment to work with employers to ensure a skilled workforce. The skills are usually measured using qualifications such as National Vocational Qualifications (NVQs), technical certificates, and/or key skills, and are enhanced by training allowances. These used to be on a par with other government benefits paid to the trainees, but now employers are encouraged to recruit unqualified staff and pay them fair salaries, whilst receiving sponsored training. This has eliminated a lot of the 'cheap labour' arguments, and offering recognised qualifications has seen value and worth develop into the provision.

Educational maintenance allowance

The Educational Maintenance Allowance (**EMA**) is a means-tested allowance paid to those over 16 who wish to remain in full-time education but are concerned about the financial implications of doing so. It pays an amount (£30.00 – 2007) to support the cost of books, travel and equipment per week, per learning programme, based on satisfactory performance. Bonuses are paid for learners who meet progress and achievement targets.

The payments are not related to monies paid through Learner Support Fund or any other financial help paid to students.

Glossary of terms

Academic relating to education, school or scholarships

Aim a broad statement of intent

Andragogy how adults learn

Domain as area or section of learning; a classification

EMA Educational Maintenance Allowance – a grant paid to learners to support their further education

Learning outcome the result of a learning session

Lesson plan a written structure for a session

Objective a specific statement of intended outcome

Programme of study a structured list of sessions

Scheme of work a document listing sessions within a programme

Session a period of learning

Syllabus the structure of a qualification

Vocational Skills related to employment

WBL work-based learning – learning that takes place predominantly in the workplace

SUMMARY

In this chapter, you have covered all of the theoretical aspects of the third learning outcome in your PTLLS qualification:

Demonstrating session planning skills; planning sessions; planning to meet individual needs; exploring the learning context.

Your Personal Development

You can explain the meaning of the expressions 'scheme of work' and 'lesson plan' and describe the key features of the documents. You can explain the difference between an aim (what the teacher hopes the session is about) and an outcome (what the learner gains from the session) and can prepare plans to meet your requirements.

You can state why planning and preparation is important in relation to variety in sessions, and differentiating activities according to the needs of your learners. You should also be aware of some of the expressions used on lesson plans.

You can identify the different types of learners that attend establishments within the post-compulsory sector and discuss the main factors that influence their delivery.

You should now be able to create documents relating to:

- Producing learning programmes/schemes of work within a specific subject area and to a particular type of learner.
- Devising lesson plans which include aims and outcomes, planned differentiation and a range of teaching and learning methods and resources appropriate to the subject being delivered, which
- Prepares you to teach in a teaching session.

CHAPTER 4
(PTLLS, UNIT 4)

Motivation and inclusion

LEARNING OBJECTIVES

In this chapter you will learn about:

- How to manage your learning environment
- What will help motivate your learners
- Giving constructive and effective feedback
- Engaging your learners in learning sessions
- The key factors in successful communication
- How to evaluate your own performance

4.1 Managing the learning environment

By the end of this section, you will be able to identify factors which influence effective classroom management skills and select strategies to practice within the classroom.

> ## The teacher is the person in charge of the classroom

This may seem obvious, but you would be surprised to see how often it does not seem to be so. Managing learning is usually associated with behaviour and is therefore referred to when dealing with younger (i.e. under 19 years old) learners. However, managing the learning environment is broader than behaviour. Remembering our rule about assumption, adults also are entitled to and will always demand a well-managed environment. The teacher is the one who, as well as teaching in a well prepared, varied, inspirational and exciting manner, addressing the needs of every individual in their group:

- Keeps control of learners
- Maintains the immediate cleanliness and tidiness of the room
- Cleans the boards
- Reports broken or dangerous equipment or furniture
- Ensures a safe and secure learning environment
- Prepares for any/all eventualities
- Is a role model for acceptable standards of behaviour
- Develops learners

- Sets and secures agreement to codes of conduct
- Ensures security is maintained
- Keeps an eye on the clock
- Determines the frequency and duration of breaks
- Offers guidance, support and counselling services.

If all of this happens, the teacher can consider themselves the 'person in charge'. By putting all of this together, the learners will learn in a manner designed to get the best and most efficient learning available. Unfortunately, I witness an increasing culture of blame and despondency:

'It was a mess when I walked in' or 'It was already broken'. Not the cries of a teenager, but a 'professional' teacher.

'The learners are getting worse' – or are they just unsure of the boundaries and nobody guides them into classroom or learning readiness?

'What time can we have a break?' – usually asked within 30 seconds of the learners entering the classroom, and repeated at two minute intervals.

'The management need to see…' You might ask yourself exactly what it is you want *them* to see?

And the classic 'I haven't got time to…'

The main issues in managing a learning environment can be classified into five sections:

1 managing the classroom;
2 managing poor behaviour;
3 managing punctuality;
4 managing the workload; and
5 creating learning readiness.

Managing the classroom	
Potential issues	*Possible solutions*
Tables and chairs in a mess	Allow a few minutes at the end of the class to put chairs under tables. Set the standard.
Rubbish everywhere	Insist culprits pick up rubbish and place it in the bin. If lesson has created rubbish allow clearing up time at end.
Writing on board	Clean board at end of lesson – set an example.
Something broken or damaged	Ensure danger does not impact on your learners and report issue to the site team, admin staff or line manager. Never assume someone has already reported it.
Coats and bags lying around	Identify and instruct learners to place bags etc. in a particular place.
Ambience of room	Display student work to create a sense of ownership and introduce a colourful area. Change displays regularly. Remove clutter. Keep it tidy and encourage learners to participate in this process.

Hint:

Always leave a room as you would wish to find it.

Managing poor behaviour
'It's war out there'
'They're out to get you'
Sue Cowley (2003: 52, 83)

Potential issues

Learners talking at the same time as you

Confrontational behaviour

Learners refuse to work

Learners don't come to class ready to work

Phones/iPods on etc.

Possible solutions

Remember that learners have opted to behave in this way. You can cope! Keep calm; be clear about what you expect by setting targets; reward good behaviour, ignore bad; be consistent; have plenty of short, varied activities; keep supplies of pens/paper; use silence or counting strategies to gain their attention, identify sanctions and rewards and initiate them when using the 'do or else' speech.

There are two stages to dealing with poor behaviour. First you should try:

1 Patience and nurturing. Setting standards by role modelling and listening to reasons, yet setting and agreeing targets and rewards. For example 'If you write (set amount), you can (listen to music for x minutes/go to break/talk).' You may wish to try peer involvement – get the group to design and agree the rules and suggest collective responsibility for adhering to them.

2 As a last resort start the 'warning cycle'. Issue a warning, then warn again with what will happen if non-compliant, a repeat means that you should follow through with the sanction (penalty). The level of sanction should reflect the seriousness of the misdemeanour.

Never look scared or argue and never shout or swear. Be assertive not aggressive. Remember 'The Look' – you know the one your mother/partner used to give you! If you still have problems, ask a colleague to observe you and offer suggestions.

Managing punctuality

Potential issues	*Possible solutions*
Learners arrive late	First of all consider the impact this has on you, the late learner and the rest of the group. This will influence the action needed.
Do you set a good example by *always* being in the classroom before the time the learners are expected?	Challenge – why are you late?
	Answer – bus, family, doctors, ugh!
Do you permit the latecomer to disrupt the lesson? Worse still, do you encourage lateness by starting the lesson again, so they can catch up!	The answer determines the action, but you should do the challenge quickly, and not allow the interruption to impact on the rest of the group. Ask the late learner to settle quickly and ignore it until an appropriate time. Then elicit more info and deal with it appropriately.
	Occasional lateness by someone who quietly enters, says sorry and settles just requires acknowledgement and no further action other than an explanation of what was missed and a target to catch up.
	The ugh! is showing disrespect and if continuous and disruptive you need to follow the warning cycle (a warning, warning and sanction issue, then sanction implementation).

Managing the workload

Potential issues	*Possible solutions*
Coping with mixed abilities in group sessions	Know your learners and plan for differentiation. (**VAK**, varied activities and resources, different tasks.)

Managing the workload	
Potential issues	*Possible solutions*
Time	Prioritise your work and keep a 'to do' list. Set yourself targets and if someone asks you to do something, be realistic in telling them when it will be done. Better to work like this than be known as unreliable.
Session Preparation	Allow time to do photocopying, printing etc., always have contingency plans in case an electrical/technological piece of equipment doesn't work.
Marking	If you set classwork or homework, you must be prepared to collect it in and mark it promptly with feedback. Try marking work sheets in the class using nominated questioning, swapping papers or issuing answer sheets to prevent the need to take it away from the room.
Disruptive learners or colleagues	You will never change the behaviour of another person, but you can change the way *you* deal with them. Try using strategies like repeat, recap, writing things down, asking for clarification or further explanation. This helps you to take control of the situation.
Organisation	Keep a diary. Note when you promise to do something. Record when marking needs to be returned or lessons must be prepared. List when deadlines are.

Creating readiness to learn	
Potential issues	*Possible solutions*
Learners do not know how to behave in the classroom. Issues around: ● attendance, punctuality ● meeting targets ● paper and pens ● respecting others ● being responsible for themselves and others ● planning their own learning ● handing in work on time ● listening ● factual comprehension/ retention	The teacher has to teach these skills (in addition to the content of their subject). Much will be done by role modelling, some by spoon-feeding and some by 1:1 tutorials to set targets. Rules and boundaries are important here to set the standard. You may need to bring a supply of paper and pens to stop the disruption of 'I can't do it because …'. Guide learners into making notes by devising handouts with white space. Encourage learners to reflect on what they have achieved at the end of the session and target their own learning in workshops.

4.2 Strategies to motivate learners

By the end of this section, you will be able to describe the key methods to improve **motivation** in learners and relate this to simple theory.

Don't smile till Easter

This was once believed to be the absolute motivator; fair, firm and focused sessions without deviation. However, this is not the 1960s and the current thinking in the post-compulsory sector is empathy, understanding and negotiation. Irrespective of your opinions with regard to these two strategies, the teacher remains the initiator of learning and to do this you need a willing and receptive audience, i.e. learners who are motivated. You the teacher, also need to be motivated; motivated to make a difference in someone's life. Motivation is concerned with the learner's desire (or need) to participate in the learning process.

One of the simplest theories associated with motivation that can be applied to learning is the work of Abraham Maslow. In 1954 he investigated the motivation of workers and this can be applied to learners. In order for a worker (or learner in our profession) to achieve their goals and aspirations, they need to go through a development of basic needs, e.g. comfort, safety, belonging and self-esteem. This is Maslow's Hierarchy of Needs. The chart is usually presented as a pyramid, with the pinnacle or goal being self-actualisation, but I would like to look at it in reverse, that is, starting at the beginning …

Let us consider the effects of this theory on the learner. In order to be receptive to learning, Maslow's theory suggests that a learner needs to address:

Figure 4A	Maslow's Hierarchy of Needs interpreted to reflect learner needs. The Back to Basics model.

Physical comfort	The basics of hunger, thirst and sleep are met. The environment is adequately lighted and heated making the surroundings comfortable

Safety and shelter	Working in an environment that has clear boundaries and rules to ensure fairness, safety and developing a confidential, trusting rapport and well-being

Love and belonging	Working in a friendly, caring environment, interacting and communicating, having a good rapport with others

Self-esteem	Feelings of pride, respect, achievement, independence, dignity, encouraged through feedback and praise

Self-actualisation	Feelings of fulfilment, encouragement, optimism, and able to transfer skills and knowledge

In the classroom this is applied usually without any conscious decisions, especially at the lower level. As teachers we talk to learners, create rules, encourage respect and value others' opinions. Our learners respond (i.e. become motivated) by doing what should be considered natural in polite society. It could therefore be argued that failure to comply with acceptable standards of behaviour could (and usually does) affect motivation and subsequent learning. Motivation is simply learners wanting to learn.

To improve motivation, the teacher should:

- Ensure that the learning environment is comfortable (temperature, light, furniture), safe and business-like.
- Ensure that breaks are regular to allow food and refreshments to be consumed. It may be worth noting here that parental support may be needed to encourage younger learners to get enough sleep and eat breakfast before commencing their learning day. Note also that some foods and drinks have been proven to have a detrimental effect on learning and behaviour.
- Create a good **rapport** with learners. Learning is a shared responsibility in so far as the learner will allow it to be so.
- Devise classroom rules for attendance, behaviour, conduct and assessment, etc.
- Know your learners. Devise teaching strategies which are of interest to them and are learner-centred.
- Explain the purpose of the lesson, creating an organised and structured learning environment.
- Plan for variety.
- Create short-term targets which are achievable. Consider incentives to reward achievement.
- Make no assumptions.
- Ensure learners are ready to learn.
- Be prepared to help learners with 'how to learn' skills.
- Support those who are struggling; offer challenges to those who are more able. Keep everyone busy.
- Praise success. Give interim feedback in a constructive manner.

- Encourage learners to identify their own goals and have ownership of their own development.

- Recognise that motivation may cause anxiety and that will also need to be dealt with.

By creating a motivational culture, the art of teaching is made easier. However, you must also expect occasional lapses. These barriers have been explained in detail in Section 2.3, but in summary will occur when learners are influenced by:

- Peer pressure

- Hormonal imbalance

- Changes in personal or domestic surroundings

- Work/life imbalance.

Motivation can be described as **intrinsic** or **extrinsic**. When a learner is inspired by learning for its own sake, or just wants to do something they are intrinsically (internally) motivated. The opposite are said to be extrinsically (externally) motivated; those learners who are learning because they need to or in order to do something. This reinforces the fact that by knowing your learners you will have an idea of why they are there, and that will result in different motivational strategies. Someone who is intrinsically motivated already has the desire to achieve, whereas the extrinsically motivated learner needs more praise in order to create the desire to continue.

Intrinsic	Extrinsic
● Recreational learners ● Career learners ● Self-directed progression	● Needs a qualification ● Needs a job ● Needs more money

There will be further opportunities to look at the theories relating to motivation as you progress in your learning.

4.3 Effective feedback

By the end of this section, you will be able to recognise the value of effective feedback and use a model of giving feedback in a constructive way.

A key to successful development of potential, increasing motivation and assessment is concerned with giving feedback. Feedback is part of the learning process, because it tells the learner how they are doing. The quality of the feedback is as important as the quality of the teaching. Feedback should be frequent and meaningful. There are two types.

The praise and criticism model is that which is based on personal judgements and is therefore subjective. The constructive feedback model is objective, because it is based on specifics and related to the assessment against standards or **criteria**. Constructive feedback can be positive, when good practice is praised. The teacher will appreciate and value what has been done and comment on how well it has been achieved. Constructive feedback can be negative when improvement needs are discussed. Giving negative feedback does not mean giving the feedback in a negative (i.e. unsupportive) way. The teacher should not use sarcasm or anger. Be helpful – start with a positive statement and then comment on the improvements that are needed.

The typical feedback conversation:

Feedback should always be planned and thought about carefully.

- State what the standard is or what the assessment was about. Describe what has been observed or reviewed, without sidetracking.
- Make a comment about what has been achieved.
- Offer alternatives like: have you considered …, you could try … Avoid 'BUT'. This muddles what you are trying to say and confuses the message. 'It was OK, but …' *(Is it OK or not?)*
- Summarise the key achievements. Make and state your judgement – you meet/don't meet the standards, you've passed or you need more practice.

Feedback should be offered on a one-to-one and as privately as possible. The feedback should be immediate or at the very least as soon as possible.

If circumstances mean that feedback cannot be immediate, then tell the learner when it will be possible. For example after the shift, when it quietens down a bit, when you get your next break, etc.

A watch point:

Don't get over enthusiastic with the praise; it is far more effective when offered as a result of something achieved, rather than responding to everything as 'brill!'

4.4 Participation and engagement in the learning environment

By the end of this section, you will be able to describe ways to **engage** learners to participate effectively in learning sessions.

Participation, and the extent to which all learners participate in the class, is the question that any observer in your classroom will comment upon. The observer, parent or employer needs to know that everyone in the class has an opportunity to contribute.

Some of the strategies for this are:

Nominated questioning

This is teacher-led questioning and aims to ensure that everyone has the opportunity to answer questions. It uses a technique of posing a question, pausing, whilst learners think of the answer and finally nominating a learner to offer the answer.

Differentiated tasks

To ensure each learner can succeed and achieve to the best of their ability

Jigsaw, snowball (pyramid) group work

Different types of activities to encourage everyone to contribute to a discussion point and be listened to. Jigsaw activities are those where different groups have different questions, the teacher then consolidates the discussion and findings to ensure everyone is aware of concepts. Snowball (also known as pyramid) is a group activity which starts in individual thought; shared with a partner; shared with another pair, until a group consensus is formed.

Buzz groups

These activities are used to consolidate individual thoughts which are transcribed, usually by the teacher, onto a board. Use a 'play or pass' strategy with learners each contributing one thought from their list until their lists (thoughts) are exhausted. You could try variations such as a 'graffiti wall', where learners write their ideas on sections of plain wallpaper which is fastened to the wall – they may use words or pictures to express their thoughts. Or try drawing a brick on an A4 sheet and photocopying it, then issue it to learners so that they can write their thoughts onto the bricks. They can then be fastened to the wipe-board as a wall of ideas and discussed by the group.

Gapped handouts and worksheets

Instead of just stuffing a handout into a file, a learner has to **interact** with it. This helps personal note-taking skills which helps with retention of knowledge. Different types or levels of handout can be designed to differentiate between learner needs.

Quizzes and games

A fun way of learning. Scrabble is good for spelling and competitiveness can be introduced by organising team Scrabble with extra points for a specialist word. Word-searches, crosswords and Sudoku are good as **openers**, concluders or while waiting for others to catch-up, and help development of functional skills. A paper dice can be made to initiate questions as recap or lesson summaries, far more interesting than a test.

ACTIVITY 1

Ask a colleague or your mentor to analyse your interactions with learners.

A simple mark (/) chart next to a learners seating position will record the number of times a learner contributes to the class, either by comment, answering a question or asking a question.

For example:

Figure 4B Interacting with your learners

Look at the contact within the main area of vision

Some of the watch points will be:

Those seated in direct eye contact will participate more than those on the periphery of your vision – so make conscious decisions to include those seated on the edges or hiding in the back row by using nominated questioning or by direct **intervention** when organising groups.

Less confident or lazy learners will soon realise that keeping their heads down will not create eye contact and that there is always someone eager to answer questions. Reduce the number of 'open to group' questions and develop nominated questions (i.e., pose the question, pause for a few seconds, then nominate your chosen learner to respond).

4.5 Effective communication

By the end of this section, you will be able to list the key factors which initiate successful **communication** and describe the main communication methods. You should also refer to the section on Barriers to Learning (Section 2.3).

Are you sure you are communicating with your learners?

Communication is the art of passing a message. If it is to be effective, the person receiving that message must understand it, and be able to respond to it, usually by sending another message. Think back to times when you have played Chinese whispers. Although that was usually a bit of fun, imagine if all communication became muddled during its transmission. Communication is generally in one of three ways, and within each there are different types:

Written	Verbal	Non-verbal
Long-hand Shorthand Text Images	Spoken: Direct – face-to-face Indirect – telephone	Sometimes called body language Dress Facial expression Proximity Touch

In any communication exchange the teacher should ensure that what has been offered has been understood. The teacher can do this by pausing to summarise things spoken and heard and by asking questions to get feedback from learners to ascertain that they have not only heard, but have understood and comprehended the topic.

Whilst we are on the topic of communication, here are some things to think about:

How much of a piece of writing do we actually read …?
It deosn't mttaer in waht oredr the ltteers in a wrod are, the olny iprmoatnt tihng is taht the frist and lsat ltteer is in the rghit pclae.

Text speak.
thx 4 ur help 2day ur gr8
(Thank you for your help today, you are great!)
ijwtk y ur l8 ru ok pcme
(I just want to know why you are late; are you okay? Please call me.)
Text messaging is a new language. It is perfectly acceptable for its intended purpose, or even within personal note-taking, but it is not appropriate in formal work, and it certainly does not aid the development of functional skills. Create rules for its use.

British Sign Language (BSL) is a specialist language for the deaf using hands and fingers to spell and create words. There are significantly fewer words in BSL than in English; sentences are expressed as a whole rather than in a series of words, so ensure that signers in your class receive lesson plans and outline scripts in advance of the session.

Why do people confide in their hairdresser, beautician, doctor, driving instructor?
Answer: because the barrier of proximity/touch is reduced or removed. Caution: these are managed acceptable instances of touch; society in general has an expectation of space around individuals. If you have to 'invade someone's space' always seek permission. Do you mind if …?

Spellings opener Tell the learners what the words of the session will be. Ask them to spell them onto the board. Ask each learner for one letter (they could nominate who will go next) and operate a play or pass strategy to reduce fear factor.

'Do you understand me' game? Sit learners back to back. Give one a picture or line drawing, and ask them to describe it to their partner, without saying what it is. The partner should make a replica drawing from the instructions given. This enhances skills of description and use of adjectives as well as creating a team spirit and is good fun!

Barriers to effective communication

Jargon, specialist terminology Demystify expressions by writing specialist or **jargon** words on the board (non-permanent) or why not start a 'new words' chart/poster (semi-permanent and visible) or use vocabulary or personal dictionaries (permanent but not always visible).

Level of language Maturity develops vocabulary. Younger learners haven't learnt the same number of words as more mature learners, nor do they use and understand 'big words'. Be mindful of this when creating handouts or using reference material.

Language and accent Each country or region of a country has its own pattern of words or accent. Some are more easily understood than others. Speak clearly and slowly until learners become familiar with your voice. Illness may also affect the tone and pitch of your voice.

Noise Background noise can be distracting. Computers, extraction units and machinery all give off a constant noise, which to some gradually disappears, but not all have this ability to cut out noise. Those with hearing impairments also have different tolerances to background noise.

Listening and writing Some learners can't do both at the same time. People with hearing impairment cannot lip-read and make notes. Add note-taking time to classroom or workshop activities. Some lessons include writing time and use music as a background ... when the music stops, teaching starts.

Talking and listening Speech should be at a speed which can be understood, and you may also need to allow thinking time. Time for learners to understand and comprehend – in their own words – between speaking time.

Beware of speaking when your back is turned, for example when writing on the board.

Eye contact is important to effective communication. When to speak (and stop speaking) is very often determined by eyes, pauses and tone of voice.

Summarise Go over what you have said regularly, use your voice to stress key points and pauses to allow thinking time. Tone of voice also adds interest to speech.

4.6 Improving your own performance

By the end of this section, you will be able to use self-evaluative strategies to reflect on your practice and initiate personal and professional development.

Recognition that your performance can be improved is accepting that whatever does (or does not) happen in the classroom is in the hands of the teacher. The teacher can, by changing their own actions, influence the behaviours of others. In order to be able to improve your practice, you have got to be able to analyse and evaluate it. This is asking you to really break down what has occurred and check critically if things went well or not.

A checklist is the simplest method of starting the process of reflection or improvement. It may be written after each lesson or a series of sessions or maybe in the form of a log or diary. Another method is to seek comments from a peer. Any feedback about a session is valuable. Sometimes an observer will see things you don't or give you an idea for an alternative method of doing something. Feedback and opinions can also come from learners. You may, for example, ask learners periodically, 'What is the best bit of my lesson?' or 'What was the bit you least enjoyed?'

Hopefully the answer to the first question is not 'the end' and the answer to the second question 'the start'. If it is, then you will need to become reflective and quickly seek advice from your mentor! The important thing is that the teacher gets into the habit of reflection.

EXAMPLE 1

An extract from a simple checklist for a post lesson **evaluation** might be:

Preparation and planning	Did I set outcomes for the session? Did I share those outcomes with learners?

The answers to these types of questions are usually YES or NO responses (i.e. closed questions). Therefore, there is no **analysis**. To analyse this preparation and planning section, you must ask the questions above, but then ask yourself a 'so what?' question or create an open question.

For example:
Did you set outcomes for the session? Answer *YES*
So what? *Because I shared the outcomes with my learners they were clear about the focus of the lesson and what they needed to do.*
OR
What was the effect of preparing measurable outcomes for the class?
It meant that my learners knew what the lesson was about.

Reflection can then occur. Reflection is about trying to improve things or understand cause and effect, i.e. to improve your practice. Taking our previous example, a reflective teacher might say *'and next time I will write them on the board and re-visit them at the end of the class to prove how much they've learnt in the session.'*

EXAMPLE 2

Question	Did you test that learners had learnt something in your lesson?
Analysis	The question sheet at the end of the lesson enabled me to check that learning had occurred
Evaluation	The question sheet was effective in checking learning because the questions were focused and aimed at the different abilities in the group, so that I could check the depth of learning
Reflection	The question sheet was effective and showed that all learners had grasped point A. The second point, however, was not understood by all and I need to recap this in detail next time

The main parts of the lesson that you should reflect on are:

- Planning and preparation
- Teaching methods, participation and differentiation
- Assessment methods and questioning
- Communication
- Resources.

You may also wish to reflect on:

- Tutorials
- Meetings
- Assignments (yours and theirs)
- Reading and research.

These occurrences are collectively known as 'critical incidents' and you will use your professional development journal to discuss and reflect upon them.

A typical **journal** page might look like this:

REFLECTIVE LOG

Incident

Describe the incident or event on which you want to reflect

Questions

What questions or issues does this raise?

Actions

What thoughts do you have to overcome/build on this experience? Who will help you?

Reflection

Reconsider the experience and any actions taken. What is the impact? Is the situation worse, same or better?

Learning to be a reflective practitioner is one of the key development areas for a teacher. It is hard to see things objectively, and it is equally hard to criticise your own practice without making excuses for occurrences. Seek the advice of your tutors, mentors and colleagues and learn to accept feedback as a genuine desire for self-improvement rather than a threat.

Glossary of terms

Analysis a detailed examination

Communication a means of sending and receiving information to share or exchange ideas

Criteria the standard of competence

Engage to participate or become involved in

Evaluation to form an idea about something by measuring its effectiveness

Extrinsic motivation motivation derived from outside the person

Interact to have an effect on

Intervention an interruption

Intrinsic motivation motivation from within the person: natural desire

Jargon language, words or expressions of a specialist occupation

Journal a diary

Motivation enthusiasm or interest

Opener an activity at the beginning of a session

Participation to take part in

Rapport a common understanding

Reflection a considered, opinion expressed in speech or writing; thoughts or considerations, developing ideas and thoughts

VAK visual, auditory and kinaesthetic learners – different ways learners like to learn

SUMMARY

In this chapter, you have covered all of theoretical aspects of the fourth learning outcome in your PTLLS qualification.

Managing the learning environment; strategies to motivate learners; participation and engagement in the learning environment; effective communication; improving own performance.

Your Personal Development

You have explored how the teacher needs to manage their environment and considered some strategies which may improve your own classroom management. You can explain how poor behaviour impacts on the class and describe some potential solutions. You can describe ways in which you will prepare your learners to be ready for learning.

You can describe how one theorist suggests that motivation can be improved and relate these suggestions to your own learning environment. You can state a number of ways in which motivation can be improved.

You can suggest ways of modifying your teaching and learning strategies to ensure that all learners have the opportunity to participate in your lessons. You may have sought advice from your mentor to analysis how you interact with your group of learners.

You can describe three different ways of communicating and suggest some ideas to improve or develop communication between you and your learners.

You are developing a reflective outlook on your performance and can describe ways that a reflective diary can support your own personal development. You understand the difference between evaluation and reflection and its impact on your performance.

You should now be able to answer questions relating to:

- How you would establish rules to support appropriate behaviour in your classroom
- The importance of developing respect and values
- Collect feedback from peers, learners and tutors to inform your personal development goals
- Use a self-reflection journal/log to evaluate the effectiveness of your own teaching
- Create an action plan related to your development as a trainee teacher and your teaching practice to improve your performance
- Offer constructive criticism to your peers on their performance.

CHAPTER 5
(PTLLS, UNIT 5)

Assessment and record keeping

EDUCATION PHOTOS / ALAMY

LEARNING OBJECTIVES

In this chapter you will learn about:

- The different types of assessment
- How to ensure effective assessment
- Recording observations
- Recording questioning
- Planning assignments
- The importance of tracking progress

5.1 Types of assessment methods

By the end of this section, you will be able to identify the ways that teachers assess learning and competence and describe the main methods used to do so.

Methods of assessment

Assessment is the term given to checking that learning has occurred. It may happen at any stage during the learner's progress through their qualification. It will help you to know when a concept is understood and therefore means you can move on to the next topic, or if you need to re-teach a topic. Carrying out an **initial assessment** helps you to plan appropriate sessions for your learners. You may use assessment to identify specific needs of learners and assessment should be an integral component of your teaching and lesson plans.

There are several different ways of assessing. The table below describes the main ones that you will come across. (See also Chapter 13)

Method	Description
Observation	Used in practical situations when a learner demonstrates their competence (natural performance) whilst being observed by their assessor. This is considered one of the best forms of assessment because there can be no doubts in the mind of the assessor that the learner knows how to do something. The observation should be recorded either on film or on paper. A phone with a camera is quite useful, but ensure that you have relevant permissions before photographing or filming a learner, especially if they or those around them are minors. There may be occasions when the verifier needs observational evidence to verify standards.

Method	Description
Simulation	This is similar to observation, but uses a simulated activity rather than natural performance. The rules associated with observation (above) apply. Whilst National Vocational Qualifications (**NVQ**s) do not generally support this type of evidence, there may be occasions when it is deemed appropriate, for example when using high-cost materials or in dangerous situations. You would not expect an airline pilot to be assessed on his ability to crash land in a natural performance scenario – this is best done under simulated conditions, which should mirror reality. Fire drills and first aid are other commonly simulated assessments.
Project and assignment	These are usually a series of activities which collect together to make a project or assignment. For example, task one may be a written description of something, task two may be a presentation of some findings and task three may be a booklet or poster. Generally, a project is designed by the learner and an assignment is designed by the teacher; both include a 'brief' which is related to the learning outcomes. There may be different assessment methods within an assignment or project depending on the tasks. The assessor will be assessing learning outcomes which relate to the proposed content of the assignment or project and are used during marking. Some qualifications also include levels of understanding, which are reflected in grading criteria.
Written questions	*Essays* A discussion type of question. The assessor will need detailed assessment marking plans to ensure fairness, especially if the essay is around opinion and therefore has no right or wrong answer. The teacher should also

▶

Method	Description
	consider what proportion of marks will be attributed to spelling and grammar, content, structure and argument etc. To be considered fair, these should be shared with your learners. Marking is quite complex.
	Short answer questions
	A series of questions where the answer is usually about a few sentences long. In some (state four reasons for…) types of question, only a few words are required. The marking plan should include all possible answers that could be offered by learners. These are quite easy to mark and are suitable for checking learning within a lesson or at the end of a module.
	Multiple choice questions
	A question with (usually) four answers to choose from. The learner has to identify which of the offered answers is correct. As a learner selects an answer there is little opportunity to expand or probe understanding. They are very simple to mark; the awarding body may use computers to scan answer sheets and calculate the number of correct answers. They are quite difficult to write in the first instance.
Verbal/oral questions	These are questions which try to establish depth of knowledge and are a useful assessment tool to complement observation in order to check understanding. For example, 'what would happen if…' questions. Verbal questioning is usually informal and sometimes unprepared in that the assessor sees something during an observation and wishes clarification or further information on a particular issue. Verbal questioning should be recorded on either tape or paper and the learner should sign to confirm accuracy of answers recorded. Good questioning should be of an 'open' type, which means that the learner has to think of the answer, as opposed to closed, where they are offered yes/no or true/false solutions – so could guess the answer.

Method	Description
	Using a nominated style ensures that questions can be offered to learners and pitched at a particular learner's known ability. Nominated style means that the teacher poses the question to the group, pauses so that they can all create their own answer, then nominates (or identifies) the learner to give the answer. It can be made fun by offering play or pass options to minimise embarrassment if learners do not know the answer. You may also try the 'ask a friend' strategy, in which a learner can elicit the help of someone else in the group.
Professional discussion	This is a semi-structured interview where the assessor and the learner discuss an issue and the assessor prompts the learner into answering questions related to subject outcomes. It is very often used to link workplace practice to standards of competence, for example in NVQs. It is an effective tool because an experienced assessor will lead the conversation to ensure all aspects are covered: however, **authenticity** could be questioned – did the assessor lead in a way that would elicit only correct answers? Is it really the learners own words/actions?
Self-assessment	As an informal strategy it is very common. Reading through a piece of work to ensure everything is covered before handing it in is self-assessment. As a formal assessment strategy it can be used in the format of personal statements or profiling. Both of these assessments require the learner to write down what they did or would do in a given situation; this is then linked to a set of standards or criteria. A student teacher will use this form of assessment to develop their reflective practice. There may be a witness testimony to authenticate the validity of the statements.

Assessment types

Assessment can occur at any time during a programme or course. Pre-course, initial, diagnostic, formative and summative are the words associated with assessment and to a certain extent identify the stage they are used. There is a lot of cross-over and similarity in the expressions and some differences in how teachers interpret the words.

Pre-course interview This is an interview process to assess potential or a learner's suitability for a course or programme. Younger learners may need to refer to schools grades or predicted grades to meet entry requirements. Adult learners may cite employment history and experience in the form of a curriculum vitae (CV). The interview should be a two-way process to ensure that learners fully understand expectations of the programme before committing themselves. The pre-course interview is therefore a means of ensuring that the right people are on the right courses. Accrediting previous experience, learning or achievement is called **APEL/APL**.

Beginning of course or programme Whether a learner is enrolled onto a full-time or part-time programme, there should be an induction. The *induction* provides the opportunity to introduce the learners to the programme, to each other, to the teacher/s and to the programme or module. The *initial assessment* will create a **profile** of the learners:

- Why are they there?
- What is their previous knowledge or experience?
- What are their strengths and weaknesses?
- How confident are they?
- Will their personal circumstances influence their progress?
- What is their character?
- What do they enjoy or dislike?
- What are their expectations and aspirations?
- Are they motivated?

It would be very easy to make assumptions at this point and break the first rule of teaching, the most common assumption being 'they're here and want to learn'. That may be so, but there will be degrees of desire and these *will* influence the learner! There are some useful yet informal strategies which can be used to find out about your learners. One of these is to use an ice-breaker activity (see section 1.2). Another even less formal way is to set a simple activity or questionnaire, maybe associated with previous knowledge, skills or experience and whilst the learners are completing it you can go around the room talking to each person on a one-to-one basis to find out something about them and why they are there. The more formal strategies are often collectively known as **diagnostic assessment**. These identify and assess learners' capabilities in order to inform the structure of the programme or scheme of work; they will also identify learning needs and therefore the support needed to ensure progress. Such diagnostic assessments include:

Learner needs analysis	To ensure that teaching methods are suited to individuals
Preferred learning styles	To find out how your learners like to learn
Initial screening	To check basic skill levels to identify level of support needed
Prior learning	To identify previous experience, learning
Skills test	To check current level of competence

As many organisations are measured and funded on their success, it raises the importance of ensuring that the right learner ⟶ is on the right course ⟶ and receiving the right support. This contributes to learners staying until the end of the course and therefore maximises their potential to achieve their learning goal. Effective initial assessment will record plans and development needs in an action plan or individual learning plan.

During the course or programme Assessment during the course is usually *formative*. This means that it is an interim judgement or decision about progress, which is reported to the learner as *feedback*. This enables them to consider what they are good at and build on their strengths, whilst informing them of improvements that need to be made to meet the requirements of the assessment or qualification. There is always 'life after formative assessment'. Careful feedback can motivate, enlighten and provide a vehicle for development. Bad feedback can destroy confidence. Feedback (sometimes called 'constructive' feedback, see section 4.3) should follow a pattern of identification of what is good or what has been achieved successfully, followed by the 'in order to improve you should' statement and finished with a praise or motivational statement to leave the learner feeling confident and willing to carry out the developments you have identified. The feedback should include the judgement made, for example: pass or refer; satisfactory or needs further development; competent or needs further training or experience, but *never* fail. Formative assessment can relate to a piece of assessed work or as a meeting to discuss progress (a tutorial). Both require skilled practice in feedback and setting of targets.

At the end of the course/module/unit Assessment at this point is usually referred to as *summative*. It is a final decision or judgement about competence or ability. Dependent on the programme, learners may be offered another chance to improve their result, but in the case of examinations it is generally a 'one-opportunity'. It is worth reminding teachers that summative judgements can have a significant impact on learners, hence their learners' apprehension before test periods. The teacher should therefore prepare learners not only by revising content but in how the examination is conducted. Past papers or simulations can provide confidence pre-exam. Some courses have assessment strategies which enable learners to be graded on their work. Clear marking criteria are required, which should be shared with learners – 'in order to receive a merit you need to …'.

After the course Some organisations will gather information to provide a statistical picture of their institution. For example the percentage of learners progressing to higher level courses or employment. This may be done at exit interviews or by customer satisfaction questionnaires. It is used to measure the effectiveness of their programmes and their contribution to economic targets.

5.2 Effective assessment

By the end of this section, you will be able to describe the key methods used to quality assure assessment techniques and the roles of people in the assessment process.

The roles of people involved in assessment are related to their part of the process. Some are primary roles, some are roles to proffer reliability and some are for quality assurance and integrity.

Figure 5A Quality assurance – roles and duties

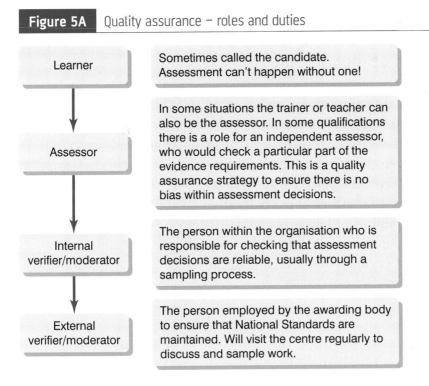

Learner	Sometimes called the candidate. Assessment can't happen without one!
Assessor	In some situations the trainer or teacher can also be the assessor. In some qualifications there is a role for an independent assessor, who would check a particular part of the evidence requirements. This is a quality assurance strategy to ensure there is no bias within assessment decisions.
Internal verifier/moderator	The person within the organisation who is responsible for checking that assessment decisions are reliable, usually through a sampling process.
External verifier/moderator	The person employed by the awarding body to ensure that National Standards are maintained. Will visit the centre regularly to discuss and sample work.

Standardisation

This is a process which is aimed at ensuring all assessment decisions are equal. It ensures that assessors are fully conversant with assessment requirements and consistently make the correct decisions. Periodically, the quality assurance team will convene meetings where everyone involved in the programme meets to discuss the assessment process, identify good practice and support new or weak assessors. Some examples of typical activities would be:

- Every assessor brings one refer, pass, merit and distinction piece of work. They justify to the group why they have marked to that level.
- Assessors submit an unmarked piece of work prior to the event, which is marked by the internal verifier or moderator. Then at the meeting everyone marks the same piece of work, the outcome being that everyone should award the same mark or grade.
- Every assessor involved in a particular unit or module brings ideas or samples of assignments etc., to the meeting to establish the expected standard for that unit or module, which is then implemented by all assessors.

Verification or moderation

This is the quality assurance process, often called internal verification (**IV**). It aims to ensure that assessments meet **validity** (relevant to what is being assessed), **reliability** (consistently marked) and **sufficiency** (covers everything) requirements. It does this by sampling assessments. Over the period of the qualification, the work of every assessor and every learner at every location should be sampled. The amount of sampling will depend on the experience of the assessor, the age of the qualification, and the number of learners and is determined at organisation level and approved by the **awarding body**.

To demonstrate best practice, for example:

An experienced assessor using an established qualification with a reasonable caseload would have about 10 per cent of their work verified.

An experienced assessor using a new qualification may increase the sample to 25–50 per cent.

A new assessor with an existing qualification might be 70 per cent plus rising to 100 per cent for a new assessor with a new qualification.

Some of the strategies used to quality assure decisions made by assessors include:

- Observing the assessor whilst carrying out a workplace observation
- Observing the assessor giving feedback to a learner about an assessment
- Interviewing assessors
- Interviewing learners
- Reviewing product evidence
- Looking at records of assessment
- Conducting an audit trail of dates.

Every organisation will have their own verification or moderation strategy, which will depend on resources. Internal verification or moderation (IV) should be part of the process of assessment rather than a product of assessment. This means verifying judgements as they occur. The worse case scenario in terms of IV is that at the end of a learner's qualification some inaccuracies are discovered, which causes a lack of confidence in all of the judgements. If this were to happen, the organisation and the assessors would lose their reputation and if this is discovered at external verification the centre is at risk of having sanctions imposed on it. Failure to comply may eventually result in a centre being closed.

One of the quality assurance roles of the awarding body is to comment on the effectiveness of the internal verification/moderation, and it measures its confidence in the organisation accordingly. Organisations will strive for 'direct claims' which means that awarding bodies are confident that they are able to quality assure with integrity, and they are authorised to apply for registrations and certificates without constantly seeking approval from external moderators and verifiers.

Further reading in terms of internal verification can be found in the Joint Awarding Body Guidance which is on most awarding body websites. For example, http://www.cityandguilds.com/documents/ind_generic_docs_policydocs/JAB_GUIDANCE_ON_IV_OF_NVQS.PDF.

Whilst this is aimed at NVQs, the good standards can be applied to many other qualifications. Those involved in assessment and verification of NVQs are required to gain approved qualifications to carry out those roles.

5.3 Tracking progress

By the end of this section, you will be able to state appropriate methods for recording the progress of learners and the importance of **tracking**. You will also be equipped to recognise some simple designs for basic record-keeping documents.

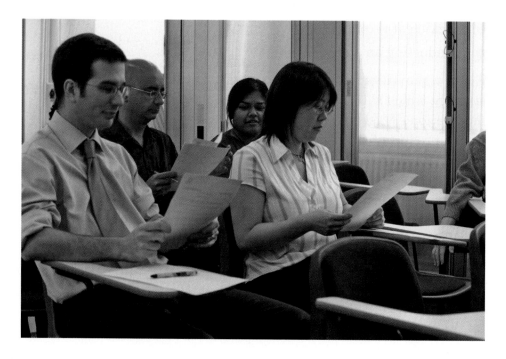

Advisory note

- Methods of recording assessments will differ according to the qualification type.
- Always use the forms agreed within the organisation.
- Suggestions for improvements should be made through the internal verifier.
- All forms should, at the very least, include the qualification title, names of the assessor and the learner and the date.

Forms below are examples of the format in order to recognise the style. They should not be considered as 'approved' documents. The forms described, which are examples and not an exhaustive list, are:

- Observations records
- Records of questioning
- Assignment front sheets
- Tracking sheets

Observation records

These forms are most commonly associated with recording of observed evidence when completing NVQs. The purpose of keeping documents relating to observation is to ensure that *what is seen is accurately matched to the assessment criteria*. Whether this is completed by the assessor or the learner will depend on how confident the learner is and how familiar with the criteria they are. In my experience it is usually the assessor's job! The observation record would be a piece of evidence to demonstrate what was seen when and should be confirmed or 'witnessed' by the parties involved – usually in the form of signatures. The most common use of observation documents is to record workplace activities. They are usually descriptive and are written as a chronological record. For example:

2 March 2007 – Reception area of Smith's Engineering,
Sometown. At 09.15, Sheila greeted the customer in a
polite manner, asking the purpose of their visit and
who they wished to see. She then used the telephone
to inform the Director's secretary that the visitor
had arrived. Sheila gave the visitor's name and the
company they represented. Whilst waiting for the visitor
to be collected, she issued a visitor's badge and
asked the visitor to sign in. Two incoming calls were
taken using the standard greeting and directed to the
extension required. At 09.20, as the secretary still
hadn't arrived to collect the visitor she invited them to
take a seat in the waiting area. A package arrived and
was signed for; rang to inform addressee of its arrival.
She smiled when the visitor left reception with the
secretary at 09.25.

ACTIVITY 1

Identify the main skills that Sheila used whilst on reception.

When writing up observations, it is useful to have a copy of the
assessment criteria to hand and to be mindful of everything that is
occurring; even if it is not directly related to the activity, it may have
significance to another task or component of the qualification.

An observation record might look like this.

Name of candidate:	Date:
Qualification:	Level:
Location of assessment:	

A description of the event or activity	Links to performance criteria

Assessor's signature:	Date:
Candidate's signature:	Date:

Records of questioning

These documents are more associated with verbal questioning rather than written questioning. Written questions automatically create a record, but verbal questions could just happen. The purpose of the document is to provide evidence of what question was asked and the answer given (whether right or wrong). This should then be linked to relevant criteria. Valid questions are those which are related to theory and underpin a practical activity.

For example, following the observation above, typical questions might be:

- What would you do if the telephone extension had been busy?
- What would you do if the addressee on the parcel had not been a member of staff?
- Why is it important to use a standard greeting when answering a telephone?
- If a visitor is very early for their appointment, what do you do?

At the end of the record of questioning, it is important that both the assessor and the learner sign to say that the document is 'a true record of questions and their responses'.

A record of questioning might look like this.

Name of candidate:		Date:
Qualification:		Level:
Unit/assessment:		
Question		Response given by candidate/learner
Assessor's signature:		Date:
Candidate's signature:		Date:

Assignment front sheets

The purpose of an assignment front sheet is to provide a standardised method of briefing learners on components of the assignment. For example, it will list the tasks to be completed and target dates; it will identify any key/basic or functional skills that are derived from the assessment; it will state the criteria for gaining pass, merit or distinction grades; and usually provide a space for assessors to give feedback on the work. It is customary that the person who designs the tasks should submit the brief to the internal verifier for approval before launching it with their group. This ensures consistency within the organisation and a double check before issuing the assignment to learners.

An assignment front sheet might look like this.

Qualification title:	
Unit title and number:	
Launch date:	Submission date:
Task	Criteria reference including links to functional skills
Feedback:	
Grade achieved:	
Assessor signature:	Date:

Tracking sheets

....

These are the forms that record progress during a qualification. They may be used so that the teacher can plot achievement of tasks within an assignment, units within an NVQ or completion of homework/ class-work activities. It is usual to record the date the unit/task/activity is completed. Best practice models include the date commenced and who assessed the work, with a space to date and initial if the work is internally verified. A similar document can be used to plan internal verification – i.e., identify which part of the qualification and which learners' work are to be sampled.

A tracking sheet might look like this.

Qualification title:									
	Unit, task or activity								
Name	1	2	3	4	5	6	7	8	ETC
Learner A									
Learner B									
ETC									

To be effective and meaningful, you should devise a simple marking code to visualise the progress. For example:

- / means a learner has started on the unit/module
- X means they have completed the unit/module.
- Always add a date when completed, together with assessor's initials.
- If verified the verifier could date and initial maybe in a different colour pen.

Glossary of terms

APEL/APL accreditation of previous experience and/or learning

Assessment to make a judgement about something, a measurement of achievement

Authenticity to establish who wrote/owns the subject

Awarding body an organisation that devises qualifications and awards

Diagnostic assessment assessment used to identify capability or skill level

Initial assessment an assessment tool to identify and establish potential or aspirations and discover facts

IV Internal verification

NVQ National Vocational Qualification

Profile an outline of the characteristic traits of a particular person

Reliability a strategy to ensure that assessment decisions are consistent

Sufficiency to check that there is enough evidence to cover the criteria

Tracking a method of recording progress

Validity a strategy to ensure that judgements are made against criteria

SUMMARY

In this chapter, you have covered all of theoretical aspects of the fifth learning outcome in your PTLLS qualification:

Types of assessment methods; effective assessment; tracking progress

▶

Your Personal Development

You have considered the many methods of assessment and understood how they may be used. You will have identified the different times within a learner's programme that assessment can be used, in particular initial assessment, as well as formative and summative judgements and how these can impact on the learner, the programme of study and the organisation. You can explain how feedback is a valuable tool in developing learning.

You can explain the roles of those within the assessment process and their contributions to the quality assurance processes. You can describe the purpose of standardisation and internal verification/moderation and identify some sampling strategies.

Finally, you have looked at some basic examples of documentation that can be used and clearly explain their purpose.

You should be able to answer questions relating to:

- Explaining different types of assessment and when they are used
- The different ways of assessing and when to give feedback
- The importance of initial assessment in developing potential and preparing programmes of study

Part Two

Planning and enabling learning

(PEL)

This is the second unit in your Certificate in Teaching in the Lifelong Learning Sector (CTLLS) qualification

CHAPTER 6
(PEL, UNIT 1)

Negotiating individual goals

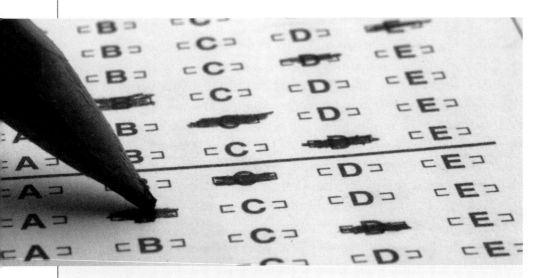

LEARNING OBJECTIVES

In this chapter you will learn about:

- The purpose of initial assessment
- Evaluating initial assessment
- Setting appropriate goals for your learners
- Negotiating and recording these learning goals

6.1 The role of initial assessment

By the end of this section, you will be able to state the role that initial assessment has and its value to the teacher, the learner and the organisation.

Initial assessment is a term given to that part of the learning process that hopes to combine the learner, the teacher and the curriculum. We know (or are learning about) ourselves and what the teacher does, we know what the curriculum sets outs to achieve, but the biggest variable is the learner, and most of us do not meet that variable until day one, week one. We may know their names and maybe their age, address and phone number, but not what they are really like. As we have already discovered (see Section 1.2), learners are individuals brought together to gain a common **goal**, but they expect and demand respect and individuality within their group setting. **Initial assessment**, therefore, is the first stage in a process designed to create an interesting and relevant programme of study for your learners. As well as finding out about personality, character and behaviour, it also measures attainment and potential and identifies skill gaps, aspirations, support needed and the level of ability. Initial assessment sets out to do quite a lot – but different individuals have come to expect different outcomes from it.

For senior managers it is used to inform strategy and funding, for teachers it identifies the person and informs the scheme of work and

Figure 6A   Purposes of initial assessment

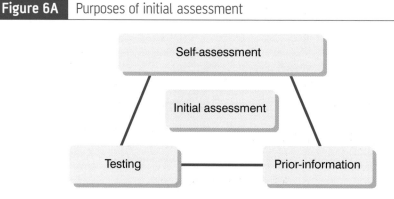

resources necessary, and for students it identifies how they will fit in and study.

Figure 6A explains how the various components of initial assessment are linked and how collectively they will create the key ingredients required to make your decisions. The process can occur at any stage of the learner's programme. At pre-entry stage it provides the opportunity to make choices, at entry it identifies level of study and needs, and **on-programme** it can inform the type of delivery.

There are many reasons to collect information; there are many uses and equally there are many things which impact on perceived or actual results. In Figure 6B, a **spider diagram** is used to visualise some of the influencing factors.

These ideas are suggestions about what kind of information to collect. Depending on the answers, and they will be as varied as your learners, the results will impact on learners and the learning environment.

Figure 6B   Factors that influence initial assessment

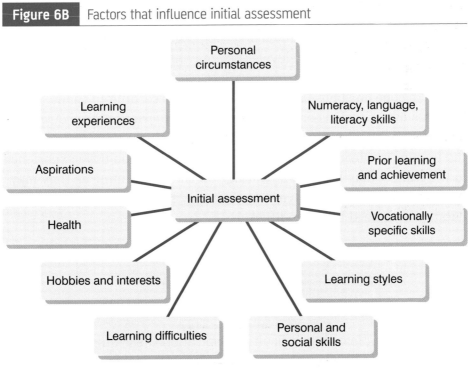

Adapted from feda.ac.uk

Attitudes

Personal circumstances, personal and social skills, hobbies and interests, health, family attitudes to learning may impact on self-esteem, confidence and motivation (see Figure 6B on the previous page). Travelling to and from the learning environment will impact on how settled a learner is at the commencement of a session, or if they can arrive on time. Family commitments and personal health may impact on attendance and punctuality or the ability to meet deadlines. Temporary illness may impact on the impression someone gives at their first meeting. If a learner has a long-standing interest in the subject it will improve motivation.

Ability

Numeracy, language and literature skills, prior learning and achievement, vocationally specific skills – a learner's ability in literacy and numeracy (and ICT) will impact on their ability to cope with the course (see Figure 6B on the previous page). There may be required levels of entry prior to commencing the programme and if learners fail to meet these required levels they may have to choose alternative learning routes. This in turn may affect motivation. A learner's ability to cope on their programme will vary according to their previous qualifications or experience. Work experience, previous employment or learning experiences will have some impact, as will the learner's reason for studying. Those learners who have experience in the subject may have an advantage on the programme as they may have more confidence: conversely, they may have developed poor habits which need to be modified.

Needs

Learning styles, learning difficulties, aspirations, learning experiences – discovering how learners prefer to learn and why they are there is an essential part of establishing how to make learning more effective, as is finding out about any other type of support needs. Trying to establish how learners got on in school, training or previous study will help a teacher to understand and overcome any barriers to learning (again see Figure 6B).

Once a teacher understands what is making their learners tick then progress can begin. It is also important that previously unrecognised traits or weaknesses are identified so that appropriate actions can be taken to support the learner.

6.2 Methods of initial assessment

By the end of this section, you will be able to list the types of initial assessment currently in use and identify the value of initial assessment.

The process of initial assessment (IA) can be formal or informal. The method of assessment and the way it is administered will influence the formality of the process. The teacher should consider the purpose of the IA and what benefits are sought. In The Chief Inspector's Report (2003), the Adult Learning Inspectorate (ALI) found that 'many providers are using a screening test but not following this up . . . the results of the assessment are not being used to inform the ILP', and continued 'different types of learners require different types of initial assessment'. This research proves that although used, initial assessment is not always effective. Much has improved since that report, but it nevertheless begs the question of purpose; if you are going to use IA, then use it well with careful consideration of what you are trying to achieve by doing it. Unless this is clear, it becomes another tedious process in **induction** from which no-one benefits, although it would 'tick a box'. Effective initial assessment is not a one-off activity but the start of an ongoing informative process.

Initial assessment should:

● Aid direction to the right course
● Help to remove barriers

- Help learners to belong
- Reduce anxiety
- Gather information about learners, their aspirations and abilities
- Identify learning needs
- Inform others about progress
- Ensure legal and moral requirements are identified, planned and implemented
- Aid the planning of an inclusive learning programme
- Inform the structure of the programme.

It may involve:

- The student
- Parents
- School teachers
- Careers Advisors
- Employers
- Former lecturers or trainers
- Carers.

It should take place:

- In comfortable surroundings
- In confidence
- In a familiar place or relaxing atmosphere.

It can be gathered using tools (or methods) which are categorised as:

1   Written tools:
    - Paper exercises
    - Application forms
    - Questionnaires
    - References – school, employer, previous course tutor
    - Screening tests – Basic Skills Agency (BSA), Key Skills Builder, Cambridge Training and Development (CTAD)
    - Self-assessment

- Free writing
- Aptitude tests
- Tutorial records

2 Electronic tools:
- Diagnostic screeners (literacy, numeracy)
- Learning style questionnaires
- Psychometric tests

3 Spoken tools:
- Interviews
- Professional discussion
- Informal discussion

4 Visual tools
- Observation
- Skills tests – mapped to National Standards.

The initial assessment should result in either an individual learning plan (ILP), the basis of a discussion to negotiate goals and targets, or planned differentiated strategies on your scheme of work.

Initial assessment in practice

Look at this scenario and, using a highlighter pen, pick out the many strategies the teacher uses to start the initial assessment of learners.

 ACTIVITY 1

- Identify the initial assessment methods.

- List the information gathered before Jamil and Fiona stated their course. How does this help to prepare them for learning and college life?

- List the information gathered during their induction to their course. How does this help their tutors to differentiate their learning?

Jamil and Fiona want to go to their local college when they have finished school. They ring up their local college and ask for a list of courses. Jamil wants to do Business Studies and fills out the application card in the prospectus to apply for a place. Fiona is not so sure: she doesn't know whether to do Tourism or Administration. She knows she wants to do something in an office, because that is the advice she got from her parents and her Careers Officer. She may also do Business Studies so that she can stay friends with Jamil. She decides to go to the open day to have a chat with teachers; her Mum comes along to find out about computer courses.

Jamil has now received a letter inviting him for an interview, which he attends, and is offered a place on the BTEC National, subject to his GCSE results. The Admissions Officer applies to the school for a reference. Fiona settles on Administration Level 2 because, following her chats, she decided that it was the most general course and her Mum says they will be good skills for whatever she wants to do.

In September they go along to the induction sessions for their chosen courses. They were surprised that they had to do some tests to check their English and mathematics. Jamil went into a blind panic: he thought he'd finished tests with his GCSEs and was very wary, especially with the English. He thinks he will not be allowed on the course if he fails. Fiona didn't see the point – she got a B in English and a C in maths in her GCSEs so gave the certificates to the teacher; she was told she didn't need to do the tests.

During this first week, they met lots of teachers and some played games to relax them. They also learned each other's names and where they came from. One teacher made them write about what they wanted to gain from going to college. Sometimes the teachers seemed to just listen and watch, at other times they sat down with each of them for little chats. Fiona said 'they tried to find out what we liked and what we wanted to do when we left college'. In some classes the teacher gave them a programme of what they would do each week, others said that they would give them more details in a few weeks. Jamil said that he preferred some teachers to others, because they were friendlier.

When they bumped into each other on Friday lunchtime, Jamil and Fiona compared notes; they had been asked to complete a questionnaire about their first week in college. They thought that there were bits that were like school, but other bits that were more grown up, they both felt as though most of their teachers were interested in them, but thought that some things weren't explained well – for example why Fiona didn't do the tests and why Jamil did, but was enrolled onto a different Business Studies group. Although Jamil enjoyed the 'getting to know you' sessions, Fiona felt very self-conscious. In general, they felt happy and looked forward to the following week.

Some things you should consider. Do you know:

- Why they chose their course?
- What their previous experience of learning is?
- How self-confident they are?
- If they have any previous experience or interests that are relevant?
- If they need any support?
- How they fit into their groups?
- What their preferred learning style is?
- What their expectations are?

How can you use the information to help Jamil and Fiona?

Initial assessment is a complex process involving pre-course assessment, diagnostic assessment and may continue throughout the programme with constant monitoring and reviewing to fine-tune needs. It results in accurate identification of individual needs, i.e. the planning of differentiation. Suggest some strategies to differentiate the learning programmes. How do you make your initial assessment work for you and your learners?

Evaluating your initial assessment

In order to gain the most from your initial assessment, it makes sense to evaluate the process. Some questions that you may ask yourself to do this are:

- What information or data comes out of the initial assessment?
- Does it impact on the programme or ILP?
- Is the information transmitted to others?
- What does the IA lead to?
- Is it collecting the right information?
- What does the data tell you?
- Who needs the information?
- Does it diagnose existing skills (e.g. basic skills)?
- Does it find out about preferred learning style?
- Does it analyse the person against the skills they require to study, learn, work or progress to higher education?

In summary, initial assessment is aiming to get the best match between your learners and their learning. It should be both backward- and forward-looking.

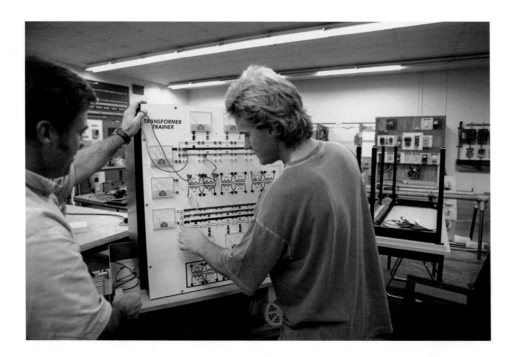

6.3 Planning, negotiating and recording learning goals

By the end of this section, you will be able to describe the difference between a goal and a **target** and develop use of expressions associated with goal setting.

A goal is what a learner plans to achieve within a course or period of learning; a target is a smaller step to help learners achieve their goals. Small, achievable targets are more easily met than longer-term goals and therefore encourage a feeling of accomplishment. Effective targets are those small, achievable outcomes that enable students to experience early success. They are not vague and they are always in context, relevant and understood by everyone. In this context goals and targets are used to refer to learners' ambitions and aspirations rather than aims and outcomes used by the teacher in sessions.

> **If you don't know where you are going you will probably end up somewhere else.**

Laurence J Peter, 1919–90, Canadian Academic and author of
The Peter Principle (1969)

Our learners arrive in post-compulsory education with many goals:

- Gaining qualifications to prepare for work or further/higher education
- Gaining qualifications to accredit existing skills
- To enhance or update skills
- For personal development or enrichment
- To achieve social integration.

They may also come:

- To meet parental/school targets
- As an alternative to school/work/unemployment benefit.

The motivational aspect of why learners enter post-compulsory education (**intrinsic** or **extrinsic**) will impact on the provision, the methods and on the relationships that emerge (see also Section 4.2). In order to exploit or capitalise on the motivational factors, teachers will need to set goals that are:

SMARTER

There are several different words associated with the **acronym**, but the meaning is clear:

Specific	Goals that clearly refer to what is expected
Measurable	Goals using verbs and phrases that can be judged
Achievable	Goals that can be succeeded
Agreed	A more powerful expression because it appears contractual
Realistic	Goals that are reasonable, practical and logical
Relevant	Goals that are appropriate and important (Avoid using achievable and realistic because they mean broadly the same thing.)
Time-bounded	Goals that express when things must be done by
Exciting	Goals that are stimulating
Enjoyable	Goals that are pleasurable
Ethical	Goals that are fair and decent
Reviewed	Goals that are revisited to check progress
Recorded	Goals that are written down

Goals are set for achievement over given periods which are usually expressed as:

- Long-term – career plans, ambitions
- Mid-term – programmes of study, assessment targets, learning outcomes
- Short-term – what to achieve in each session.

Goals are the building blocks of progression. They aim to move someone (in this instance a learner) forward. The size of these goals varies, and good teachers know their learners well enough to know how large or small a target or goal needs to be to ensure achievement. Some like the big picture; some are daunted by too large a goal and are motivated by lots of smaller targets and thus achievements. Whether large or small, a goal needs to be expressed in a statement that the learner understands and the goals need to be stated in the context of the overall ambition.

Expressions you may hear:

- *Goal-oriented* – this means that a learner responds to knowing what can be done now that couldn't be done before.
- *Negotiated* – this refers to a discussion about how the learner wants to achieve their goals, for example: in what way, by when.

ACTIVITY 2

Convert these targets into 'SMARTER targets'.

For example 'improve writing skills' could be written as 'always use capital letters for family names when filling in forms'.

Hand in assignments on time
Come to lessons ready to work
To revise for the exam
To pass your driving test

Discuss this activity with your mentor.

● *Medal/mission* – a method of motivating and praise associated with setting targets and rewarding achievement (Petty 2004: 65).

Goals and targets, usually recorded on the ILP, are best negotiated. This will aid ownership of the targets and create useful discussions to inform the most appropriate targets for the learner.

Glossary of terms

Acronym an abbreviation or series of initial letters which together make a word

Extrinsic motivation motivation derived from outside the person

Goal an aim or desired result

Induction a formal introduction to a programme/role

Initial assessment an assessment tool to identify and establish potential or aspirations or discover facts

Intrinsic motivation motivation from within the person; natural desire

On-programme a term to describe a period of learning

Spider diagram a visual form of note-taking to collect thoughts

Target an objective or focused path towards a specified outcome

 # SUMMARY

In this chapter, you have covered all of the theoretical aspects in relation to the first learning outcome of the second unit in your CTLLS qualification:

The role of initial assessment; methods of initial assessment; planning, negotiating and recording learning goals.

Your Personal Development

You will have further developed the skills and knowledge acquired through the PTLLS stage of your qualification and built on skills associated with initial assessment.

You have investigated the various stages and methods of initial assessment and the reasons why teachers need to collect and use the information. You have completed a case study to identify what initial assessment looks like in the context of induction and considered how information can be used to benefit learning. You have evaluated your own initial assessment strategies by completing a self-assessment questionnaire and adapting your practice in the light of your discussions with a mentor. Finally, you have practiced writing SMARTER targets for learners.

You should be able to answer questions relating to:

- The role and purpose of initial assessment
- Negotiating with learners
- Initial assessment strategies
- Agreeing goals and targets.

You should be able to demonstrate use of initial assessment in your planning of programmes and lessons.

CHAPTER 7
(PEL, UNIT 2)

Planning for inclusivity

SALLY AND RICHARD GREENHILL / ALAMY

LEARNING OBJECTIVES

In this chapter you will learn about:

- The importance of implementing an inclusive learning environment
- How to devise schemes of work which meet learner needs
- The key components and importance of a lesson plan
- How to adopt plans and schemes for different learners
- The impact of delivering inclusive learning
- How to gather and respond to learners' feedback

7.1 Establishing and maintaining inclusive learning environments

By the end of this section, you will be able to describe what is meant by **inclusion** and have an understanding of the importance of implementing an inclusive environment within your own teaching area.

Providing opportunities for everyone in the community is not a new idea; equality of opportunity appeared in the 1970s and Helena Kennedy QC wrote about widening participation in 1996 (Further Education Funding Council 1996). Several revisions, in the format of legislation and government reports, have culminated in the current notion (or label) of inclusivity. In this context, we are looking at educational inclusion, specifically in post-compulsory education, rather than social inclusion. Organisations have to plan strategically to deliver equality, diversity and inclusion and are being inspected against their ability to provide opportunities. This has resulted in active marketing towards groups that would not normally enter FE. At the classroom level, every teacher has a responsibility to ensure that everyone is included.

The opposite of inclusion is exclusion; not something that happens regularly or without a great deal of anxiety, but in FE one of the changes recently introduced is the delivery of learning to those who have been excluded from compulsory education.

In a report initiated by the Scottish Funding Council (2006: 4), one senior manager in an FE college said:

> There are people here who would not have been here five years ago. Their circumstances have not changed. They are still living difficult lives; still living in poverty; still have a serious disability or health issue. We can't change these things but we can adapt what we do to help them get here, turn up, feel okay about what they are learning, and leave with what they aspired to.

He continued:

> Good learning does not reinforce previous negative
> experiences and may remove many barriers.

When inclusion is effective it will:

- Motivate by celebrating success and inspiring learners
- Develop and maintain positive attitudes
- Foster interest
- Encourage reflection
- Offer small chunks of learning with progressively more challenging goals
- Create positive relationships between teachers and learners
- Create an effective transition towards employment or relevance to further study
- Use individual learning plans to plan and record progress
- Offer a wide range of provision, delivered at times and locations to meet learners' needs.

When inclusion is not effective, it will:

- Provide poor use of modern technologies to enhance learning
- Offer a narrow range of teaching approaches
- Have insufficient assessment of learning or lack effective feedback
- Withhold development of functional (basic) skills
- Lack adequate methods to collect data or feedback to develop learners or provision.

Inclusion, therefore, is about creating interesting, varied and inspiring learning opportunities for *all* learners; ensuring all learners contribute and are never disadvantaged by methods, language or resources. This is described in other ways such as **differentiation** or 'meeting individual needs': both of these terms tend to refer to the mechanics of inclusion.

ACTIVITY 1

Reflective practice

How do you ensure an inclusive learning environment for your learners?

Think about the actions you take in planning, delivery, support and assessment.

7.2 Devising schemes of work to meet learner needs

By the end of this section, you will be able to recognise the importance and key components of a scheme of work and state how schemes are written to meet individual need.

REVISION

In Part One (PTLLS), Chapter 3, we looked at schemes of work and how important it is to create a logical sequence of learning. We examined why planning and preparation of the content of the programme is essential and considered what needed to be included in the document. A scheme of work (or programme of study) includes a general description of who the group is and the timing of the sessions, it states the aims and outcomes of the programme and gives a brief breakdown of the topics to be covered in each session with an indication of how assessment will occur. For a complete review, refer to Section 3.1.

When devising schemes to meet learner needs, the teacher needs to consider the outcome of any initial assessment that has been carried out. In many cases the scheme is devised before the learners commence their course and the specific details to meet learner needs are implemented in the session or lesson plans. However, there are some things to think about which mean that you can both forward plan your programme and be proactive in meeting the outcomes of learner needs identified in your initial assessments.

Remember that a scheme of work is a broad outline of the overall programme and should be considered a working document. I would challenge anyone who maintains that it is a final statement, and especially someone who wheels the same document out year after

ACTIVITY 2

When planning your programme you may want to consider the following questions:

What are you comfortable with?

What are your own strengths?

What do you perceive the difficulties to be?

What do you want your learners to learn?

What resources are available? Can you use them?

Do you know where to get equipment from if it is not already in the room?

Do you know how to prepare the type of resource?

What are the physical surroundings like?

How much material do you need to cover (think about what learners must know, could know, nice to know)?

Can you negotiate learning or is it already set?

Do you understand the curriculum requirements?

How does it fit with other learning on the course?

year, to justify how it can possibly be a working, responsive document aimed at creating the best learning opportunity possible. At the very least, technology changes, curriculum content, current practice and legislation is updated, and good teachers take the best of what has happened before and make improvements!

The questions in Activity 2 will give you an idea of the way you are able to teach your subject, Plus broad ideas about methods and resource needs. By asking a few additional questions Activity 3 or considering a few other points you will begin to be able to create a more learner-responsive programme.

 ## ACTIVITY 3

How will the teaching methods, resources and assessments you have chosen meet individual needs?

Is there something in every lesson for visual, auditory and kinaesthetic learners?

Is the environment suitable for all types of activities in terms of furnishings, accessibility and mobility?

Is there a balance of teacher– and learner–centred activities?

Have you included an introduction to the course, your module or this subject?

How ready are your learners to learn? Do you need to create the rules, set standards and identify boundaries?

How will you know that learners are learning? Build in time to do reviews, tutorials, catch-up sessions and revision.

By preparing your scheme in this way, you will have made significant progress in (generally) meeting everyone's needs and hence be able to concentrate on the specific needs of learners. There will always be unforeseen factors, but see them as challenges and face them confidently knowing that your scheme is fluid enough to cope with them, rather than a tablet of stone which cannot be moved.

7.3 Devising lesson plans to meet learner needs

By the end of this section, you will be able to recall the importance and key components of a lesson plan and state how plans are written to meet individual need.

REVISION

In Part One (PTLLS), we looked at lesson plans and how important it is to specify the fine points of your proposed teaching and learning strategies. We looked at why the planning and preparation of the content of the lesson is essential and considered what needed to be included in this aide-memoire. A lesson plan includes details about the group – how many, date of lesson, etc. It states the aims and outcomes of the lesson and gives a detailed breakdown of the topics to be covered, how they will be delivered and an indication of how you will know whether the learners have learned the topic. For a complete review, refer to Section 3.1.

In your lesson plan you will identify the session outcomes, content, resources and assessment methods. You may also annotate it to justify choices made, for example stating methods against visual, auditory and kinaesthetic (VAK) learning styles, or teaching/learning styles (e.g. active (learner-centred) /passive (teacher-centred), listening, note-taking, speaking etc). When you are teaching you are using differentiated strategies, but sometimes these just happen, they are not planned. By matching what you know about your learners to the topics being learned, you will be able to improve your teaching and thus the effectiveness of the learning experience.

What can you differentiate?

- Learning outcomes
- Tasks and activities
- Teaching methods
- Resources
- Group work
- Assessment
- Support

Amended to suit specific individuals or groups.

These are very broad statements, so let us break them down into actual things that can be done. Some examples of strategies used to differentiate include:

1 Learning outcomes:
   - ILP targets
   - Varying targets
2 Tasks and activities:
   - Balanced VAK activities
   - Varying complexity of task/s
   - Providing for gifted and less able learners
3 Teaching methods:
   - Nominated questioning
   - Language and expression, communication styles
   - Changing seating positions
   - Supporting learner readiness to learn/study/work etc.
4 Resources:
   - Enlarging handouts
   - Altering font types and sizes
   - Assistive technology – keyboards, mouse alternatives etc.
   - Introducing visual images
   - Using modern technology, e.g. the Internet, virtual learning environment (**VLE**), Intranet

5   Group work:
  ● Pyramid group activities
6   Assessment:
  ● Questioning techniques
  ● Complexity of written questions
7   Support:
  ● 1:1 support
  ● Peer support
  ● Use of support assistants for reading, writing and comprehension
  ● Memory aids, recording devices or note frames.

 ## ACTIVITY 4

....

How do you maximise your learners' potential?

Make a list of some of the things you do in the classroom to meet your learners' needs. Keep this to hand when planning future sessions and prepare to differentiate.

Be proactive and reactive!

Being *proactive* means that you prepare for all eventualities: being *reactive* means that you will listen to your learners and modify accordingly.

7.4 Adapting plans and schemes

By the end of this section, you will be able to identify ways that you can adapt programmes and lessons to meet needs, and understand the theory behind the process.

REVISION

In Part One (PTLLS), we looked at planning to meet individual needs (Section 3.2) and different ways of teaching that will meet those needs (Section 2.1). We discussed how learners have different ways of learning (Section 1.2). We can therefore conclude that effective teaching and learning responds to the individual needs of learners and this is expressed as an idea in the scheme of work, as an intention in a lesson plan and demonstrated in the delivery of learning.

Adapting plans and schemes means modifying your teaching and learning activities to meet the needs of those assembled in your group. Teaching 'mixed ability groups' is not new; it is another instance of labelling. Differentiating or adapting is usually modifying or doing something differently, maybe changing the way you (usually) deliver something, or it can be about a specific action you make for an individual or small group. Adaptations in sessions are usually by task, by outcome or by support. Each is responsive to the ability of your learners. The adaptations or differentiation are always about what is in the best interests of the learner. Yes, it does take more time to prepare for everyone in the session, but this will be rewarded when your lessons are interesting, keep everyone occupied and don't become a fraught battle of wills. Time will fly because learner-centred activities are more exciting and although they may take longer to achieve the final goal than teacher-centred ones (because they may involve more group exploration and experiential learning), the learners are active so they don't get bored, and you don't become exhausted. Before you know it the lesson is over and outcomes are achieved successfully. Learner-centred activities are invaluable in creating learner autonomy, developing study skills and the skills of critical analysis and reflective thinking.

To bring in some theory, Benjamin Bloom (1913–1999), created a classification of learning which he called a 'taxonomy'. Further work by Bloom, David Krathwohl and R. H. Dave extended this work.

Particularly in respect of the third category (psychomotor domain) you will see variations. For example, Elizabeth Simpson and Anita Harrow have both extended Bloom's original work and devised their own terminology. Each has in common a progression leading from basic actions to standard or habitual practice. The theory can be usefully applied when devising differentiated outcomes, because the classifications provide levels of learning. It was originally devised as a means of explaining 'mastery' in tasks, but has been used widely in educational terms in a variety of ways. Although published around 50 years ago, it is timeless and has become one of the classic models of theory.

The first stage of the classification is associated with three skills or **domains**:

- **Cognitive** (intellectual or thinking skills)
- **Affective** (attitudes, beliefs and values)
- **Psychomotor** (physical, practical and co-ordination skills)

Bloom (and others) advocate that all learning can be classified into these three domains. He then subdivides them, which is where it starts to become useful to the teacher.

The **low order** skills are usually those in the short-term or shallow memory. If you tell your learners a fact or opinion today, they will be able to remember it tomorrow; they won't be able to do anything with the information or transfer its meaning to another context, but they can call to mind the basic fact or recall the skill. This is **shallow learning**.

With the **high order** skill, the learner truly understands the fact – the learning is deeper, they can apply it in different situations and argue its worth against other peoples' thinking. It represents second nature. This is **deep learning**. For the teacher, this theory means that you can develop learning and understanding either in a phased way (using Bloom to structure learning development in your scheme of work) or by ability (using Bloom to provide different levels of task according to the capabilities of your learners). You can stretch learners to meet their full potential. Assessment and questioning can be differentiated using Bloom's theory, either to offer appropriate questions according to ability or to challenge more able learners to think and apply their knowledge. Bloom's Taxonomy, therefore, is a useful tool.

Cognitive domain

Level	Taxonomy	Learners will be able to:
Low order skill	Knowledge	State, list, recognise, draw,
	Comprehension	Describe, explain, identify
	Application	Use, apply, construct, solve
	Analysis	List, compare, contrast,
	Synthesis	Summarise, argue, explain
High order skill	Evaluation	Judge, evaluate, criticise

Based on Bloom (1956).

EXAMPLE

Map reading. At its lowest level a learner can recognise a red line on a map as a road.

At the next level they can identify the red roads and maybe see that other roads are blue and yellow; the next level would be to use a map to work out what road goes from A to B. The next level would have the learner using a map to plot a route between locations, listing alternative options.

At the higher levels learners would be able to plot locations using grid referencing and scale and finally apply their knowledge to other map formats to evaluate the difference between the formats.

Affective domain

Level	Taxonomy	Learners will be able to:
Low order skill	Receiving (being aware)	Choose, describe, use, select
	Responding (reacting)	Answer, discuss, perform, write
	Valuing (understanding)	Demonstrate, argue, debate, explain
	Organisation and Conceptualisation	Compare, contrast, generalise, modify
High order skill	Characterisation (behaviour)	Acts, displays, practices, solves, verifies

Based on Bloom and Krathwohl (1964).

EXAMPLE

Health and safety. At its lowest level, if I say 'don't run' a learner slows down to a walk. At the next level, they usually walk along corridors; in the next level the learner realises why running is not allowed; at organisation level they probably tells others around them about running versus walking in corridors, and finally at the highest level they would probably be putting up notices warning others about running in corridors!

Psychomotor domain

Level	Taxonomy	Learners will be able to:
Low order skill	Imitation	Repeat, copy, follow, replicate
	Manipulation	Re-create, perform, implement
	Precision	Demonstrate, complete, show
	Articulation	Solve, integrate, adapt, modify
High order skill	Naturalisation	Design, specify, invent

Based on Dave (1967).

EXAMPLE

Driving a car. At its lowest level, when the instructor says 'brake and clutch', that's what the learner driver does; at the next level, the learner driver repeats the process without always being told, say at traffic lights; next the learner confidently brakes, probably without stalling the car.

At 'articulation', the learner driver can control the speed of the car using brakes, gears and acceleration and finally, as second nature they drive in any situation without thinking, clutch control in a traffic jam or on a hill are examples of that.

Useful online resources

http://www.learningandteaching.info/learning/bloomtax.htm
http://www.nwlink.com/~donclark/hrd/bloom.html
http://www.businessballs.com
http://www.teachers.ash.org.au/researchskills/dalton/htm

ACTIVITY 5

In order to help you think about differentiating to meet individual needs, look at the following scenarios and decide how you might aid that individual's learning. You may find it advantageous to revise from Part One and the previous sections in this chapter before trying this activity.

1   Susan has difficulty in concentrating in group activities

2   Carly struggles with note-taking

3   Shara and Petra were absent last week

4   Matthew has a visual impairment

5 Everyone calls out answers to questions at the same time

6 Barney is dyslexic

7 Four of the group are doing Level 1 within the Level 2 computer class

8 Leroy gets bored but always produces really good pieces of work

9 The transport bus is always late which means learners turn up in dribs and drabs for the first 10 minutes of the morning class

How would you plan to differentiate for these learners?

Possible solutions (these are my offerings, you may have others):

1 Susan – ensure that there are plenty of short activities in the lesson. Research suggests that even the most highly motivated learner starts to lose concentration after about 10 minutes, so that should be the length of these short, snappy activities. When working with others, help her to remain on task by preparing a 'focus sheet' or writing frame giving ideas, with plenty of room to write and some questions or prompts. Maybe she could be the scribe for the group.

2 Carly – you need to find out how she likes to make notes. Does she like everything neatly arranged in a linear format, or does she like bullet points? Does she like themes with brief notes (nuclear) or a thought pattern style e.g. a spider diagram or clouds? (See Appendix C on Study Skills). Once you've discovered her preferred way of making notes you can help her with pre-prepared note sheets. If she is meticulous and struggles because she really likes you to speak at dictation speed, then I recommend she either uses a tape recorder or other recording device, or you prepare handouts from your notes to offer to her at the end of the session. A support assistant could make notes on her behalf. Perhaps during induction you should talk through note-taking styles and make it part of your initial assessment, rather than waiting for it to become a progress problem for one of your learners.

3   Shara and Petra – obviously you can't repeat the lesson for them, but you do need to get them up to speed. When they arrive, give them an **opener** type of activity to complete whilst you are setting off the rest of the group in a recap or similar activity. An opener can be a quiz designed to recap previous learning, or a word search, crossword activity or a brain gym activity (http://www.braingym.org). You could ask them to read through your teaching notes or handouts from last week (or another learner's notes). Whilst the remainder of the group are completing their activity, you can do a 1:2 session with Shara and Petra to get them to the same level as the rest. You really can see why differentiation should be planned in this scenario; there is no way that you could do this kind of session without preparation.

4   Matthew – this is quite an easy one to deal with, yet Matthew should be respected in terms of which one of the following he is more comfortable with. You can either ask Matthew to move closer to the front so that other learners' heads aren't bobbing about in front of him; however he may prefer to remain where he is. Therefore you would need to copy handouts or presentation notes in a **font** style and size that is legible for him and offer them to him for his use in class. Dependent on the degree of sight impairment you may have specialist support staff accompanying him, in which case you should brief them at the beginning of the class about what help you need.

5   Questioning – this is about how *you* ask the questions. If you are asking questions generally to the whole group it is not surprising that there is a mass answer. The learners don't know that you only want one person to answer! You need to change your approach to a nominated style, but in doing so you must also teach your learners to use the same style, because again they don't know what you are trying to do. A nominated style is discussed in more detail in the assessment unit, but basically it involves you asking your question, allowing time for all learners to think about the answer and then you nominate one person to share their thoughts with the rest of the group. This is called pose, pause, nominate. I've also heard it called pose, pause, pounce – but that sounds a little aggressive! This is a great way of differentiating because you can pose questions at the level you know your learners can cope with, perhaps using Bloom's theory to devise your questions.

6 Barney – has Barney been officially assessed as dyslexic or is that what he says? If an assessment has been done, the Statement will give you clear guidance about what the dyslexia professional considers relevant to aid Barney's learning. You may need to check with another teacher or his tutor to find out what diagnostic assessments have been done. If you suspect dyslexia then seek guidance about how to organise an assessment, again through his tutor if appropriate. If it is Barney's own opinion then you should be a little more suspicious about what is wrong: he may be correct – an assessment will confirm this, but he may be covering another barrier to learning, so that needs investigating. Some of the strategies to support dyslexia might involve use of coloured paper or overlays, font type, reading ability level guidance, specialist support, time allowances etc.

7 Mixed ability – this involves some compare and contrast research as part of your planning. You must look at the levels of qualifications offered within your class and see where the similarities are. It could be the level of explanation that is given can be amended, i.e. giving your Level 1 learners info sheets or **screen shot** worksheets to enable them to carry out the tasks. It may be that you have access to a support assistant, in which case brief them on the level of support you want them to offer, which would be enhanced with a subject specialist support (very rare, but maybe possible to organise – if you don't ask…). You may have to structure group work in such a way as to differentiate tasks or use peers to support or integrate learners. In some qualifications it is part of the curriculum that Level 3 learners have to 'supervise' Level 1 or 2 learners in order to prepare them for working within industry.

8 Leroy – he is obviously able if he is submitting good work, unless he is copying from someone else or getting family help. This needs to be checked out. A few questions about the topic in a one-to-one meeting will tell you whether he knows his stuff or whether his work is someone else's. His boredom is probably down to one of two problems; either your lesson *is* boring, in which case think about alternative teaching and learning methods, or Leroy is very intelligent, grasps thing quickly and you are not challenging or stretching him enough, in which case you need to think about alternative teaching and learning methods. A clear case for some reflection about what you are doing here.

9   Transport – the same answer as number 3, using openers to give
     you some breathing space, but this time everyone does the
     activities or recaps as they arrive, with the main class topic being
     introduced when everyone has got there. The danger with this is
     that those learners that are there on time will gradually get later,
     so something relevant must happen in the class from the official
     start time. If transport is late then so be it. You may wish to report
     this to the group tutor, or the person who organises the transport.
     If it is public transport, then you could suggest an earlier
     bus/train! You could always talk about this in a team meeting:
     does it happen in every morning lesson? Are the affected learners
     'cause for concern'? Should the start time of the class be delayed?
     (See also Dealing with punctuality in Section 4.1.)

7.5 Delivering inclusive learning

By the end of this section, you will be able to state the impact of
delivering in an inclusive learning environment, with reference to
disability, teaching and learning and support for learners. You will be
able to list key roles that support an inclusive delivery.

In terms of teaching and learning, this is where we are **empowered** to most effect. We can control what we do and to a certain extent what our learners do and can achieve. In the previous section, we considered how to plan for inclusion, but we can also modify our teaching style and methods, our resources and our assessment techniques either as the programme or lesson progresses or to become routinely inclusive. Some general inclusive learning strategies that you can try are:

Teaching and learning styles

Ensure that every lesson includes methods that appeal to visual, auditory and kinaesthetic learners. Follow a structured style – introduction, middle and an end, with a balanced amount of teacher talk and plenty of things to look at and do. Look out for who is making the contributions in the class and make a conscious effort to ensure that all learners take part in the class. Support your less able learners and stretch the imagination of the gifted ones. Vary activities and make learning fun! Use different outcomes and/or assessment activities to differentiate need.

Resources – paper-based learning aids

If you have to do a lot of talking create a handout for your visual learners to follow. Better still, make it interactive for your kinaesthetic learners by requiring words to be inserted or questions to be considered. I once saw an interactive PowerPoint presentation – the teacher's presentation included all of the facts, but the learners' printed handouts had a modified copy with words, numbers etc. missed out, so although they were following teacher talk, supported by PowerPoint, they also had something to do – therefore meeting all VAK types. Other paper-based activities include self-study packs that provide either catch-up, extra help for those that need help or those that can extend learning or revision uses. Resources to use as openers, fillers or closure activities include word search, crossword or quiz-word or matching games.

Resources – font type and presentation

Use at least a 14 pt font, larger in display formats such as PowerPoint or overhead transparencies. Use a clear font style such as Arial, **Berlin Sans**, Tahoma, or Comic Sans. These plain *sans serif* styles are good. Fonts such as Harrington, *handwriting styles*, or Old English are not very legible, because they are too fussy. I particularly like fonts that represent the letter a as 'a', because I think it is easier on the eyes. Whilst on the subject, blue print on pale yellow paper is quite easy on the eyes – but I appreciate that photocopiers are not generally set up for this, so you may wish to experiment, especially if a learner is suffering from eye strain. Avoid a **justified text** as it distributes words unevenly across the page. When developing study skills with your learners you should also advocate a similar set of rules for when your learners present their word processed work to you for marking – it helps your eyes as well!

The Royal Institute for the Blind publishes a Clear Print Guideline, which is very informative and is available at http://www.rnib.org.uk/xpedio/groups/public/documents/publicwebsite/public_printdesign.hcsp.

Accommodation

Prepare the room for the activities to be completed in the session, think about what you will be doing and what your learners are expected to do. Different types of group work require alterations to the room layout (see Section 2.4). You may need to include provision for wheelchair users – which could be height adjustable benches, tables or workstations or just space to move around safely in the classroom.

Support

Differentiation is not just the ability to provide support in the form of a Learning Support Assistant, but can include documents to support study. The most common types are assignment frames, writing frames or research frames. Each of these 'frames' has the ability to set questions which will help focus learners ideas and structure work. They are especially useful when supporting independent learners. (See Appendix C: Study Skills p. 369.)

Assessment

In the same way that teaching and learning is differentiated to meet everyone's needs it follows that assessment must also do so. It is too easy to forget that this is also something which needs to be considered, especially as many assessments are prescribed or preset by the awarding bodies. Any learner receiving learning support can usually apply for special arrangements in any kind of test or timed examination.

Some further ideas include:

● Verbal questioning can be differentiated using nominated styles; written question sheets can include a mixture of multiple-choice questions, yes/no type and short answer type in the same test.

Homework and class-work assessments could be varied to include things for all learner types:

● *Visual learners* like to write in bullet points and use images; labelling things; making posters or booklets.
● *Auditory learners* like to verbalise their answers; write essays; do research.
● *Kinaesthetic learners* like to make things; do role play; presentations.

Using classroom support workers

Generally, there are three types of support workers that you will come across, but there are as many different job titles as there are organisations in which they work. You will need to find out what the titles and associated job roles are within your organisation. Some of those titles are:

Classroom Support Assistant

Classroom Assistant

Learning Support Assistant

Learning Assistant

Basic Skills Support

Support Assistant

Support Tutor

Support Lecturer

Care Assistant

Student Support Worker

Type one is there to support the physical needs of learners. They will help learners with personal care needs and at mealtimes: in the classroom they will help by holding things or fetching and carrying to ensure a safe learning experience. Together with the learner they will identify and control what they do.

Type two is there to support the academic learning needs of an individual or group of individuals – probably functional skills support. They will help learners to make notes, recall facts and comprehend information, write things down, help with literacy and numeracy needs. They are not usually a trained teacher, although they may be trained in supporting the work of teachers or be volunteers or paid employees. They are a group of people that are most valuable in the room, yet very often they are undirected and therefore their value is not fully utilised. The more experienced they are or the longer they work with a particular teacher or group, the more self-sufficient they become.

Type three is there to support vocational and academic learning needs or behavioural support. They are probably a trained teacher, perhaps from the same subject specialism and assist the teacher, probably team teaching at times. If they are qualified and from the same subject, they can very much pre-empt what the teacher is trying to achieve and are usually an effective support mechanism.

Whatever the type of support worker, communication is the key to the effectiveness of that support. I would suggest that when a teacher plans their lesson they consider how they want the support worker to work with the learner. If this is annotated onto the lesson plan and offered to the support worker then the support worker will be able to see what is going to happen, how you think it will be done and what outcomes you are expecting and use their skills and experience to help you make it happen. Too often I have seen support workers either doing very little, because they do not know what is expected of them or the activities aren't clear so they are unsure of how to support their learner, or in some cases they just do everything for the learner, who forgets to learn how to do things for themselves. A support worker cannot support unless they know what you are trying to achieve; telepathy is not yet in their job description! In an ideal world it would be good to have a conversation about what support is required before the lesson and de-brief on how it went afterwards, but rarely is that feasible. A shared coffee break occasionally is not too demanding though!

Support workers can make valuable contributions:

- in consultations about causes for concern
- when used in an advisory capacity to think about appropriateness of resources and teaching strategies
- in team meetings
- at reporting periods
- as a resource
- when embedding functional skills
- to differentiate teaching.

Who will benefit from support worker assistance?

- learners with mobility, hearing or visual impairments
- learners with special educational needs (SENs)
- learners identified with weak literacy and/or numeracy skills
- teachers with very large or diverse groups
- teachers of learners with behavioural problems.

Research carried out in 1997 found that 'students on learning support were more likely to achieve than those who did not need the support in the first place' (Petty 2004: 513). Accessing learning support and working with support workers must be seen as an opportunity and not as something which confirms that a learner is not very good. This is a cultural shift and is changing positively as teachers, learners and managers see the resulting value. Unfortunately, those of you working in the community or the workplace may not have such staff to support you. However, if you are experiencing situations which regularly need support arrangements you should discuss this with your line manager. Because you work in more isolated situations you may not be familiar with procedures for accessing support or not realise that funding and mechanisms are available. Support, in any circumstance, is not usually systematically employed unless demand or need is assessed.

The role of the class tutor

When operating within an inclusive environment, monitoring progress and providing continuity is paramount. The role of the class tutor and the provision of tutorial time are vital in creating a learning experience that is beneficial to everyone. In this context I am referring to the role of the tutor as someone who provides academic and **pastoral** support, rather than the generic term of tutor which is sometimes used as an alternative to teacher or assessor.

The role of the tutor and purpose of tutorials is one of supporting learning and will manifest itself in a variety of ways:

- Preparing for and monitoring learners whilst they learn and study
- Providing pastoral and emotional support – supporting the well-being of the learner
- Initiating introductory and diagnostic support – induction, study skills, ILP, initial assessment, preparing for inclusive learning
- Completing progress reviews and personal development reviews
- Addressing retention – looking for and pre-empting cause for concern, offering solutions to issues, and monitoring actions
- Providing opportunities for teacher and learner to communicate on a one-to-one basis
- Providing group development e.g., citizenship, wider key skills
- Advising other teachers about characteristics of learners which are likely to impact on teaching and learning activities

- Completing target-setting discussions towards achievement
- Developing communication skills of learners
- Developing learners' autonomy
- Addressing individual problems or concerns
- Showing that you care at the individual level.

However, tutorials can be costly to operate, especially when delivering one-to-one tutorials. This is due to the time needed to ensure that every learner has a tutorial, thus making them very time-consuming. Seeking accommodation that is appropriate to tutorials can also be problematic: small private rooms are not always available and if you are trying to do one-to-one interviews at the same time as being responsible for the whole group it is very challenging – what does the rest of the group do whilst you are chatting to one individual?

Another consideration when tutoring concerns learners' perceptions of the tutorial; some may consider it to put pressure on them (both staff and learners) or appear threatening. However, if tutors demonstrate the value of tutorials and always express confidence in the process, it will result in a positive perception, rather than a negative one. This reinforces the need to teach learners about tutoring and its purposes. The benefits of operating a tutorial system significantly outweigh the disadvantages, and are usually a key part of a learning programme. Effective tutoring systems aid retention and achievement, which of course are the key processes measured in education and training.

In carrying out this role it is essential that tutors are selected and trained in the specific skills of being a tutor. It should not be assumed that everyone can tutor. As well as training in the documentation used by an organisation to record the process, a tutor needs many other skills. Walklin (2000: 254) lists functions that can be attributed to the role of the tutor as: catalyst and advisor, fact finder, auditor, technical expert, problem solver, advocate, reflector, solution provider, enabler, facilitator, influencer and implementer. Let us look at some of the skills needed to carry out these roles:

- Active listening. A tutor should *really* listen: don't interrupt other than to seek clarification or summarise. Look interested but not nosey. Value their opinion – even if it differs to yours – and do not voice opinion or inflict your values on the learner, even when asked 'what shall I do?' or 'what would you do?' Respect pauses in the conversation because silence is usually thinking time, especially if your questioning is open and initiates reflection.

- Questioning and explaining. Use open questions to encourage learners to reflect on their actions, considering cause and effect. Effective communication is essential: both parties need to be able to talk and understand, listen and hear. Non-verbal communication is also very important. In terms of questioning think about how those questions are asked:

(a) Open: What do you find difficult?

(b) Closed: Do you find assignments difficult?

(c) Leading: You are having difficulty with assignments ...

(d) Hypothetical: What would happen if ...?

(e) Reflective: How will you approach the assignment next time?

- Record keeping. Usually called reviews, plans or similar. The purpose of the document should be to prompt the discussion, record what is said and what the agreed outcomes are.

- Planning. Both the tutor and the learner should plan the tutorial. The tutor should have a fairly good idea of progress and pastoral issues relating to their learners and be able to recount them in tutorials; learners should know the types of discussion topics that will be mentioned so that they can begin to formulate their strategies to develop.

- Time management. Ensure that everyone understands how much time is allowed. Manage that period well and if things look like being delayed or over-running take action to control it. A learner may also seek guidance on how to plan and use their time effectively.

- Praise, feedback, discipline. Commenting about how well things are going, offering constructive feedback on progress and taking responsibility in dealing with problems is required to maintain rapport and the effectiveness of the process.

- Motivational interviewing or discussion. This is a strategy involving techniques to guide the learner into identifying and dealing with their own issues based on intrinsic learning values.

- Anti-discriminatory practice. Tutoring without any bias or discrimination.

- Enabling the development of problem-solving skills by encouraging learners to solve their own problems in a supported way.

- Discretion and confidentiality. The tutor may be privy to information which is expressed within a private discussion. You may have to use your discretion about responding to what is said; if what you are told is best shared then the owner of the information should be the one to share it. Exceptions to this may occur if abuse is suspected or if an illegal practice is identified. (See also Section 1.4.)

- Empathy (not sympathy), non-judgemental. The tutor should try to understand how things make the learners feel and keep opinions to themselves.

- Respectful and socially correct. Respect should be mutual and aids the development of a good relationship (rapport). There are social parameters to think about when conducting tutorials; respect of personal space, sitting to the side rather than opposite the learner.

- Flexibility. Tutoring demands different styles and expectations to meet different learners that are consistent in methodology and equality.

- Codes of practice and ethics. Working within your Duty of Care (see Section 1.3).

The tutor may or may not teach the group, there are no particular guidelines on this; it may be beneficial to remain independent or be advantageous to get truly involved in the learner's personal and academic development. You should follow your organisation's methods and remember that there are boundaries between the roles of the teacher, the tutor and the counsellor which should be clear in everyone's minds.

Tutoring, like any other part of teaching, is not without its problems. Tutors who do not prepare for tutorials are likely to end up with unfocused sessions without any meaningful outcomes; crossing the boundaries of tutoring and counselling can lead to ill-informed actions, imprudent use of time and is unprofessional, the tutor should know when to refer the issue to someone more qualified to deal with it. The tutor should balance their approach: not too authoritarian or too nonchalant. If it is found that the support provided is ineffective an evaluation should establish the cause: is it too supportive, meaning that your learner is not challenged to develop their own support mechanisms? You may need to question whether the support is (still) relevant.

Disability Discrimination Act 1995 (c50)

The Act gives disabled people the right to employment, education, access to goods, facilities and services, and access to buying or renting land or property. Part Three (which was amended in October 2004) requires businesses and organisations to take reasonable steps to modify physical features that act as a barrier to disabled people who wish to access their services. Part Four (which was amended in September 2002) specifically relates to education and states that providers should take steps to ensure that the disabled are not treated less favourably than other students.

The primary instruction is that colleges, training providers and other organisations make 'reasonable' adjustments to include everyone, for example:

- by installing ramps or lifts to replace steps
- ensuring facilities assist access
- creating signage appropriate to needs
- improving toilet facilities
- ensure rooms are accessible
- undertake health and safety risk assessment
- create plans and progress towards accessibility
- publish disability statements and entitlements
- provide support, for example – sighted support, sign language interpreters, note-takers, specialist equipment, rest breaks
- prepare for assessment to ensure that testing is fair and accessible for all. This may involve negotiating extra time in written examinations to meet specific needs, or, offering one-to-one support, or providing scribes for written work
- Assistive technologies – a range of equipment can be purchased to make a more comfortable or ergonomic environment, for example, arm supports, pen grips, voice recognition devices.

Useful information

The Open University provides an extensive list of ideas at: http://www.open.ac.uk/inclusiveteaching/pages/inclusive-teaching/learning-environments.php

In summary, delivering an inclusive learning package means considering what is appropriate and needed. It is a balance of activities, using support staff and guidance to ensure that everyone who wants to access learning can do so that and those who do not usually feel comfortable in accessing learning are confident that your organisation will meet their needs and aspirations.

7.6 Acquiring and responding to learners' feedback

By the end of this section, you will be able to describe the mechanisms which collect information about learners and express ideas to respond to their feedback.

There are a number of informal and formal methods of collecting views of students. Learner responsiveness is another of the current buzz words.

Informal	Formal
Post-it notes	Surveys
Discussion	Evaluation sheets
Verbal Q&A	Questionnaires Focus groups

Covert feedback:
    Attendance
    Behaviour
	Tutorials
	Complaints cards

The purpose of all of these methods is to collect information and feedback from learners. The Post-it notes, for example, mean that learners can make a comment at the time it becomes apparent, without interrupting the flow of the lesson (things like 'I don't understand that' will be written on the Post-it). The discussion will have an emerging agenda, usually initiated from a single question and then moving on in whichever direction the conversation develops. Focus groups are similar, except that they are slightly more managed and the interviewer has a clear idea of what they are trying to find out and will lead questioning in that direction.

Most organisations delivering training use 'happy sheets' to capture the first reactions to the course or training activity. They are useful to a certain degree. (Did the course match its publicity? Did you achieve your planned objectives? How do you propose to use the learning gained?). However, in terms of evaluating the effectiveness of the learning it comes too soon: learners have not had the opportunity to use the learning or discuss it with anyone. Surveys are another frequently used part of the curriculum to establish student satisfaction. There are companies that carry this task out for an organisation and then match performance to other organisations it works with; this helps to **benchmark** performance against other providers.

Whatever the method of collecting information, it is of no use and would be a waste of time unless something is done about what is gathered from the information. You must close the loop.

You may collect information for a number of reasons:

1   To confirm that learners are happy on their chosen programme of study

2   To audit that processes have occurred, for example: induction paperwork completed, assessment processes are completed

3   To find out if learners' own objectives have been met

4   To check that differentiated learning methods are suitable

5   To inform quality assurance processes – course review, self-assessment, internal verification, satisfaction surveys

6   To confirm understanding.

The final stage of collecting information and receiving feedback from learners is to use it to the benefit of the organisation, the teacher or the learners.

 ## ACTIVITY 6

Look at the following results from learner feedback strategies. What would you do if this came to your attention?

- You find out from class Post-it notes that three learners did not understand a key theory you were trying to explain.
- The induction review form shows that not all learners received copies of the Student Charter.
- The course evaluations from today's course confirmed that many learners thought the course would give them ideas to use when they returned to their own establishment.
- The annual student survey said that 37 per cent of learners felt that the prices in the café were too expensive, 87 per cent would recommend their programme to someone else and 67 per cent said that they thought the staff delivering on their programme were helpful and friendly.
- The attendance during Miss B's lesson is rarely above 40 per cent. Other teachers of that programme have attendance averages of 80–100 per cent.

Glossary of terms

Affective – concerned with emotions and values

Benchmark – a standard or point of reference to compare performance

Cognitive – concerned with thinking skills

▶

Deep learning – learning which is memorised and fully understood

Differentiation – catering for the needs of all learners to reduce barriers to learning

Domain – an area or section of learning; a classification

Empowered – given responsibility for something

Font – a type or style of lettering in a printed document

High order – most thorough level of learning

Inclusion – finding opportunities to integrate all learners

Justified text – even distribution of words across the page within fixed margins

Low order – a superficial level of learning

Opener – an activity at the beginning of a session

Pastoral – concerned with the well-being of learners

Psychomotor – concerned with physical, practical and co-ordination skills

Screen shot – a visual image from a software program reproduced into a document to support understanding

Shallow learning – learning which is retained for a short period

Taxonomy – a classification

VLE – virtual learning environment

 SUMMARY

In this chapter, you have covered all of the theoretical aspects in relation to the second learning outcome of the second unit in your CTLLS qualification:

Establishing and maintaining inclusive learning environments; devising schemes of work to meet learner needs; devising lesson plans to meet learner needs; adapting plans and schemes; delivering inclusive learning; acquiring and responding to learners' feedback.

Your Personal Development

You will have learned about inclusion – what it is, why we do it and what you can do as a teacher to ensure an inclusive environment. You have understood about differentiation and what this means to both the teacher and the learner and the importance of differentiating to create high-quality learning experiences. You have completed activities that develop your ability to create schemes of work; reflected on how to select activities deemed to support inclusion and maximise learners' potential; made suggestions about how to differentiate in a range of situations; and finally, considered the impact of learners' responses and how they may affect your actions.

You should be able to answer questions relating to:

● The use of different delivery methods, resources and adapting session plans to create an inclusive learning environment;

In your teaching practice this will develop your ability to:

● Prepare schemes of work and session plans which meet individual needs and demonstrate inclusive learning strategies.

CHAPTER 8
(PEL, UNIT 3)

Using inclusive strategies

LEARNING OBJECTIVES

In this chapter you will learn about:

- Planning inclusive learning sessions which motivate and enthuse
- The strength and limitations of different learning resources
- Effective use of new and emerging technologies
- The importance of promoting equality while supporting diversity
- How to match functional skills required of the curriculum to the ability of your learners
- Modifying resources to fit individual needs

8.1 Designing inclusive learning activities which motivate and enthuse learners

By the end of this section, you will be able to identify learning activities and list factors that motivate learners. You will be able to describe how these **concepts** link to produce inclusive learning sessions that enthuse your learners and encourage them to meet their full potential.

REVISION

In Part One, you identified a variety of relevant teaching and learning activities (Section 2.1) and how they are used to meet individuals' needs in your curriculum area. This was also described as differentiation. You also looked at Maslow's opinions on motivation, how to engage learners (Section 4.2) and identified ways to improve motivation in the classroom.

Inclusive practice, reviewed in the previous chapter (Section 7.5), concentrated on the necessity of differentiating to meet individual need. To a certain extent this will increase the motivation and therefore make the learning session more rewarding for learners. It is not, however, a rule. As the teacher, you may have devised various activities, resources and assessment tools to meet everyone's needs, but notice that there is still something missing. So what is it? Well, it is likely to be that you have overlooked the fact that people have characters; they have moods, distractions and emotions. Whilst you may be able to deal with changes in these if they are ongoing, if they emerge during your lesson, it relies upon you to 'think on your feet'. It may or may not be possible to sort out the issue or modify your lesson, and in my experience when you can get around to dealing with it – i.e. for next lesson, everything has changed anyway! Younger learners in particular do have quite sudden changes in their behaviour as a result of mood swings and adults may be concerned about other facets of their lives, for example work or family, which temporarily distracts them. So the advice is that you need to understand what motivates and remember the importance of knowing your learners.

Types of learners – some expressions you may hear:

- VAK – visual, auditory and kinaesthetic learners – different ways learners like to learn
- Disaffected learners – no longer satisfied with the learning environment
- Disengaged learners – detached or not involved in learning
- Dysfunctional – unable to deal with normal social behaviours
- Gifted and talented learners – highly skilled or adept in particular things
- SEN – special educational needs
- ADHD – attention deficit hyperactivity disorder

We will look at the different needs of these types of learners later.

Motivation Theory

Motivation Theory, described by Abraham Maslow (1970), focuses on needs, arguing that basic needs must be met before a learner can enter a state of mind in which to learn. This is not the only theory relating to motivation; all describe ways of trying to find out why someone wants to learn and how best to make it happen. (See also Section 4.2.)

Intrinsic and extrinsic motivators Everyone is motivated in one of these ways. Those said to be intrinsically motivated are developing because they want to; they have an inbuilt desire to progress and want to learn because they can. Those who are extrinsically motivated are developing because somebody or something wants them to or they need to. Maybe they have the offer of financial reward or better job prospects. Whatever the reason for the motivation, it is necessary and it is crucial that the teacher knows what their motivational driver is. If, for example, someone is extrinsically motivated they will improve their motivation if their work is displayed on the wall, or other similar outward expression of their achievement: equally, someone intrinsically motivated will get satisfaction from study time to research a topic. Once again, the teacher should play to the strengths of the learner when trying to raise enthusiasm in learning.

 ACTIVITY 1

Why are you doing the Certificate in Teaching in the Lifelong Learning Sector qualification/course?

List the reasons and decide whether you are intrinsically or extrinsically motivated.
What would help you to become more motivated?
Why does reflecting on your own levels of motivation enable development?

Discuss your answers with another member of the course.

Medals and mission This is a goal-oriented theory, based on the desire to be rewarded for achievement. A learner is given a clear direction or task and when it is reached there is a reward. The reward may be money, for example a pay rise on gaining a qualification, it may be a certificate, which could be proudly displayed or it could be acknowledgment from a colleague or teacher in a statement indicating 'well done'. The 'mission' can be a series of small targets or a single target, depending on the preferences of the learners. The 'medal' may also be phased.

Vicious and virtuous circles As the name suggests, this focuses on the fact that when things start to happen (positively or negatively) a learner enters a circle. The vicious circle is spiralling downwards; conversely, the virtuous circle is spiralling upwards. In motivational terms, if you start to achieve things you are more likely to want to continue. A learner enters a Can Do – Will Do mindset.

Turner (1990) promoted a model demonstrating the need for praise to promote a better standard of performance:

Figure 8A Motivation in training

Competence ←——————→ Training

Pride ←————————————→ Performance

Petty then adopted Turner's model to show how success forms the motivator to further achievement, creating a virtuous circle (Figure 8B); this is the upward spiral.

Conversly in the vicious circle, the statements are in the negative and so the motivation lessens because as a learner fails they are not inclined to progress or do more work.

Figure 8B The virtuous circle (Petty 2004: 47)

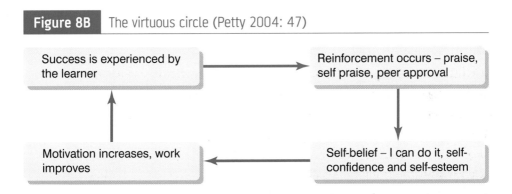

Success is experienced by the learner ——————→ Reinforcement occurs – praise, self praise, peer approval

Motivation increases, work improves ←—————— Self-belief – I can do it, self-confidence and self-esteem

Bandura and self-efficacy Albert Bandura (1994) suggested that an individual's belief in themselves and their ability is related to what they can achieve. The mindset here is 'if I believe I can, then I must be able to.' This is self-efficacy, which in this context means that belief in yourself will aid motivation. When you apply this in the classroom it concerns how you address the learner who says 'I can't do this'. This learner needs to be encouraged to try, you will re-explain the topic and through coaching and reassurance you will enable that learner to achieve.

Herzberg's Satisfaction Theory Frederick Herzberg (1959) was one of the early writers on motivation. This was originally associated with the workplace, but can be attributed to learning. He suggested that people need personal growth and interest and that a person's level of satisfaction determines how motivated they are. This is a 'needs' model in that everyone needs the right conditions, status and security in order to develop.

Positive and negative reinforcement These ideas come from the behaviourist theories originally suggested in research on animal behaviour (Pavlov's dog responding by salivating). In learning terms this is about offering positive or negative rewards to motivate. The motivation has a value. Positive reinforcement is rooted in the desire to seek a reward for achievement or good work. Negative reinforcement works on the threat or fear factor of not doing well.

The two examples that come to mind are: 'If you complete the work you may go to break' or 'If you don't complete your work, you can't have a break.' Both phrases suggest the same outcome, but the method of delivering is totally different. Pay bonuses work on this theory, as do the bonus payments in EMA (The Educational Maintenance Award).

 ACTIVITY 2

How to learn about motivation

One activity you may try centres on the personalities of TV and film characters. Some video/DVD scenes you may want to think about are:

David Brent in *The Office*
Basil Fawlty and Manuel in *Fawlty Towers*
Caine and Walters' relationship in *Educating Rita*

How does each of these people motivate their staff or protégés?
List the positive and negative methods each uses and relate those ideas to motivational theory. What can you learn by these examples?

The teacher should consider the advantages of using positive reinforcement as a motivator. Remember, though, that what you offer (or threaten) must be carried out, or it becomes empty reinforcement.

Useful online resources

en.wikipedia.org/wiki/motivation
http://tip.psychology.org/motivate.html
http://www.businessballs.com/maslow.htm
http://webspace.ship.edu/cgboer/maslow.html
http://changingminds.org/explanations/theories/
http://www.geoffpetty.com/downloads/WORD/reinforcement.doc

A simple search through a search engine using the following key words will reveal a lot of information: motivation, Maslow, intrinsic, extrinsic, Herzberg, Petty.

Specialist areas of motivational need

There are groups of learners who have particular issues. Whilst not wishing to stereotype needs, a teacher should be mindful of the support these groups may need to offer to improve motivation. If you follow your own rule of assuming nothing, yet seek to find out how individuals access useful learning strategies, you will create an inclusive environment.

Attention deficit hyperactivity disorder (ADHD). Some learners
may be diagnosed with ADHD. If you have such a learner in your class you should seek advice on their particular needs, but in general learners need to be in a position where they cannot be distracted or distract and see positive role models around them. You should not play to their need to gain your attention, but remember that they easily lose focus and their attention span is poor, so planning is essential when preparing lessons to meet their needs.

In lessons, try to:

- prepare material that is of interest
- create responsibility for their own learning
- initiate peer support systems
- design short, sharp activities
- use plenty of varied activities
- maintain a routine in the classroom
- create clear concise handouts
- offer reminders and praise.

Gifted and talented learners These are a group of learners who need to be motivated in the same way as every other learner, although it is tempting to assume that because they are able and usually intrinsically motivated they are OK left to their own devices. This group is at risk of becoming bored by learning that lacks challenge in the same way that any other learner lacks motivation; the teacher needs to respond and act upon it by differentiated teaching.

'Gifted' refers to those learners that excel in core subjects, whereas 'talented' usually refers to those skilled in more practical or artistic subjects. More recently 'gifted and talented' has become a general term for those learners who demonstrate high abilities in a number of areas.

Characteristics of **gifted and talented learners**:

- Quick thinking
- Methodical
- Creative
- Flexible
- Communicative
- Dexterous
- Team players.

Strategies to challenge the group:

- Offering opportunities to investigate and research
- Setting high order objectives (Bloom, section 7.4)
- Using open questions to seek opinion or argument
- Question opinions and ask what if … ? questions
- Providing opportunities to negotiate own targets
- Develop learner and learning **autonomy**.

Specific language needs groups There are groups for whom education is needed to support the ability to either become employed in the UK or work effectively in the UK. These are groups who are not native English speakers. They may struggle to comprehend the language and it must not be assumed that they possess some specific educational need. There are differences in academic ability as with any group of learners; their need is for language support to enable the groups to participate fully in education. The groups that come into this category include asylum seekers, English as a foreign language (EFL) and English for speakers of other language (ESOL).

The motivation for this group will come from activities in the classroom that are appropriate to their academic level, yet mindful of their ability to understand the concept in a different language.

In lessons, try to:

- prepare material that relates to hobbies or the learner's vocational area
- create responsibility for their own learning
- initiate peer support systems
- maintain a routine in the classroom language
- create clear concise handouts, using images
- use personal dictionaries.

Motivation and generating enthusiasm are the most challenging tasks that a teacher is faced with. My suggestion is always to go back to basics: assume nothing and find out what makes your learners tick. Remember that things happen around us and that will change how learners feel about their surroundings, targets and aspirations. Respond logically, encourage and remember that it is easier to criticise than praise; we all like a 'well done' or 'thank you'.

8.2 Resources – strengths and limitations

By the end of this section, you will be able to analyse the advantages and disadvantages of using a range of resources and how they contribute to effective learning.

REVISION

In Part One, Section 2.5, you listed the types of resources available to teachers, for example: boards, projectors, paper-based, games and audiovisual resources, and justified and evaluated their use in your lessons.

The resources most commonly used in the classroom are:

- Wipe board
- Flip chart
- Interactive board
- PowerPoint presentation
- Handouts
- Overhead transparencies
- Games
- Models
- Video/DVD

Resources generally enhance the verbal (auditory) teaching methods by providing a visual stimulus. Some resources can engage learners when being used so they meet kinaesthetic learning preferences.

Resource	Strengths	Limitations
Wipe board	Role models note-taking skills, notes key words and spellings, can be colourful, widely available, easy to use, can pre-prepare headlines, visible, cheap, doesn't break down	Non-permanent record, need to keep cleaning board to make space, slippery surface may make handwriting illegible, sustained use makes them difficult to keep clean, fixed position, encourages teacher to have back to room
Flip chart	Paper can be distributed around learners for interactive group work/display, moveable, can double as small wipe board, pads can be pre-prepared	Paper not always available, bulky if moved any distance, small writing space
Interactive board	Writings can be saved/printed, modern, professional, versatile as write-on board or display board, anything visible on computer screen can be displayed in a group setting and retrieved at a later date	Semi-permanent record, very expensive to purchase, not widely available, training needed before effective use, needs a special pen to write with, writing looks odd
PowerPoint presentation	Updated version of overhead projector and slides, graphics and animations aid interest, speed of use can dictate pace of lesson, modern, professional delivery with large audiences	Projection equipment needed which is expensive and noisy, tends to be over-used or poorly used, reliant on hardware which may not work, not widely available in community or workplace environments

▶

Resource	Strengths	Limitations
Handouts	Easy to create, copy and use, versatile, wide variety of formats, permanent record to take away, printed versions make good quality editions, can be laminated to preserve, easy to adapt for differentiation, wide range of styles and uses	Overused at times, learners don't always read them fully, can get tatty when continually reproduced, especially copying from copies or reusing, need to consider copyright when copying from texts
Overhead transparencies	Widely available, portable, can build up pictures and diagrams, colourful, relatively easy to create, can be retained for future use if stored in dust-free area, can be used to pace lesson, good with large audiences	Slightly outdated, slides difficult to keep in pristine condition, different types of transparency needed for write-on, copiers and printers, projector is noisy and relies on power source
Games	Fun activities, tabular/text formats can easily be made into games for group work	Time-consuming to create or expensive to purchase
Models	Three dimensional, either life-sized or scale versions, good to feel/see/smell, ideal in 1:1 or small group settings, ideal to use/prepare for dangerous or expensive situations	Difficult to store, expensive to purchase or difficult to make
Video/DVD	Good method of aiding comprehension, appeals to all age groups, visual	Display equipment required which is expensive, not widely available and reliant on power sources

Resources are used either to aid teaching or to aid learning. The most effective resources stimulate a number of senses, are versatile and easy to use, achieve what they set out to achieve and are simple. There is no single resource that is purely advantageous to prepare and use, so the teacher must weigh up the strengths and limitations, and consider their learners and the environment in which they work. Then they can make informed decisions about what resources they should use.

8.3 New and emerging technologies

By the end of this section, you will be able to describe some of the new technologies which support learning and analyse how they enhance learning.

Most new and emerging technologies are associated with either computers or microchip technologies. It is obvious that teachers will use these (sometimes) labour-saving devices to appeal to their modern learners.

However, there is still a place for tried and tested methods and the key to successful teaching is a blended approach, that is, complementing traditional and modern technologies to aid effective learning. The interaction between the modern and the traditional adds variety, meets different needs and doesn't compromise the skills of the teacher. Inspectorates such as Ofsted advocate that poor learning is linked to lack of use of modern learning technologies (Ofsted, Annual Report 2004/05).

Some of the modern technologies, very often referred to as ILT (information learning technology) or ICT (information and communication technology), are listed below:

● World Wide Web (www)/Internet – a vast array of useful (and useless) information. Learners can be directed to sites for further reading or research or the sites can be downloaded (displayed) for use in class and for learners to engage with the activities contained within the sites. Copyright laws apply to how the

Internet is used and transmitted. The teacher should be cautious about its use: a web page can be written by anyone and there are no guarantees about the accuracy of the information they contain; sometimes a very innocent word used in a search engine has different connotations – check it out first, especially with younger or vulnerable learners. Use of 'cut and paste' sometimes incites the learner to plagiarise work by inaccurate referencing

- Intranet – organisational-based web pages, similar to the Internet. Specific readings or information pages can be uploaded (put onto the Intranet) to support learning

- VLE – (virtual learning environment) provides alternative learning strategies, without the need for direct contact. Brands commonly seen are Moodle, Blackboard, and LearnWise etc. They can support distance learning packages, support material, tracking systems, chat areas and email functions. Usually accessed and protected through password protection software

- Mobile phones – to text, email or surf the Internet, make video clips

- Digital cameras – a permanent record of practical activities

- Presentation software – PowerPoint

- Interactive boards – used as a board or display screen, touch or mouse-controlled through a PC or laptop or with a DVD player

- Electronic voting systems – an up-to-date version of multiple choice questioning seen on TV as audience-interactive answer systems

- Weblogs (blogs) – personal diary and chat facilities. Their educational use is not yet proven, although it has potential, it is not reliable in terms of content or accessibility.

Resources needed to facilitate the use of modern technologies:

- A computer (PC or laptop)
- A screen
- A projector
- Speakers
- Peripherals (devices associated with a computer: keyboard, mouse etc.)
- Software

When incorporating ILT or ICT into your teaching you should bear in mind how it is accessed. Not everyone has a computer, nor does every learning environment support the use of modern technologies. Thus a totally ILT/ICT-based learning medium would not be inclusive. This further supports the earlier suggestion of a blended approach. By all means offer it as an alternative means of learning and include it in teaching if you can, but remember that it doesn't suit everyone, nor is every teacher comfortable with its use and by offering both traditional and modern strategies you will be able to differentiate and vary your teaching.

8.4 Promoting equality, supporting diversity

By the end of this section, you will be able to explain the terms **equality** and **diversity** and why these agendas are required. You will be able to evaluate your own methods, comparing them to standards and identify strategies for promoting and improving practice.

REVISION

In Part One, Section 1.5, we looked at the legislation brought into being to support equality and diversity. We also considered some of the things that the teacher can do in the classroom to enhance their practice.

Society is diverse. Some people are old, some are young. Some are disabled, some black, some have children, some are male – everyone is different but everyone is valued and respected.

Some stats:

By 2010 only 20 per cent of the UK working population will be white, male, able-bodied and under 45.

Ethnic minorities make up 7.9 per cent of the population; in London it is 31 per cent.

National Council Voluntary Organisations – Defining Diversity
http://www.ncvo-vol.org.uk – accessed 30.06.07

Equality and diversity are terms which are expressed quite frequently, yet usually without a clear explanation of what the terms mean. So, here goes …

Equality means more about compliance with the law than diversity. It pre-empts discrimination by adhering to a systematic policy approach to ensure organisations stay within the boundaries of the legislation. It covers gender, race, disability, age, religion and sexual orientation.

Diversity recognises and celebrates differences; it supports equality by respecting rights, valuing individual talents and advocating that everyone's skills are fully utilised. Failing to promote diversity has an expensive outcome; there is a risk of litigation by dissatisfied customers, there is a risk that funding by public bodies will be discontinued and there is the possibility that the organisation's reputation may be harmed.

The equality agenda is more about conformity to laws and policy interpretations. It helps to ensure that the organisation supports equality by advising staff, learners and other stakeholders about its standards. The diversity agenda, in seeking to celebrate the differences in society, looks at the culture of the organisation to check that it promotes equality throughout its business practices.

- Expressed beliefs – that practices do not stereotype or make assumptions
- Cultural forms – that books and media are appropriate and jokes are not biased
- Knowledge systems – that learning resources and the curriculum offer is relevant and appropriate.

It will operate at three levels:

1 Individual – checking for verbal, physical abuse and discriminatory acts
2 Organisational – that practices, policies and procedures are *in situ*
3 Structural – that buildings support an inclusive regime.

Equality and diversity not only affects teachers' practices, but requires the teacher to advocate equality and diversity in their learners. For example, comments of an unfair nature must be challenged rather than ignored and, irrespective of the **demography** of the learning environment, learners are prepared for the national balance.

ACTIVITY 3

Self-evaluation: How equal and diverse is your practice?

How well do you do in terms of equality and diversity? Use this evaluation table, but try to avoid yes/no answers by making a comment that discusses how it is and/or how it ought to be.

Have you attended equality and diversity training?	
How diverse are your learners?	
Can your learners explain about bullying and harassment?	
Do the placement providers that you use have equality and diversity procedures in place?	
What is the demography of the community you serve?	
Do you monitor applications, retention and achievement in terms of gender, age, ethnicity etc.?	
Is your course generally taken up by a particular group of people?	
How are complaints dealt with?	
Do social and enrichment events celebrate the diverse society?	
Are all religious festivals recorded on the business calendar?	
Do your resources and teaching methods promote equality and diversity?	

From your answers, you should now write down ideas about how you can develop your inclusive practice to ensure equality and diversity.

8.5 Identifying functional skill abilities of learners

By the end of this section, you will be able to compare and contrast the functional skill abilities of your learners with the functional skill needs of your curriculum, state the importance and methods of identifying **functional skills** in both contexts and how to develop literacy, numeracy and information communication technology skills.

REVISION

In Part One, Section 2.2, you were introduced to the meaning and purpose of functional skills, reviewed their location within the National Qualifications Framework (NQF), and looked at how functional skills could be embedded into the curriculum.

In 1998, the Moser Report highlighted the poor basic skills in society, saying that one in five people were functionally illiterate. The Leitch Review in 2005 stated that one-third of adults do not have basic school leaving qualifications. Functional skills are a key element of the 14–19 reforms as set out in the 14–19 Education and Skills White Paper (DfES 2005), which defines functional skills as:

> Core elements of English, mathematics, and ICT that provide an individual with essential knowledge, skills and understanding that will enable them to operate confidently, effectively and independently in life and work.

> 14–19 Education and Skills: Implementation Plan
> (Feb 2005) www.dfes.gov.uk

The Basic Skills Agency (2001) writes:

> The ability to read, write and speak English and to use mathematics at a level necessary to function and progress at work and in society in general.

> http://www.basic–skills.co.uk

In the post-compulsory sector, we are constantly faced with meeting the people these reports refer to. The reasons behind these levels of ability are varied and subjective, but suffice to say, they are real and may inhibit our learners' abilities to achieve their potential. It may be appropriate here to describe what a learner should be expected to be able to do at the various levels as a means of setting the benchmark for identifying the skills required of learners entering your specific career or vocational area.

Literacy	Numeracy
At Level 1, someone can:	
• Take part in an interview for a job or course or follow a simple procedure in a manual • Fill out an application form for a driving licence or passport	• Read bus and train timetables correctly • Follow direction to mix, dilute substances in proportion • Estimate distances using scales printed on a map
At Entry 3, someone can:	
• Obtain information or advice from a telephone helpline • Read a job advert in a local paper or job centre • Write a short letter to a family member or friend	• Understand price labels on prepacked food • Check the receipt and money when paying for goods • Use a map to find a location, e.g., for an interview
At Entry 2, someone can:	
• Respond to a question and know when to ask for help • Follow simple instructions on a vending machine • Fill in a simple form	• Understand measurements and sizes on labels • Use simple measuring equipment, e.g., scales • Understand expiry dates and renewal dates, e.g., food labels, road tax

Literacy	Numeracy
At Entry 1, someone can:	
<ul><li>Follow a one-step verbal instruction</li><li>Understand common signs in their local area and at work, e.g., toilets, no smoking</li><li>Write their own name and address on an official form</li></ul>	<ul><li>Select the correct numbered button in a lift</li><li>Count the correct number of drinks for visitors</li><li>Key in a telephone number</li></ul>

http://www.advice-resources.co.uk/adviceresources/general/guides/bsa/bsa.pdf

 ACTIVITY 4

In the context of your subject, what functional skills do learners of that subject need in order to be proficient?

It may help to break those skills down:

Literacy:
Speaking
Listening
Writing
Reading

Mathematics:
Numbers
Measurement and shape
Handling data

You should think about the skills required to achieve technical or knowledge abilities AND skills to aid learning.

Three levels of functional skills are needed:

1   Those who need a quick update to get their skills to the required level
2   Those who need minimal support in functional literacy or numeracy
3   Those who need specific targeted help to develop their skills.

There is a fourth group who may need support and that is those whose first language is not English. In this group they may be literate and numerate in their mother tongue but not able to transfer those skills into a second language.

Identifying problems in functional skills

Screening The obvious thing to do as part of your enrolment or selection process is to check that your learners have the minimum requirements for entering your programme. For example: entry to a National Diploma requires 5 GCSEs at C or above (or equivalent). It is the 'equivalent' that usually causes problems, but the NQF (see Section 2.2), guides you to academic and vocational equivalents and a CV will help you decide about the skill levels of mature learners.

Initial assessment The next check is likely to be at induction. You can observe and/or interview your learners. You can look at set pieces of writing and ask questions to identify ability levels. Learners with poor functional skills, especially the more mature ones, are adept at disguising those skills. Some things that may alert you to problems are:

● 'I forgot my glasses, so I can't do it'
● 'I'm in a rush, can I take it home and do it later?'
● Patchy completion of the enrolment or application form.
● Distracting conversations or behaviours.

Some strategies that help to reassure learners about why you need to do these initial assessments include:

● Talking about improving skills rather than poor skills
● Raise self-esteem; motivate by looking at values and reasons

- Explanations
- Discussing outcomes and support.

Diagnostic The final method of checking ability is usually either a routine strategy of induction or a response if you suspect that there may be inadequacies in functional skills. There are a range of tests, both paper-based and online, to ascertain the level of ability. Some learners with poor functional skills benefit from computer-aided resources. It is highly likely that learners will have what is called a 'spiky profile'. This means that they are good at some aspects and weaker in others, causing them to be at different levels on the NQF.

Useful online resources

http://www.basic-skills.co.uk/resourcecentre
http://www.learndirect-advice.co.uk/helpwithyourcareer/jobprofiles/
http://www.move-on.org.uk

8.6 Adapting resources

By the end of this section, you will be able to suggest ways of modifying resources to meet individual needs of learners and to suit curriculum requirements whilst maintaining an inclusive learning environment.

REVISION

In Part One, Section 2.5, you reviewed a range of resources and were able to identify how to use them in the context of your own teaching subject.

Adapting resources to meet needs, both yours and your learners, is similar to adapting methods of presentation and assessment to benefit learners. Resources are not only the equipment and paper you take into the classroom, but you and your support mechanisms. A resource is anything which aids either the teaching or learning. There are some very simple rules when making sure that your resources are fit for purpose:

● Keep it simple, both in its creation and use.

● Ensure purposefulness – why create a resource that does not offer any value to the learning process?

● Be confident – practice how you will use the resource, especially if using it for the first time.

● Equipment – have you got access to what you need to use your resource?

Why do we use resources?

● To create interest

● To explain things visually

● To provide information

● As a memory aid

● To collect information

● To create active learners

● To promote autonomy

● To offer variety

● To promote equality

● To communicate

● To differentiate.

The adaptations that are made depend on what resources you use, how you use resources, and when you use resources. Earlier chapters and sections within this chapter have detailed some ideas about adapting resources. These involve considering your learners, what they are studying, how they are studying and all the variables that emerge as you get to know your learners. Some of the simplest and more common adaptations that can be made are:

● To include white space – learners can add notes during your presentation, thus engaging with the resource

- To include images – to enhance visual appearance and create interest
- To word process handouts and OHTs, with appropriate font styles and sizes
- To miss out words – again to engage learners with the handout or PowerPoint
- To address inclusivity (paper/print colour, size, language, expression, etc.)
- To slow down your speed of writing on the board which helps to improve legibility
- To use reveal and overlay techniques to create pace in the lesson
- To use key points or bullet points rather than lots of text.

To consolidate this section, try this activity to analyse one of your resources:

 ACTIVITY 5

Adapting resources

Take one handout or print out from a PowerPoint presentation or web page (or similar text-based resource) that you have used in the last few weeks.

Analyse the following:

What percentage of the resource is white space?	
Is it read-only or is the learner required to interact with the resource?	
How many images are in the resource?	
What is the presentation style?	

▶

Is the resource prose, subtitle/text, bullet point or key word?	
What is the balance between the presentation style (same/varied)	
What is the font style and font size?	
How do you know if the information contained within the resource is understood?	

How can you improve the resource to meet the needs of:

● Visual learners?

● Kinaesthetic learners?

● ESOL learners?

● Entry Level learners?

● Level 3+ learners?

Is the resource fully referenced?

Are there additional links to further information or websites?

Can the resource be effectively used as:

● A teacher's aid?

● A learning aid?

● A revision tool?

● An assessment tool?

Review the resource and *adapt* it accordingly. Keep before and after versions to show your personal development, and *reflect* on this activity with a colleague or tutor.

Glossary of terms

ADHD Attention deficit/hyperactivity disorder

Autonomy independence in the ability to learn

Concept an idea

Demography a study of population trends

Diversity valuing and celebrating the differences in people

Equality ensuring fairness

Functional skills basic skills of literacy and numeracy

Gifted and talented learners highly skilled or adept

NQF National Qualifications Framework

VLE virtual learning environment – a modern teaching and learning style using computer technologies

 # SUMMARY

In this chapter, you have covered all of the theoretical aspects of the third learning outcome of the second unit in your CTLLS qualification:

Designing inclusive learning activities which motivate and enthuse learners; resources – strengths and limitations; new and emerging technologies; promoting equality, supporting diversity; identifying functional skill abilities of learners; adapting resources.

Your Personal Development

You will have looked at motivation theories, considered your own level of motivation and reflected on how this affects your learning and what could be done to improve motivation.

You have reviewed a range of resources and compared the advantages and disadvantages of their uses, commenting on how they can be adapted in order to be fit for purpose. You have analysed a resource, commenting on possible adaptations. You have evaluated and reflected upon how new technologies are appropriate and relevant in the learning environment.

You have developed your awareness of equality and diversity and how and why it is important. You have undertaken a self-assessment of your own practices, identifying areas for development and improvement.

In the final section, you have revisited functional skills needs and started to explore how functional skills are important in your specific curriculum area in preparing your learners for study and work.

You should be able to answer questions relating to:

- Equality and diversity in the classroom
- Adapting resources for inclusive learning
- Development of functional skills.

And demonstrate:

- Appropriate selection of resources in your teaching situations.

CHAPTER 9
(PEL, UNIT 4)

Effective communication skills

LEARNING OBJECTIVES

In this chapter you will learn about:

- Theories of communication
- Different communication methods
- Communication in teaching
- How to improve communication
- Potential barriers to communication
- How to liaise effectively with learners, peers and other stakeholders

9.1 Communication methods

By the end of this section, you will be able to state the main theoretical ideas surrounding **communication** models and describe methods that create effective communication.

REVISION

In Part One, Section 4.5, you discovered that communication is the art of passing messages and can occur mainly by written, verbal and non-verbal methods. You also considered how some things will turn out to be a barrier to **effective** communication.

Communication theory – Shannon and Weaver model

One easy to understand model of communication was suggested by Shannon and Weaver in 1949. This is a basic model in which they say that all communication needs:

- An encoder – the means of sending the message (speaking/writing)
- A message – something to say
- A channel – a way of sending the message
- A decoder – a means of receiving the message (listening/reading)
- A receiver – the person to send the message to.

They further add that communication is hindered by noise.

This model is satisfactory in so far that it explains how communication is transmitted; however, it does not suggest how messages need to be understood in order to be effective. Nor does it address how individuals put their own interpretation on messages and that those interpretations sometimes confuse the issue.

Figure 9A Communication model – Claude Shannon and Warren Weaver 1949/ David Berlo (1960)

Remember our first rule of teaching
ASSUME NOTHING

Just because we have said or written something, it does not mean that it has been received and understood. This leads us to consider the many skills required when communicating.

- *Listening* – The ability to hear what is being said
- *Comprehension* – The ability to understand what is being said
- *Speaking* – The ability to express thoughts and messages clearly
- *Writing* – The ability to express thoughts and messages legibly
- *Negotiating* – The ability to agree or compromise with others in discussions
- *Reading* – The ability to understand written text
- *Empathising* – The ability to understand and share feelings and emotions
- *Using numeracy* – The ability to use numbers to express ideas
- *Persuading* – The ability to reason or argue your beliefs in discussion
- *Networking* – The ability to work in a group to share ideas
- *Assertiveness* – The ability to be forceful and confident
- *Sharing information* – The ability to contribute to or take part in discussions
- *Speaking and writing in a foreign language* – The ability to express ideas to those whose language is different to your own.

This is critical to:

● Workplace harmony
● Effective teaching and learning
● Productivity

Communication theory – Transactional Analysis

Eric Berne developed his theories of Transactional Analysis in the 1950s; they are more associated with relationships than the actual process of communicating, which offers another perspective. He was inspired by Freud and the scientific developments of the era. His theories are widely accepted today, but are being modified to meet the modern environment. You will find that they are applied in a wide variety of contexts including medical research, personality analysis and management development as well as communication theory. Not surprisingly, he ascertained that communication was at the centre of human relationships and that communication was natural. He argues that it is a stimulus: thus, we will always speak when spoken to. He does quantify this by saying that those responses will vary according to our 'alter ego states'. Each person is made up of three alter **ego** states: parent, adult and child.

Parent ego state This is our voice of authority, very often typified by tried and tested statements, learned from our parents, For example the parent would say: 'under no circumstances', 'always', and advocate values such as don't lie, cheat etc. The **body language** may show impatience and the verbal language includes patronising expressions.

Child ego state This is our dependent state. This is typified by us seeking assurances, or at its worse displaying immature behaviours. It may display temper tantrums, whining voices, baby talk, excuses and big words used incorrectly.

Adult ego state This is our independent state; the ability to think and act responsibly and maturely. The physical appearance is attentive and non-threatening. Sentences include reasons and negotiated styles.

The styles are not limited to words and also include non-verbal expressions.

Berne states that effective communication is when the states are equal. For example, when someone in the parent state talks to someone in the child state, it is only effective if it is returned in the same style, i.e. the child accepts they are communicating with a parent. Thus the dialogue with younger learners who may be seeking guidance and reassurance as they enter post-compulsory education is usually a parent-child type. As learners mature you are more likely to see adult to adult communications. In short, Berne argues that effective communication is more about relationships than the act of sending and receiving messages.

 ACTIVITY 1

Scenario

It is the beginning of a new term and the inexperienced teacher is working with a group of 14-year-olds in a vocational setting. Communication is failing and as a result creates a poor behaviour management situation. The teacher thinks that they cannot teach or manage this group and becomes confrontational.

Using Berne's theories of Transactional Analysis, explain the underlying causes of this communication problem. How could the teacher improve this scenario?

The teacher probably made the assumption that the learners wanted to learn the subject, would be motivated and probably enjoy an environment different to that of the methods seen in schools. Using Berne's theory, you may be likely to see the teacher initially trying to communicate in an adult-child position. Unfortunately, this was the first mistake. Younger learners have to learn how to communicate in an adult way. From the day they were born, they (the learners) have communicated in parent-child positions and this is mirrored in schools. In a confrontational situation a child-child position emerges and usually goes nowhere! It is part of the transition between compulsory and post-compulsory education that a parent-child style is maintained and as trust and maturity develop, then a more adult-adult position can be adopted.

Communication in teaching

Communication occurs in every teaching and learning interaction.

- *A presentation* – speaking, listening, reading and writing occur in the preparation and delivery of every presentation. Both learners and teacher present information during their programme.
- *Assignments* – learners will communicate to you through their writing and they will have engaged in communication throughout the gathering of information. The ability to express themselves accurately in their written work is essential to language development.
- *Questioning* – either verbal or written; teachers and learners have to speak or write and listen or read in order to understand and respond to the question.
- *Verbal exposition* – teachers are offering information, learners are listening, comprehending and hopefully rephrasing into their own notes. Again accuracy in spelling, grammar and punctuation is essential to ensure meaning and correct interpretation.
- *Feedback* – teachers and learners need to be able to communicate effectively in order to support learning.

Modern communication channels Teaching and learning is being modernised as communication develops and evolves using modern technologies. We email each other frequently, our learners text us to let us know they will be late, we can receive and mark work online, learning programmes can be 'taught' remotely using distance learning and self-study packs, possibly linked to virtual learning environments (VLEs). Increasingly we blog and chat about things in our lives and participate in forums to ask questions and discuss issues. We need not now attend meetings (or lessons!) if we can use video conferencing, web cams and conference calls. Our learners might even catch up with missed lessons by downloading a webcast or podcast! Whilst these technologies continue to improve and become more interactive, there is nothing which beats a blended approach to learning. So don't get too carried away yet, there is still considerable value in communicating face to face and of course, we should not disadvantage those learners who are technophobes or simply do not have access to such resources.

Authenticity In communicating with learners and other stakeholders it is essential to validate the authenticity of what is spoken and written. Whilst it is easy to identify whose thoughts are being expressed when using direct assessment methods such as observation and questioning, it is not so easy through some of the other assessment methods, for example assignments and essays. Unfortunately, whilst the Internet is valuable to research, it is also easy to express other people's ideas and claim them as your own. This is plagiarism. See Appendix C: Study Skills, p. 376.

9.2 Improving communication; barriers to learning

By the end of this section, you will be able to express ideas which will enhance communication skills in your learners and yourself. You will be able to state why communication is not always effective and describe the effects this has on learning.

REVISION

In Part One, Sections 2.3 and 4.5, you discovered that there are numerous reasons for communication not to work. Using DELTA (disability, emotional, language, technology and ability) classifications and considering language tone and style you discovered that you are able to modify your teaching to overcome these barriers.

Improving communication

Negotiating is one of the keys to effective communication. Finding out why learners want to do something (or not), and establishing compromise is when and how a more favourable environment will emerge; a more adult relationship. This will not occur overnight, just because a 16-year-old has started college and thinks they are grown up, it does not necessarily follow that they are adult. This maturity may take up to six months (or longer) to develop before that 16-year-old starts to understand the needs, language and behaviours associated with post-compulsory education. Try not to give up too soon!

Communication is essential in the learning environment and it becomes more effective when enhanced by active learning strategies:

Oral skills can be developed by talking in class, discussions and questioning. By offering learners time to 'solo free write' you are giving all of them time to consider their answers, and this will develop how they participate in constructive talking by increasing their confidence in speaking. Similarly, allowing pair time or small group time to discuss issues and then a feedback slot improves knowledge and thus confidence.

Writing skills can be enhanced by note-taking, class and homework exercises, written assessments. In any activity that you do you should encourage writing skills, even if the writing is in note form. It could be a handout where the learner has to complete missing words, or ideas expressed in writing using note, report and essay formats.

Listening skills can be enhanced by discussion groups, role play activities and teacher talk sessions. These sessions develop listening skills by creating opportunities during which learners have to listen to other ideas; those ideas can be consolidated into their own evaluative work. Asking learners to present mini seminars about a subject will result in them responding to questions posed by others in the group, which results in comprehension activities. ICT skills may also be developed if presenting information using software packages.

Reading skills can be enhanced by paraphrasing, case studies and comprehension activities. By giving a learner something to read and asking them to do something as a result, it demonstrates their understanding of the subject.

These active learning ideas both develop the basics of communication as well as creating lively things to do in class. Even the most passive activity of listening can be enlivened by asking learners to do something with the information just received. The responses from learners will confirm the effectiveness of your communication – that is: is the message received and understood?

How do you know if communication is effective?

There are some simple watch points:

- Facial expressions
- Loss of attention
- Noise level rises
- Leaning back on seats.

There are some simple checks:

- Ask open questions
- Gather feedback
- Recap asking for explanations
- Listen to conversations in group activities.

By watching out for change you will soon pick up vibes about effectiveness.

CHECKLIST FOR COMMUNICATION EFFECTIVENESS	
Language used was clear and used tone and expression to create mood	
Technical words and jargon terms were explained	
Learners' body language demonstrated interest in the speaker	

▶

CHECKLIST FOR COMMUNICATION EFFECTIVENESS (*continued*)

Facilities created for writing, listening and effective recording of information	
Questions were relevant and were open in style (demanding answer – not yes/no response)	
Clarification was sought if unsure about intended meanings – by teacher, by learner, by support assistants	
Feedback was unambiguous	
Activity and learning summaries were clear and highlighted key issues	
Suitable communication strategies were used to ensure all learners participated	
Background noise is minimised	

Communication assessment

How was communication effectiveness assessed?

By self, peers, learners, tutors, other: _____

Reflections about how communication can be improved:

Barriers to learning

Petty explains communication as a chain of events, in which a message is developed, transmitted, heard and comprehended. He expresses this as:

> What I mean → what I say → what they hear → what they understand.

> Petty 2004, p. 38

He refers to the game of Chinese whispers as a means of proving that communication as a messaging system can sometimes go a little awry. This, however, is a linear model, a one-way process: effective communication is formed from a two-way process. That is, there needs to be some form of check to ensure that what is said has been understood.

Just because you are a good teacher and everything around you is conducive to learning, it does not necessarily follow that your learners will be able to learn. Sometimes, their previous experiences in learning will form a barrier which will prevent learning occurring; with widening participation in learning comes a variety of behaviours which, if inappropriate, can interrupt or constrain the learning process, resulting in **disengaged** learners and problems with attendance and punctuality. Additionally, staff may be reluctant to meet the new challenges in the curriculum, and be expected to cope with learners who bring their many characteristics and individualities. These obstacles must be managed.

Some of the main issues that you will see in learners are: lack of confidence; lack of vocational/basic skills; lack of understanding about expectations and ineffective transition from the previous to the current learning programme. These can be overcome by:

- Access to preparatory courses
- Learning at a level/pace relevant to need
- Modes of attendance to meet need
- Negotiated learning
- Targeted learning
- Supported learning
- Structured tutorials.

Increasingly, the principle of putting the learners first when designing programmes is being demonstrated in schemes and session plans. This can be achieved by:

- Delivering topics practically before underpinning with theory;
- Designing the curriculum to meet learner needs rather than staffing needs;

- Addressing deficiencies on functional skills by differentiating, discrete provision, flexible learning materials, learning support, but always embedding the skills and supporting the development of learners;
- Using **holistic** learning strategies to minimise repetition in programmes;
- Preparing learners for learning;
- Spreading out assessment over duration of course;
- Assessing with consideration of other commitments of learners.

Equally, you might not be good at getting the message across, in which case you need to review your methods and adapt your strategies accordingly.

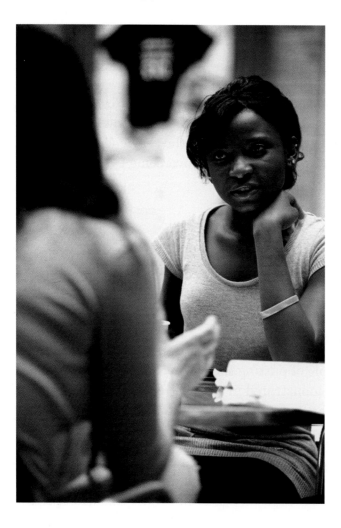

9.3 Liaising with learners, peers and other stakeholders

By the end of this section, you will be able to describe the role and communication lines between the various stakeholders in the education process and state the importance of liaison.

Liaising means to co-operate. It is important that everyone in the educational **context** is working to the same outcome, even if they are motivated by different drivers. Let us consider the various people (the stakeholders) involved:

The learner

The learner wants to achieve their learning aim or ambition. There are sometimes periods when this is not their primary goal (other factors may influence their progress), but generally they are enrolled to reach a specific goal. They will liaise with their teachers and employers – or if under 18, their parents.

The learners' parents or guardians

Learners aged below 18 remain the responsibility of their parents or guardians. As such they care about the progress of their wards and may contribute to that process (to varying degrees). They will liaise with teachers and learners.

Teachers or tutors

They are involved in the process of helping their learners develop. They will be a team of people, each responsible for a specific part of their curriculum. They will liaise with learners, parents or employers (dependent upon age of learner), other teaching staff and managers.

Management teams

They oversee the work of teachers and undertake quality assurance arrangements. They will liaise with teachers, governors and funding bodies.

Governors/board of directors

They have overall responsibility for the running of the organisation. They will liaise with the management team and funding bodies.

Employers

Employers will either send their staff for training or receive people at the end of their training and education. They want to ensure that training offered in either case is relevant to their needs and is up to date. They liaise with learners and teachers and funding bodies.

Funding bodies

They provide the money to pay for courses and training and therefore want assurances that the monies are well spent. Funding may be from public or private sources. They will liaise with employers, managers and the governorship or directorate.

Other people in the process are:

- Corporate services (finance, personnel, admissions),
- Careers, employment agencies
- Awarding bodies, regulatory bodies
- Inspectorates
- Government bodies, and
- Care and support services.

Whilst each has a valuable role, their contact is usually restricted to one of the group of primary stakeholders, listed above.

The co-operation between all of these groups of people is vital to the smooth running of the organisation. Communication between the parties ensures that learners receive the most **efficient** and effective learning that can possibly be provided. The learner is at the **hub**. Without learners, teachers wouldn't have anyone to teach, parents and employers would not need or be able to promote training as a means of economic survival, funding bodies would not need to support learning and managers and governors would not have organisations to strategically direct. Therefore, it is not surprising that most educational initiatives are responsive to learner needs, yet oddly they (the learners) are very often the smallest voice in educational development.

By representing this sequence visually, you will see the possible reason for the learner voice not having a strong impact on how education happens. It may be a cynical viewpoint, but the people who control education have the least dealings with those who participate in it, which means it befalls the teacher, who has a greater role in the liaising between those involved in the process of education, to ensure meaning and value is provided for all stakeholders. So, whilst the learner is the centre of the education, the teacher is the centre of the communication.

Figure 9B   Communication channels

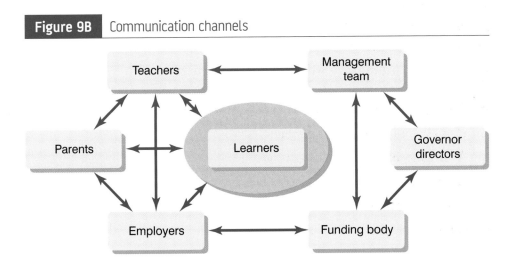

Whilst discussing stakeholders, it may be appropriate to mention 'the learning contract'. It is becoming more and more frequent that learners are asked to sign documents committing to achievement, attendance or compliance to rules.

Arguments for:

- Learner is clear about expectations
- Learner commits to a learning agenda.

Arguments against:

- Value to learner or organisation
- Legal requirement or moral value.

It is quite acceptable that these documents are used; however, how binding they are remains an issue.

Glossary of terms

Body language using conscious or unconscious gesture to express feelings

Communication a means of sending and receiving information to share or exchange ideas

Context the setting in which learning occurs

Disengaged uninvolved with learning

Effective to produce the intended or desired result or outcome

Efficient productive working without waste

Ego self-importance or personal identity

Holistic the big picture; the whole curriculum

Hub the centre

Negotiation agreement and compromise towards outcome

SUMMARY

In this chapter, you have covered all of the theoretical aspects in relation to the fourth learning outcome of the second unit in your CTLLS qualification:

Communication methods; improving communication; barriers to communication; liaising with learners, peers and other stakeholders.

Your Personal Development

You will have looked at theories of communication and seen how they can be applied to the dialogue between teacher and learner. You have considered ways that communication can be made more effective and the impact that effective communication has on the learning process. Finally, you have reviewed the roles of people associated with learning and identified how they must liaise with each other to improve the learning environment.

You should be able to answer questions relating to:

- Effective communication
- Methods of communication
- Communication theory
- Active learning to develop communication
- Efficient liaison between stakeholders.

CHAPTER 10 (PEL, UNIT 5)

The minimum core

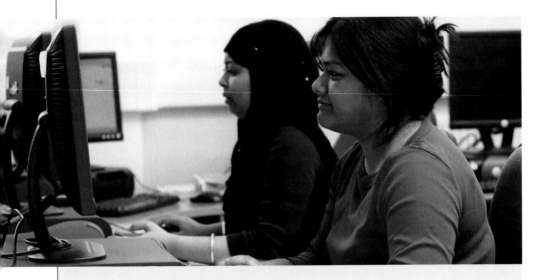

LEARNING OBJECTIVES

In this chapter you will learn about:

- The skills which constitute the minimum core
- How you can develop literacy and language skills
- How to develop your skills and understanding of numeracy
- How to develop skills in information communication technologies

10.1 Overview of the minimum core

This chapter considers the ways in which you can develop your skills of **literacy**, **language**, number and information and communication technologies. It should be read in conjunction with the latest guidance from the Lifelong Learning UK (**LLUK**) skills council about literacy, language, **numeracy** and **ICT** (**minimum core**) standards. This is available from http://www.lluk.org.

One of the first things that should be done as part of your qualification is to find out your current ability in the minimum core themes and then identify how you will develop them. This will probably be done by initially asking you to produce any previous certificates in the subjects, for example, GCSEs, O levels, A levels or adult literacy or numeracy tests. If you do not have such certificates, or can't find them, you may be asked to sit **diagnostic assessments** to confirm your level of competence. This information will then be transferred to your individual learning plan (**ILP**). Most providers of teacher training will specify the minimum level of competence required to enter their programmes. Generally, if you do not hold at least a Level 2 qualification in English or literacy, you will struggle to meet the requirements of the assessment of the programme and risk not being confident to teach or assess your learners. You should seek additional support should this be the case.

Summary of the minimum core elements

Language and literacy:

- Personal, social and cultural factors influencing language and literacy learning and development
- Explicit knowledge about language and the four skills: speaking, listening, reading and writing
- Personal language skills.

Numeracy:

- Personal, social and cultural factors influencing numeracy learning and development
- Explicit knowledge about numeracy communication and processes
- Personal numeracy skills.

Information and communication technology (ICT):

- Personal, social and cultural factors influencing ICT learning and development
- Explicit knowledge about ICT
- Personal ICT skills.

Each section of the minimum core requires you to have both the skills and understanding to develop the functional skills of your learners and your own personal functional skills. In Preparing to Teach in the Lifelong Learning Sector (PTLLS) there is no requirement to meet the minimum core, although you may find that it is at this point that your own skills are first analysed. In the Certificate in Teaching in the Lifelong Learning Sector (CTLLS) the focus is on the development of personal skills. There will not be any assessment other than for the purpose of proving that development. Your programme will include opportunities to develop the skills either embedded into the programme, as part of your teaching experience, within a continuing professional development programme or as a stand-alone class.

The Diploma in Teaching in the Lifelong Learning Sector (DTLLS) will include both personal skill development and developing knowledge and understanding elements. This will be reviewed regularly and targeted developments made. The minimum core is initially to be assessed through **self-assessment**. Whilst in its introductory stage there are no formal assessment requirements. It is anticipated, however, that external testing will soon be introduced to measure the development and outcomes.

Note: The coding system used within the standards below is unique to this publication and is used to link the suggested activities with the standards.

Some of the activities listed below are more effective when carried out under the supervision of a literacy, numeracy or ICT specialist.

10.2 Developing literacy and language skills

By the end of this section, you will be able to identify some opportunities to develop your skills and understanding of literacy and language. Through referencing teaching and learning activities and your personal development to the standards below you will demonstrate your progress and development.

In the same way that you may be developing your learners' functional skill needs, your own personal skills may benefit from a similar exercise. For the teacher these skills will be development from Level 2 skills (at entry) to Level 3 skills (on exit). These skills are known as the *minimum core*. That means the standard of literacy, language, numeracy and ICT required of teachers. There is still much national development in this subject insofar as it will apply to teachers – are the skills embedded and evidenced through the role or is there a need for testing? It really is watch this space at the moment, but this section concentrates on developing skills as part of the role, rather than attempting to 'teach' Level 3 functional skills in literacy, language, numeracy and ICT.

Listed below are the standards of competence required of teachers. They will probably seem complex and confusing at first – it is normal to think that. Your tutor will guide you through the process by creating an individual learning plan to identify exactly what you need to do to develop the skills. This may vary according to the skills you possess as you start the programme and changes in policy and assessment of functional skills.

The minimum core standards (literacy)

Part A   Knowledge and understanding

Personal, social and cultural factors influencing language and literacy learning and development

- The different factors affecting the acquisition and development of language and literacy skills (LAK1)

- The importance of English language and literacy in enabling users to participate in public life, society and the modern economy (LAK2)
- Potential barriers that can hinder development of language skills (LAK3)
- The main learning disabilities and difficulties relating to language learning and skill development (LAK4)
- Multilingualism and the role of the first language in the acquisition of additional languages (LAK5)
- Issues that arise when learning another language or translating from one language to another (LAK6)
- Issues relating to varieties of English, including standard English, dialects and attitudes towards them (LAK7)
- The importance of context in language use and the influence of the communicative situation (LAK8)

Speaking

- Making appropriate choices in oral communication episodes (LAS1)
- Having a knowledge of fluency, accuracy and competence for ESOL learners (LAS2)
- Using spoken English effectively (LAS3)

Listening

- Listening effectively (LAL1)

Reading

- Interpreting written texts (LAR1)
- Knowledge of how textual features support reading (LAR2)
- Understanding the barriers to accessing text (LAR3)

Writing

- Communicating the writing process (LAW1)
- Using genre to develop writing (LAW2)
- Developing spelling and punctuation skills (LAW3)

Part B   Personal language skills

Speaking

- Expressing yourself clearly, using communication techniques to help convey meaning and to enhance the delivery and accessibility of the message (LBS1)
- Showing the ability to use language, style and tone in ways that suit the intended audience, and to recognise their use by others (LBS2)
- Using appropriate techniques to reinforce oral communication, check how well the information is received and support the understanding of those listening (LBS3)
- Using non-verbal communication to assist in conveying meaning and receiving information, and recognising its use by others (LBS4)

Listening

- Listening attentively and responding sensitively to contributions made by others (LBL1)

Reading

- Find, and select from, a range of reference material and sources of information, including the Internet (LBR1)
- Use and reflect on a range of reading strategies to interpret texts and to locate information or meaning (LBR2)
- Identify and record the key information or messages contained within reading material using note-taking techniques (LBR3)

Writing

- Write fluently, accurately and legibly on a range of topics (LBW1)
- Select appropriate format and style of writing for different purposes and different readers (LBW2)
- Use spelling and punctuation accurately in order to make meaning clear (LBW3)
- Understand and use the conventions of grammar (the forms and structures of words, phrases, clauses, sentences and texts) consistently when producing written text (LBW4)

Some activities that will develop your knowledge, understanding and skills:

A case study

Identify an individual or group of individuals and identify their educational and cultural backgrounds, their barriers to learning and any specific learning need relating to literacy (LAK1, LAK2, LAK3, LAK4, LAK7). What are their aspirations and how does literacy form part of their development? (LAK2, LAK8).

The lesson

Conduct a typical lesson and map it to the minimum core.

Alternatively, observe a session and comment upon the speaking, listening, reading and writing activities of the teacher and learners (LBS1, LBS2, LBS3, LBS4, LBL1, LBR1, LBR2, LBR3, LBW1, LBW2, LBW3, LBW4).

Reference the objectives or outcomes of the session/s to literacy (and numeracy) national standards (Core Curriculum Entry/L1/L2).

This activity is also effective when the analysis is related to learning styles and teaching methods, thus (hopefully) demonstrating a balanced, inclusive style (e.g. visual, auditory, kinaesthetic; active/passive).

Understanding material

Analyse a handout, worksheet or assignment task in relation to the complexity of the language, the activities it requires (writing something or reading and comprehending etc.), and reference it to national standards/core curricula (LAR1, LAR2, LAR3, LAW1, LAW2, LAW3).

Comprehension – research

Interview someone whose first language is not English, and find out how they cope with learning and teaching in a second or foreign language. How has their language choice changed and are there external influences on language choice: (LAK2, LAK3, LAK5, LAK6, LAS1, LAS2, LAS3, LAL1, LBS1, LBS2, LBS3, LBS4, LBL1).

An alternative activity is to listen to about five minutes of a person speaking in a foreign language. Then discuss your feelings, and identify if you understood anything through expression or gesture (LAL1, LBL1, LBS4).

Another similar activity is to attempt to decode some text using a different alphabet system, shorthand or Wingdings font (LAR1, LAR2, LAR3, LAW1, LBR2).

Shadow drawing

Two people sit back to back. One person (A) has a simple picture; the other (B) has a blank sheet of paper and a pen. (A) gives instructions to (B) in the hope that (B) will replicate the picture. (B) is allowed to check the instructions, but may not look at the original picture (LBS1, LBS2, LBS3, LBL1).

Colour – action research

- Use a range of coloured overlays and place over the top of white handouts.
- Experiment with coloured pens on boards and overhead transparencies.
- Select a different colour when writing on the interactive board.
- Photocopy handouts onto different coloured paper.
- Print handouts using a different font colour.

Compare and contrast the clarity of the colours and decide which are more easily read. This strategy of colour clarity is particularly useful in supporting learners with **dyslexia** (LAK3, LAK4, LAR2, LAR3, LAW1, LAW2, LBR2).

These activities will demonstrate your understanding of literacy and language (and in some cases numeracy) and how it impacts on learning. It will show that you are aware of barriers which impede language and literacy development. In writing the reports your own skills of reading and writing will be developed, especially in terms of spelling, grammar and punctuation and paraphrasing. (LBW1, LBW2, LBW3, LBW4). When interviewing or speaking to learners to elicit the information, your own oral communication and listening skills are developed (LBS1, LBS2, LBS3, LBS4, LBL1).

10.3 Developing mathematical skills

By the end of this section, you will be able to identify some opportunities to develop your skills and understanding of numeracy. Through referencing teaching and learning activities to the standards below you will demonstrate your progress and development.

The minimum core standards (numeracy)

Part A   Knowledge and understanding

Personal, social and cultural factors influencing numeracy learning and development

- The different factors affecting the acquisition and development of numeracy skills (NAK1)
- The importance of numeracy in enabling users to participate in, and gain access to, society and the modern economy (NAK2)
- Potential barriers that can hinder development of numeracy skills (NAK3)

- The main learning difficulties and disabilities relating to numeracy skills learning and development (NAK4)
- The common misconceptions and confusions related to number-associated difficulties (NAK5)

Communication

- Making and using judgements about understanding (NAC1)
- Communication processes and understandings (NAC2)

Processes

- A knowledge of the capacity of numeracy skills to support problem-solving (NAP1)
- Making sense of situations and representing them (NAP2)
- Processing and analysis (NAP3)
- Using numeracy skills and content knowledge (NAP4)
- Interpreting and evaluating results (NAP5)
- Communicating and reflecting on findings (NAP6)

Part B   Personal numeracy skills

Communication

- Communicate with others about numeracy in an open and supportive manner (NBC1)
- Assess your own, and other people's, understanding (NBC2)
- Express yourself clearly and accurately (NBC3)
- Communicate about numeracy in a variety of ways that suit and support the intended audience, and recognise such use by others (NBC4)
- Use appropriate techniques to reinforce oral communication, check how well the information is received and support the understanding of those listening (NBC5)

Processes

- Use strategies to make sense of a situation requiring the application of numeracy (NBP1)
- Process and analyse data (NBP2)

- Use generic content knowledge and skills (NBP3)
- Make decisions concerning content knowledge and skills (NBP4)
- Understand the validity of different methods (NBP5)
- Consider accuracy, efficiency and effectiveness when solving problems and reflect on what has been learnt (NBP6)
- Make sense of data (NBP7)
- Select appropriate format and style for communicating findings (NBP8)

Whereas dyslexia is associated with a difficulty in interpreting words and symbols, **dyscalculia** is associated with difficulties in making sense of numbers and calculations. Some people just seem to panic when faced with maths, whereas others really enjoy working with numbers. Hence there seems to be emphasis in the numeracy standards on 'supporting' and 'sensitivity'.

A case study

Identify an individual or group of individuals and identify their educational and cultural backgrounds, their barriers to learning and any specific learning need relating to numeracy (NAK1, NAK2, NAK3, NAK4). What are their aspirations, and how does numeracy form part of their development? (NAK2, NAK5).

Data-related activities

Many of the things a teacher is required to do will relate to analysing numbers. How many passed their course (**achievement data/success rate**), how many stayed until the end (**retention**), what is the average pass mark etc. You need to learn how to follow these simple formulas and present your own statistics.

For example, look at the following register:

	Week number										
	1	2	3	4	5	6	7	8	9	10	%
A	/	/	/	/	/	0	0	/	/	/	80
B	/	/	0	0	0	/	/	0	0	0	40
C	/	0	/	/	/	/	/	/	/	/	90
D	/	/	0	/	0	/	0	0	0	0	40
E	0	0	/	/	/	/	0	/	/	/	70

A has attended 8 out of 10 sessions. To calculate the percentage: $8 \div 10 \times 100$. This will give you 80 per cent. The **formula** is always the number of sessions attended, divided by the number of sessions possible, multiplied by 100.

What else does this table tell you?

- The average attendance is 64 per cent.
- There were 60 per cent of learners who completed their course.
- E started late; did this impact on achievement?
- What happened in week 7?
- Is there a link between the absences of B and D?

Analyse the attendance at your classes in number and percentage format.

What is the average (mean) attendance?

(NBP1, NBP2, NBP4, NBP7, NBP8)

Numeracy ice-breaker

Using five or six random numbers and the basic mathematical signs of add ($+$), minus ($-$), divide ($\div$) and multiply ($\times$), make a given number.

You do not have to use every number or sign, but may only use any number once. Give a time limit of 20–30 seconds. For example:

4, 10, 3, 7, 8. Make 559.

(Based on *Countdown*, Channel 4).

(NBP2, NBP3)

Discussion about how you felt when presented with a calculation should conclude this activity. Did you understand the instructions? What is the link between communication and number?

(NAK3, NAK4, NAK5, NAC2, NBC1, NBC4, NBC5)

Answer: $(7 \times 8 = 56 \times 10 = 560)$ $(4 - 3 = 1)$, $560 - 1 = 559$

Interpreting and evaluating results

Carry out a survey with your learners. Use a questionnaire that responds to questions in a quantitative way. For example, yes/no, strongly agree/agree/disagree/strongly disagree, true/false. Analyse the results and present the findings as 'x per cent of students agreed that…' etc. What does the information tell you?

(NBP1, NBP2, NBP3, NBP5, NBP7, NBP8)

See also mean, median and mode activity in Principles and Practice of Assessment, Section 16.3, p. 339.

10.4 Developing skills in information communication technologies

By the end of this section, you will be able to identify some opportunities to develop your skills and understanding of ICT. Through referencing teaching and learning activities to the standards below you will demonstrate your progress and development.

The minimum core standards (information and communication technology – ICT)

Part A   Knowledge and understanding

Personal, social and cultural factors influencing ICT learning and development

- The different factors affecting the acquisition and development of ICT skills (IAK1)
- The importance of ICT in enabling users to participate in, and gain access to, society and the modern economy (IAK2)
- Understanding the range of learners' technological and educational backgrounds (IAK3)
- The main learning disabilities and difficulties relating to ICT learning and skill development (IAK4)
- Potential barriers that inhibit ICT skills development (IAK5)

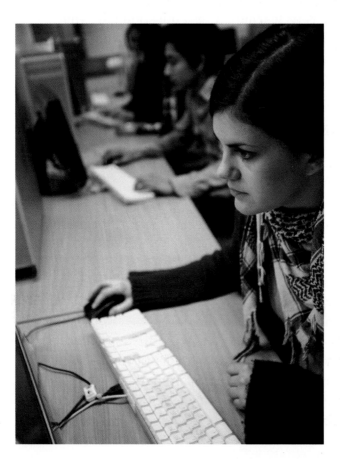

Communication

- Making and using decisions about understanding (IAC1)
- Communicating processes and understandings (IAC2)

Processes

- Purposeful use of ICT (IAP1)
- Essential characteristics of ICT (IAP2)
- How learners develop ICT skills (IAP3)

Part B   Personal ICT skills

Communication

- Communicate with others with/about ICT in an open and supportive manner (IBC1)
- Assess your own, and other people's, understanding (IBC2)
- Express yourself clearly and accurately (IBC3)
- Communicate about/with ICT in a variety of ways that suit and support the intended audience, and recognise such use by others (IBC4)
- Use appropriate techniques to reinforce oral communication, check how well the information is received and support the understanding of those listening (IBC5)

Processes

- Using ICT systems (IBP1)
- Finding, selecting and exchanging information (IBP2)
- Developing and presenting information (IBP3)

Technology is moving so quickly that it is sometimes difficult to keep up to date, both with equipment and skills. Teaching involves using technology to aid learning. Handouts are clearer when freshly printed. Interactive boards can save what you write on them and print off copies for learners. But have you ever 'lost the will to live' in front of a poorly delivered PowerPoint presentation? Using ICT needs to present a balanced approach and therefore every teacher needs to know and develop their skills in ICT.

A case study

Identify an individual or group of individuals and their educational and cultural backgrounds, barriers to learning and any specific learning need relating to ICT (IAK1, IAK2, IAK3, IAK4, IAK5). What are their aspirations and how does ICT form part of their development? (IAK1, IAK2).

The lesson

Conduct a typical lesson and map it to the minimum core.

Alternatively, observe a session and comment upon the ICT activities of the teacher and learners (IBC3, IBC4, IBC5, IBP1, IBP2, IBP3).

Group or individual activities or discussion points

List the ways that computers, the Internet and email influence our lives (IAK2).

List the resources that include technology (IAC2, IAP1, IAP2).

How comfortable are you with ICT? (IAK2, IAK5, IAC1, IAC2, IAP1, IAP3).

What is legal and what is not in terms of accessing and using material on the Internet? (IAK1, IBP1, IBP2).

Are learners disadvantaged in any way by the use of ICT? (IAK4, IAK5).

Self-assessment

Can you use: a word processing package, a presentation package, a spreadsheet application, a database package, a publishing package, an email application, a search engine?

For each would you consider that you are proficient, acceptable, OK with the basics, or nor very good?

Can you open, save, print and retrieve documents?

Do you know what all the icons mean and what shortcuts there are?

Do you understand terms like virus, spam, surfing, download, blogging? (IAC1, IBC2, IBP1, IBP2, IBP3)

Recording progress of the minimum core

It is important that you are able to demonstrate your progress against the minimum core standards. It is not sufficient that you 'think' the tutor has done this, so 'it must be covered'. Here are some suggestions about how you may record (sometimes called tracking, referencing or mapping) your progress.

Idea 1

Use this column to either write the standards in full or use a coding system as suggested above for each of the literacy, numeracy and ICT standards	Use this column to explain how you have met the standard
≡XAMPL≡ Part B Personal language skills SPEAKING Expressing yourself clearly, using communication techniques to help convey meaning and to enhance the delivery and accessibility of the message (LBS1)	I communicate to my learners verbally, through handouts and through my PowerPoint presentations. I use body language to express my feelings and to interpret theirs. I communicate to my peers and managers using spoken and written formats, which include email. My lessons are structured to have a clear beginning, middle and ending and each session progresses from the previous; I use recap to show explicit progress. Whenever I can, I relate the subject to examples from my own experience and try to engage learners in discussions about their own experiences. I have used visual images in handouts and have created models to demonstrate the topic.

Idea 2

Standard	Task 1	Task 2	Task 3	Task 4	Task 5	Task 6	Task 7	Task 8	Etc.
	Each task should be described								
Write the standards or use a coding system	Use a ✓ to show when done								
LAK1	✓	✓		✓					
LAK2	✓			✓					
LAK3		✓	✓	✓					
LAK4	✓		✓						
LAK5	✓		✓						
etc									

Sources

1   *Addressing literacy, language, numeracy and ICT needs in education and training: defining the minimum core of teachers' knowledge, understanding and personal skills. A guide for teacher education programmes*, June 2007, The Sector Skills Council for Lifelong Learning.

2   *Addressing literacy, language, numeracy and ICT needs in education and training: defining the minimum core of teachers' knowledge, understanding and personal skills. A guide for teacher education programmes*, July 2004, Lifelong Learning UK/Further Education National Training Organisation (**FEnto**).

3   *Including language, literacy and numeracy learning in all post-16 education: Guidance on curriculum and methodology for generic initial teacher education programmes*, March 2004, Further Education National Training Organisation/National Research and Development Centre for Adult Literacy and Numeracy.

Glossary of terms

Achievement data the number of students who achieved their qualification, usually expressed as a percentage of those who completed

Dyscalculia associated with difficulties in making sense of numbers and calculations

Dyslexia associated with a difficulty in reading and interpreting words and symbols

FEnto Further Education National Training Organisation

Formula a mathematical rule

ICT information and communication technology

ILP individual learning plan

Language Written or spoken communication

Literacy the ability to read and write

LLUK Lifelong Learning (UK) Sector Skills Council

Minimum core standards of competence in language, literacy, numeracy and ICT

Numeracy the ability to use numbers

Retention the number of students who complete their programme

Self-assessment an organisation's ability to monitor and quality assure its provision

Success rate the number of students who complete and achieve their qualification, usually expressed as a percentage of those who commenced

SUMMARY

In this chapter, you have covered all of the theoretical aspects in relation to the fifth learning outcome of the second unit in your CTLLS qualification:

Developing literacy skills; developing language skills; developing mathematical skills; developing skills in ICT.

Your Personal Development

You will have looked at the overview of the Standards and matched some of the jobs you do as a teacher to those Standards. You have also had an opportunity to complete some exercises which meet the Standards. Finally, you will have created a system of recording your progress towards completion of the Standards and presented these to your mentor or tutor for assessment and guidance.

Assessment of the minimum core is through self-assessment. Many of the activities, essays, presentations and discussions you have done in class will demonstrate and provide opportunities to collect evidence of competence. The sessions you have with learners and conversations with peers and managers will also provide evidence.

Note:

The numbering/coding system used in this chapter is unique to this publication and therefore may not be widely recognised.

CHAPTER 11
(PEL, UNIT 6)

Reflection, evaluation and feedback

JENNY MATTHEWS / ALAMY

LEARNING OBJECTIVES

In this chapter you will learn about:

....

- The benefits of reflection and reflective practice
- How and when reflections occur
- The theories of reflection
- Direct and indirect strategies for acquiring feedback
- Taking a proactive approach to personal development

11.1 Reflection and reflective practice

By the end of this section, you will be able to explain what reflection is and describe some of the theories that underpin **reflective practice**.

Is reflection a benefit or a chore?

Reflection means learning from experience, mistakes and success. It is a process of self-awareness, through **critical analysis**, leading to informed decisions about development. The ability to reflect must be learned; a teacher must learn to be honest, constructive and remain impartial when reflecting. It may not be a systematic, intuitive personal skill. If it is too critical, too congratulatory, too shy, or too confident it will not answer the key question when reflecting: 'How was it for you?'

When analysing yourself or receiving feedback from a colleague, it is important not to feel threatened. All judgements are made for a purpose, and for you, the recipient, the purpose is to improve, develop and become a better teacher. A reflective practitioner does not operate in a blame culture; they wonder about the impact of their actions and what they can do or change to make things easier, better, more efficient and more effective. The important emotions are not concerned with failure but with how to regard each experience as a learning opportunity.

It is important to remember on what and why a teacher reflects, and that is the core business value: the learning process.

What can be reflected upon?

- Lessons – methods, resources, assessment etc.
- Communication
- Behaviour
- Success and **attainment**

- Self: skills and knowledge
- Learners.

In fact any event or occurrence is worth reflection.

How does reflection occur?

- Questioning
- Discussions and chats
- Questionnaires
- Interviews
- Observation
- Observing
- Feedback.

When does reflection occur?

Never or always.

That seems an odd answer, I hear you say. Reflection is something that good teachers engage with and coasting teachers don't bother about. The choice is yours! The argument here is the nature-nurture debate. Is good teaching natural or is it developed?

Theories associated with reflective practice

As with any other part of teaching, there are a number of models, created by **philosophers** and research, which help to explain the process of reflection and the reasons why it is important.

John Dewey wrote about reflective thinking in 1933. He suggested a five-stage model that takes someone through a problem to a solution. It broadly follows a route of:

- Identifying the problem,
- Thinking about answers, and
- Experimenting with solutions.

In this simplified version, it expresses the notion of 'thinking about answers' in order to create the reflection, and thus identify a solution.

One theorist, David Kolb (1984), is used frequently to explain learning processes. He describes how people learn from their experiences, using trial and error. In this way, he explains how reflective practice builds upon things that happen (concrete experience) and develop through understanding why into a 'have another go' scenario. This, he suggests, is a logical cycle of development which constantly (through repetition) leads to better practice.

| **Figure 11A** | Kolb's learning cycle (1984) |

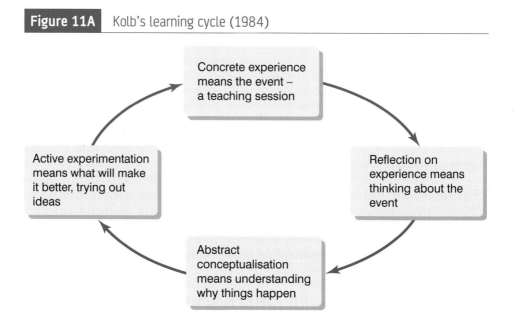

The year before this, Donald Schön (1983) had categorised theory into two types:

1   Official theory – tried and tested strategies, passed down through the ages,

2   Unofficial theory – personal ideas used to problem-solve.

This was developed further when he considered reflection and suggested that reflection also occurred in one of two ways:

1   In-action – when thoughts (reflections) are made immediately and adjustments are made which react quickly to a problem. That is,

those which could be described as thinking on your feet or, more cruelly, winging it!

2   On-action – when considerations (reflections) are made after the event. A more analytical and thought-out process in which future practice is amended. This is very similar to Kolb's opinions.

In 1985, Stephen Brookfield added his contributions to the beliefs of others. In his theory, Critical Lenses, he thinks about how we respond to assumptions. He states that what we are told can work (in theory), but that it may differ in practice. The analysis of this reminds us that a teacher's development is influenced by that which is around us, by the assumptions we make and by the events we experience. Do we always see what is in front of us?

More recently, David Boud (1995) adds to the theories, suggesting a clear link between self-assessment and reflection; learning only occurs as a result of both processes. This is similar to the thoughts of motivation theorist Bandura (1994) (see Section 8.1), who said that in order to develop, someone must want to do so. Applying this back to Boud, in order to learn (and improve), you have to be sufficiently motivated to want to analyse your own performance and spend time thinking about improving.

11.2 Using feedback

By the end of this section, you will be able to describe **direct** and **indirect** strategies for acquiring **feedback** in order to support skills in reflective practice. You will evaluate formal and informal processes which lead to personal development.

Feedback will come from a variety of sources:

Direct:

- Self-assessment
- Peer assessment
- Performance assessment
- Student feedback.

Indirect:

- Diaries and logs
- Action research
- Professional development planners.

Self-assessment is a way of analysing the thoughts you have either at the time or later: it may be a very informal process. It may be that on the journey home at the end of the day you wonder why Jodie reacted like that in the session, or wondered how you could have delivered that bit of information in a better way, because it was clear that it wasn't fully understood, or how you could improve your use of a particular resource to make it more interactive – lots of things may go through your mind. It is important to realise, however, that you did what you did because it seemed right at the time, but with hindsight you could have …. It may be that you did what you did because that's all you knew; you may not know what else you could do.

To develop your performance using self-assessment and reflection, especially in the more informal style described above, it is important that you move towards a more formal style in order to make it more valuable. To do this, it is better to write things down so that you can look at them later, in the cold light of day, perhaps with someone. List the facts, be descriptive, write down your immediate thoughts, feelings, reactions (i.e. start the evaluation) and then close the book until later.

In a more formal self-assessment process, you may decide to consider each part of your lesson systematically. You will certainly be asked to do this frequently as a student teacher or newly qualified teacher (**NQT**). It is part of the way you will learn teaching skills.

A suggestion for a self-assessment checklist to use after a lesson:

Session:	
Date:	Time:
Group:	
Planning and preparation Documentation, outcomes, variety, timing	
Delivery Methods, differentiation, resources, balance, structure	
Learning Engagement, participation, motivation	
Environment Room layout, safety, temperature, facilities	
Rapport Communication, behaviour, discipline, attendance	
Assessment Variety, achievement of outcomes, Q&A style, homework	
Overall comments	

Remember that checklists like this are to remind you about events; they will aid later reflections and enable adaptations for future sessions. Look at how this might be completed:

Session:	
Date: February	Time: 10 – 12
Group: ND Second Year Level 3	
Planning and preparation Documentation, outcomes, variety, timing I had a written copy of my plan on the desk. I found it useful there because at one point I forgot where I was,	

and had to refer to it to get me back on track. The timings were mixed, I allowed too much time to introduce the topic but when we went into the discussion group it was longer than I expected. Never imagined that the feedback would be so detailed, everyone wanted their say, even though others had said the same things. My writing of outcomes is much better now, maybe move them now to differentiated ones for some students.

Delivery
Methods, differentiation, resources, balance, structure

I followed the advice of my tutor and used a very structured approach (had a beginning, a middle and an ending). In the main body of the lesson I introduced the topic with teacher talk and I didn't really do another teacher bit until the end. The middle was a mix of group activities using pyramid and jigsaw group strategies. The pyramid got a little manic, I don't think I managed it very well, especially as the groups got bigger. I remembered to photocopy my notes for AB, but then others wanted them – I think they may want them to prevent making notes themselves. Must speak to their tutor – do they know how to take notes? My ending was not good, because I had run out of time.

Learning
Engagement, participation, motivation

They seemed to like this way of learning, plenty of time to think about answers to problems. I think everyone joined in, but can't be sure.

Environment
Room layout, safety, temperature, facilities

I'm used to this room now, so I know what it's got and how to use everything. Wasted time setting out room when learners were in, I could have got in earlier (it is empty during the break). Didn't put it back when I'd finished cos I'd run out of time – should I? Noticed the OHP is missing.

Rapport
Communication, behaviour, discipline, attendance

Some good discussions going on, this must be useful in their communications class. I asked them to write key words in their personal dictionaries. No problems with behaviour this week – was that because I did more group work? Archie was off again today.

Assessment
Variety, achievement of outcomes, Q&A style, homework

Didn't really assess today, I listened and I think that they all met the outcomes because they took part in the discussion groups and we all got the same information from the groups

Overall comments
I was happy with the lesson, although the timing was still not right. Need to copy notes in case Archie is in next week. Group work was good.

 ACTIVITY 1

If this was your lesson evaluation, what reflections would you make?

How would you change the session if you had to repeat it?

What feedback would you give to the teacher if you had observed this session?

Peer assessment is another feedback tool. It will be used during the early parts of your teacher training to support micro-teaching sessions. In this case you will deliver a small teaching session to your peers and ask for their comments. According to what they write or say, you will make decisions about future practice. As you develop as a teacher, you will initiate support and comments from other teachers, or mentors. The chances are that they will use a document similar to the one used for self-assessment and together you will discuss the things that emerge. You may ask someone to come in and help you because you are struggling with a particular issue, or it may be part of your organisation's procedures that colleagues engage in peer assessment in order to initiate useful conversations about teaching and learning. It may be part of your development that you work with a mentor.

The conversation that follows a peer observation, which is not judgemental, is called feedback. It is the same thing as the feedback you give to your learners to develop their skills and knowledge. The feedback itself should consist of comments, personal opinions, advice and suggestions. As with all feedback, it is up to you what you do with the suggestions and advice. Hopefully it will give you ideas, but good feedback will 'listen' to your justifications and together develop ideas for improvement.

Performance assessment is something that will probably occur either as part of your assessment on a teacher training qualification or as part of your organisation's quality assurance processes. In Appendix D: Teaching Observations it describes some of the things you should do before and during an observation. A performance assessment will make a judgement on your abilities. If it is an observation from your tutor, then the purpose, whilst assessing your competence, will also be to initiate conversations about skills and give developmental feedback. The outcome will probably be 'satisfactory' or 'needs further practice' – the wording may vary, but they are the usual outcomes of a teacher training assessment.

If the assessment is part of the quality process by an inspection team, then the feedback is probably going to be more of a judgement than feedback. You will be told your particular strengths and weaknesses, from which you should be able to ascertain your grade. The observers are making judgements about the learning experience, to which you contribute, but may not control. Not all observers will tell you your grade and any feedback may last only a few seconds. The grades in this process are likely to be:

- *Grade 1 outstanding.* There are many strengths and few, if any, weaknesses, much of the teaching is exceptional and promotes a positive learning experience for all learners.
- *Grade 2 good.* The strengths outweigh the weaknesses. The learning experience is sound with many examples of good practice.
- *Grade 3 satisfactory.* There are a balance of strengths and weaknesses, leading to satisfactory learning experiences.
- *Grade 4 inadequate.* The weaknesses outweigh the strengths, resulting in learners who do not succeed in their goals and targets.

These grades are used by internal and external inspection teams to make judgements about the organisation's performance.

Student feedback is one of the most valuable, yet least used feedback tools. Who better to ask about the quality of the teaching than those in receipt of it? Feedback from learners can be gathered through questionnaires or interviews, formally and informally.

 ACTIVITY 2

List the ways you do/could collect information from learners about:

- The teaching
- Their course or programme
- The learning environment
- The support they receive.

ACTIVITY 3

Devise a questionnaire to use with a group of learners to find out if they enjoy and learn in your lessons. Note in your journal when you issued it, and undertake a self-assessment of the lesson.

Analyse the results of the questionnaire, writing the results in your journal.

Compare your self-assessment with the analysis of the student questionnaire.

Complete a table like this:

Main self-assessment outcomes: List the main points you thought were good/bad in the session.	**Main student questionnaire outcomes:** List the main points your learners thought were good/bad in the session.

State the similarities between your self-assessment and the student questionnaire _____

State any differences between your self-assessment and the student questionnaire _____

Comment on the perceptionsof your learners' experiences and compare them to your own _____

Reflection:

Justify why any differing opinions have occurred. Make suggestions about how your performance could be modified in the light of these findings.

Diaries, logs and journals

These are means of recording events. They are used with a self-assessment process to help you to remember what happened. A suggestion for a log is offered in Section 4.6. Although an indirect form of feedback, it creates the opportunity for feedback through records. The feedback comes when you re-read the logs. One of the advantages of keeping logs, particularly about **critical incidents**, is that the reasons for things happening may not be explained until much later. If a student is playing up in class, you may think at the time 'oh, that's unusual', but carry on nevertheless. It may not be until weeks later that you find out about something that happened in that learner's life that caused the unusual outburst. The reflection may be that next time you might initiate an 'are you OK' discussion (at an appropriate time). Just remember that they may say 'Yes', which wouldn't move anything forward at the time.

Action **research** is quite a detailed investigation into something. It is when you undertake a systematic trial of a new or different strategy and analyse the effects – thus giving you feedback on future development.

Professional development planners are a means of recording your development and learning, but may tell you about what else you need to do. For example:

Activity	Learning outcome	Future development
4 July 2007 Attended event in B149, to learn how to access data about how many learners pass their course. Organised by MIS team. 2 hours cpd.	Learned how to use the management information system to find out how many learners started, stayed and completed course. I now understand the importance of completing forms and responding to requests about numbers.	Found out that retention was not very good, especially for learners who start late on their programmes. Need to work with team to create an online induction to support late starters and ensure through tutorial and initial assessment that they settle into their course. Discuss at team meeting next week. Talk to lead tutor and student services.

From this chart several things can be noted:

- Events attended
- Number of continuing professional development (**CPD**) hours
- What you got out of the development activity
- What further training is required.

The feedback in this instance is concerned with the teacher finding out that there is a retention issue on the course; probably during the course the trainers were able to give ideas about why and this enabled the teacher to plan some more development to overcome this secondary discovery.

11.3 Proactive personal development

By the end of this section, you will be able to explain the effects of non-reflective practice and efficient reflective practice. You will be able to describe the types of personal development and how this can benefit the teacher.

It is suggested that there are links between theories associated with reflection and those of motivation; a teacher must have the desire to develop themself. This is demonstrated as a development model, in which the teaching life is mapped.

A non-reflective practitioner:

Figure 11B   Model showing decline resulting in lack of development

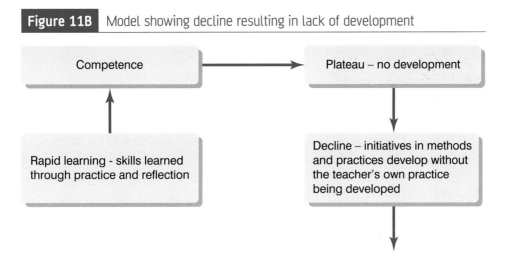

The second model (Figure 11C) shows how someone enters into constant improvement and development, thus keeping up-to-date with everything around the sector, through engagement with reflective practices.

This reinforces the point that development is determined by the individual teacher: thus it is within the power of the teacher to state when that development will occur. Does the teacher wait until they need to develop or do they develop to prepare themselves for what is to come? To a certain extent, this decision has been taken out of the hands of the teacher by the introduction of legislation demanding that teachers engage in continuous professional development.

Figure 11C Model showing improvement as a result of reflection

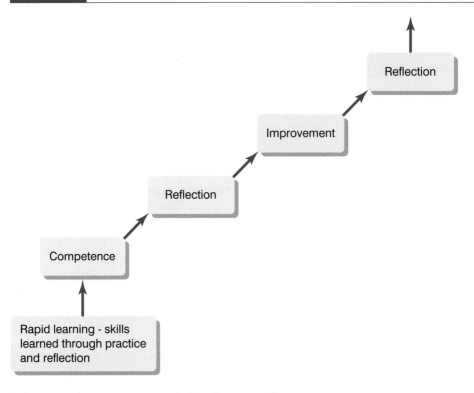

What constitutes personal development?

The simplest answer to that is: anything which develops the person. That can be:

- Teaching skills to make a better teacher
- Functional skills to support minimum levels of literacy, numeracy and ICT
- Study skills to enable efficient learning
- IT skills to enhance skills in using computers
- Tutor skills to support learners' development
- Assessment skills to improve the reliability of judgements
- Theoretical skills to improve understanding of roles
- Character skills, time/stress/relaxation, to support the teacher under pressure
- Legislation updates to ensure compliance
- Research skills to maintain up-to-date practice and knowledge.

There are probably other categories. In short, development = progress.

Progress will then lead to efficient and effective teachers, which in turn will lead to a successful learning environment – which is our key priority.

Recommended reading

Hillier, Y. (2005) *Reflective teaching in further and adult education.* London: Continuum.

Glossary of terms

Attainment reaching the goal or qualification aim

CPD continuous professional development

Critical analysis a detailed examination resulting in an opinion or argument

Critical incidents events that have a significant effect

Direct feedback/communication clear and unambiguous link

Feedback verbal or written comments about the assessment intended to bring about improvement

Indirect feedback/communication a link via a secondary method

Justify explain and prove something

NQT newly qualified teacher

Philosopher someone who studies theories, attitudes or beliefs

Reflection a considered opinion, expressed in speech or writing; thoughts or considerations, developing ideas and thoughts

Reflective practice thoughtful practice to develop skills

Research an investigation

SUMMARY

In this chapter, you have covered all of the theoretical aspects in relation to the sixth learning outcome of the second unit in your CTLLS qualification:

Reflection and reflective practice; using feedback; proactive personal development.

Your Personal Development

You will have considered what reflection is and how to use it to develop your own practice. You have looked at the theory associated with reflection. You have carried out self-assessment of your own teaching, practicing reflection and feedback skills. You have developed your ability to question learners in order to find out about their learning and used the answers to develop your own practice. You have improved your skills in using personal development to improve your teaching, stating the importance of using a positive approach to development.

You should be able to answer questions relating to:

How and why you should evaluate and reflect on your performance and, following your teaching sessions, will demonstrate an ability to make reflections and prepare your development plans, in order to improve your practice.

Part Three

Principles and practice of assessment

(PPA)

This is the third unit in your Certificate in Teaching in the Lifelong Learning Sector (CTLLS) qualification

CHAPTER 12
(PPA, UNIT 1)

Concepts and principles of assessment

PHOTOFUSION PICTURE LIBRARY / ALAMY

LEARNING OBJECTIVES

In this chapter you will learn about:

....

- Assessment basics
- The language of assessment
- Key concepts of assessment
- The principles of assessment

12.1 Concepts and principles of assessment

By the end of this section, you will be able to describe the meaning of words associated with assessment and explain the main concepts (ideas) and principles (values) relating to assessment. This chapter builds on the ideas in both the PTLLS and PEL units.

REVISION

In Part One (PTLLS), you reviewed the main methods of assessment and the types of assessment, looking at the main points at which assessment is carried out (Section 5.1). In Section 6.1 you considered the role and methods of initial assessment and the importance of goals and targets.

This section also links to other sections of this unit:

● Section 14.2, The rules of assessment, and
● Section 16.1, The purpose of assessment.

Assessment basics

Assessment is the term given to the process of checking that learning has occurred. It is the way teachers know whether or not they have been effective in their sessions.

> Assessment is the process by which evidence of student achievement is obtained and judged. Ecclestone (1996) points out that assessment requires two things: evidence and a standard or scale.
>
> Gray et al 2005: 50

Some of the first things you need to grasp in assessment are: how, what, when, where, why. You cannot assess somebody or something without telling them about it or setting the standard. The standard may be role modelled, industry-based, competence-based or theoretically driven. Whichever applies, the standard should come from the syllabus. However, in recreational courses there is unlikely to be a syllabus, so the **standard** becomes the teacher's and/or the learner's goals. Therefore standards and goals are the keys to successful assessment.

> ## If you know where you are going, you'll be able to tell when you've got there.

The output of assessment is 'evidence'; evidence is the confirmation that assessment has occurred and the way it is proven. To summarise, assessment in educational terms usually means 'a method of confirming learning'.

Why assess?

Look at the table in Activity 1: it notes key parts of the learning process and asks you to think about your current practice by using how and why statements.

 ## ACTIVITY 1

Where are you now in terms of how you assess learning?

Key stages of learning	How do you currently assess this stage?	Why do you do this? (Self, learners, managers)
Initial assessment of skills at entry to programme		

▶

Key stages of learning	How do you currently assess this stage?	Why do you do this? (Self, learners, managers)
Getting to know your learners		
Planning learning for groups: for individuals:		
Check that the content of the lessons is learned		
Check that the content of the topic/module/unit is learned		
Learning is understood and can be transferred to other contexts or situations		
Dealing with emerging issues and needs		

The purpose of this exercise is to see where you are now.

Assessment is an essential part of learning, and you can use this initial self-assessment to think about where you need to develop. You may refer to this in a reflective journal or diary.

The language of assessment

Assessment can be carried out before recruitment (at interview), at commencement (diagnostic and initial assessment), during and at the end of the lesson and at the end of the module, unit or programme. It may be pertinent at this point to look at how qualifications are structured, as this will lead us to the points at which assessment should occur.

Programme of study

A collection of qualifications usually associated with full-time attendance which create a framework or course: the curriculum.

Qualification

A certificated qualification, endorsed by an awarding body and approved through the National Qualifications Framework (NQF – see Section 2.2, p. 43), for example:

C&G Cert in Teaching

BTEC First Dip in Health and Social Care

NVQ Level 1 in Hairdressing

NCFE Cert for entry to the Public Services

HND in Business Studies

Level 3 Application of Number

A qualification consists of the standards of performance, ability or competence i.e. the syllabus

Unit/module

The smaller subsections of the qualification which focus on a particular aspect. There will usually be several units or modules in a qualification. Each unit or module will have its own specified outcomes and evidence requirements. Some qualifications have a further breakdown of the unit/module which is called an element.

Content/performance criteria

Each unit, module or element will have statements relating to what has to be covered in order to achieve the unit. These statements about content are written in terms of what the learner will know or do at the end of the unit/module/element.

In NVQs these are called performance criteria: statements of competence – what the learner will be able to do at the end of the unit/module/element.

Lessons are arranged around these frameworks: thus you may be employed to teach a particular unit or module or you may work within a team of people to train towards a whole qualification. Whichever strategy is used, the teacher will have to assess whether learning has occurred. In some qualifications this learning is referred to as demonstrating **competence**.

Unfortunately, assessment is such a wide topic and the qualification frameworks so varied that many different terms are used (assessment **jargon**) and it sometimes takes a while to learn the words; usually when you do discover their meaning it is broadly the same as another similar word used by a different qualification team. Let us look at some of those terms.

Term	Alternative expressions
Qualification	Standards, specifications, course, syllabus
Learning outcome	Objective, range statements, content, statements of competence
Evidence requirements	Assessment guidance, evidence, portfolio, assignment, assessment criteria
Grading	Grading criteria are the level at which the outcomes are met – e.g., pass merit/credit or distinction
Verification	Moderation, standardisation
Assessment	Test, exam, evidence (proof)

 ## ACTIVITY 2

Make a list of any similar jargon terms you use in your lessons when explaining the subject or how it will be assessed.

- ●
- ●
- ●
- ●
- ●
- ●

- ●
- ●
- ●
- ●
- ●
- ●

Consider:
Wording in assignments or instructions to complete question sheets.

Development point:
Create a dictionary of terms that your learners may find helpful.

See also Appendix C: Study Skills, Command Words p. 376

Concepts of assessment

A concept is an idea, in this instance, about assessment. The concepts that you will commonly see are:

- Norm referencing (or normative)
- Criterion referencing
- Ipsative assessment
- Formative assessment
- Summative assessment.

Norm referencing is when learners are assessed against each other. It is quite an old fashioned concept. For example, if you were to set a test where the top 10 per cent were able to progress to a higher level or rewarded in some way, and the lowest 10 per cent were penalised in some way, perhaps by going down a **grade** of class, then this would be norm **referencing**. The learner's ability is measured (and compared) against other learners. This is very common in educational establishments, when learners are split into classes according to ability rather than year or house groups. The percentiles can also be varied: for example if there were a lot of students who gained high marks in their test, but you only had reward spaces for half of them, it is possible to raise the pass mark to match the figure of 'top 10 per cent of learners,' equally if the tests were very difficult, you can lower the pass mark to reward the 'top 10 per cent'. In this way, you will consistently have a top 10 per cent, although their pass marks may have been different.

Criterion referencing is when a learner achieves a standard, they either can (or can't) do the task, question or competence. They can continue in their attempts until the criterion is achieved (plural is criteria). Therefore in this style of assessment it is measuring what a learner can do. Whilst it is generally associated with a 'can do–can't do' (pass–fail) assessment, it may be linked to a grading scale which determines how well a learner can do something. In this strategy a learner can pass, pass with credit or pass with distinction.

Ipsative assessment is relatively new in assessment concepts. It is used within self-assessment when an individual is matching their performance, knowledge or ability against a set of standards. It is a useful way of undertaking an initial assessment or, alternatively, a way of summarising learning; it can also be used whilst learners are on their programme of study to encourage reviews of progress. **Profiling** is a method of recording **ipsative** assessment.

If you were to measure your performance as a teacher against the 'New overarching professional standards for teachers, tutors and trainers in the lifelong learning sector' (LLUK 2006), you would be undertaking an assessment using an ipsative model.

For example, this is an extract from Domain E – Assessment for Learning, using criteria related to professional practice (LLUK 2006: pp. 11, 12).

Assess your own performance against the statements of competence:

EP1.1	Use appropriate forms of assessment and evaluate their effectiveness in producing information useful to the teacher and the learner
EP1.2	Devise, select, use and appraise assessment tools, including where appropriate, those which exploit new and emerging technologies
EP2.1	Apply appropriate methods of assessment fairly and effectively
EP2.3	Design appropriate assessment activities for own specialist area
EP3.2	Ensure that access to assessment is appropriate to learner need
EP4.2	Use feedback to evaluate and improve own skills in assessment
EP5.3	Communicate relevant assessment information to those with a legitimate interest in learner achievement, as necessary/appropriate

In the boxes on the right you will write statements, make lists, justify your choices and opinions, describe strategies and give examples of instances when the competence is demonstrated. In ipsative assessment, as it is usually a self-assessment and therefore only an individual's opinion of their ability, the judgements will usually be supported by other assessments.

Formative assessment is an interim judgement. It is also known as 'continuous assessment'. It has the advantage of being an ideal opportunity to tell a learner how they are progressing and giving them the chance to improve. This type of assessment is very motivational because it is seen as a review rather than an assessment. It helps learners to progress and maximise their potential. There is life after **formative** assessment! One of the disadvantages of formative assessment (although significantly outweighed by the advantages) is that continuous assessment may feel like *continual* assessment. Kolb's learning cycle (see Section 11.1, Figure 11A, p. 254) advocates the concepts of formative assessment and feedback within the cycle, indicating their value in personal development and progression. Formative assessment aids learning.

Summative assessment is usually associated with tests and exams. It aids the assessment of learning and is quite formal. In **summative** assessment styles, a learner progresses through their qualification until the time comes that learning is complete and they are tested on their knowledge or skills. A judgement is made, which is then expressed on a certificate. If a learner wishes to improve they usually have to 'sit' the examination again. This does put enormous pressure on learners as the outcomes may determine their future, however with teaching that prepares a learner well for their test, such apprehension and anxiety can be lessened.

Principles of assessment

A principle is a rule that you will follow; it is an underlying standard that you will not compromise. Some of the principles that you should advocate are:

- Consistency. You will always ensure that the methods and timeliness of your assessment are at a level standard, making certain that irrespective of how and when your learners are assessed, the outcomes are constant.

- Accessibility. You will always ensure that all of your learners are able to access your assessments and follow systems of equality and inclusion.

- Detailed. You will always ensure that your assessments cover your curriculum or unit fairly and evenly, leaving no part undecided.

- Earned. You will always ensure that your learners have achieved their qualifications with rigour and others will respect the integrity of the assessment.

- Transparency. You will always ensure that everyone involved in the assessment is crystal clear about its purpose and meaning.

These principles form the **acronym** CADET.

C	Consistent
A	Accessible
D	Detailed
E	Earned
T	Transparent

So, these are the values and principles that you follow when preparing, implementing and evaluating assessment. It will be these values that will help to determine the effectiveness of your assessment.

It should be remembered that assessment is not merely something which occurs in a modular format or end of year test. In every lesson that you do you will set learning outcomes, deliver your topic and then close the lesson. You must remember that to truly know if you have achieved the learning outcomes you must set an assessment activity. If the close of your lesson is: 'Well, today folks we've looked at x y and z, is everybody clear now?' you may be able to claim that you have 'taught' your topic, but you cannot claim that your learners have learned anything! You must, therefore, include small assessment activities in the structure of your lesson, to help you confirm learning. The easiest to prepare are verbal or written questions – but make sure everyone contributes and remember that you can use similar activities in the next class to recap, before moving forward to the next topic. In the next chapter we will review the different ways that this can be achieved.

Glossary of terms

Acronym a abbreviation or series of initial letters which together make another word

BTEC Business and Technology Education Council; a qualification title part of Edexcel; an awarding body

C&G City and Guilds; an awarding body

Competence the knowledge of or ability to do something

Formative continuous assessment

Grade a level or degree of competence

HND Higher National Diploma

Ipsative self-assessment against standards of competence

Jargon language, words or expressions of a specialist occupation

Level 3 A position within the NQF indicating the value of a qualification

NCFE Northern Council for Further Education; an awarding body

NQF National Qualifications Framework

NVQ National Vocational Qualification

Profile how information about a thing or person is recorded

Referencing a source of information

Standard an agreed level of competence

Summative final or summary assessment

SUMMARY

In this chapter, you have covered all of the theoretical aspects in relation to the first learning outcome of the third unit in your CTLLS qualification:

Concepts and principles of assessment.

Your Personal Development

You have completed a couple of activities to identify your starting points in understanding assessment and developed your knowledge of assessment in the context of current curriculum. You have looked at the main concepts of assessment and what is meant by the terms norm and criterion referencing, ipsative, formative and summative assessments. Finally you have looked at principles of assessment and decided on the values you advocate when carrying out assessments.

You should be able to answer questions relating to your understanding of:

● Concepts and principles of assessment.

CHAPTER 13 (PPA, UNIT 2)

Types of assessment

LEARNING OBJECTIVES

In this chapter you will learn about:

....

- The advantages and disadvantages of different methods of assessment
- How to provide effective assessment
- Qualifications for assessors

13.1 Methods of assessment

By the end of this section, you will be able to describe the advantages and disadvantages of each assessment method and make informed decisions about which to choose.

REVISION

In Chapter 5 you looked at the methods of assessment more commonly used in the post-compulsory sector – these were observation, simulation, project, assignment, written questions, verbal questions, professional discussion and self-assessment. Each method was described with some instances of how it might be used.

In this section, we are going to extend your knowledge of assessment methods so that you are able to make decisions about which methods to choose for your purposes.

Methods of assessment can be classified into two main types:

1   **Direct** – evidence of the learner's work

2   **Indirect** – evidence or opinion from others

Assessment method	Advantages	Disadvantages
Observation Direct	Primary assessment method for practical skills	No permanent record of performance
	Able to see naturally occurring practice	Expensive
	Ideal opportunity to see if theory is applied in a practical situation*	Needs to be verified to confirm judgements
		Can be intrusive
	Can be used formatively or summatively	Can't check theory or underpinning knowledge
	'Can do' or 'can't do' outcomes	Detailed preparation and organisation required
		May be subjective

Assessment method	Advantages	Disadvantages
Simulation Direct	Can be used to assess when circumstances involve dangerous or expensive resources Can be used formatively or summatively	Does not match the real thing in terms of senses and emotions
Project and assignment Direct	Can be used formatively or summatively Allows individual creativity to develop Develops research skills Collection of tasks which can be differentiated easily Assesses wide range of skills and knowledge*	Confused in meaning – project is learner-derived, assignment is tutor derived Poorly used – preparation only concerned with single subject, whereas it may be applicable across a broader range of topics Time-consuming
Written reports/ case studies Indirect/direct	Less formal than an essay Allows description, comprehension and analysis of facts* Opportunity to answer 'what if' scenarios Aids reflection Can include personal values and opinions	Need detailed marking grids
Written questions Direct	**Essays** Assesses understanding and high order cognitive skills* Can gain insight to opinions/arguments relating to an issue Can assess literacy Can be closed (no reference), open book, or open (later submission) styles	**Essays** Takes time to write and mark No single answer Easy to prepare Limited coverage of the subject/syllabus Prone to subjectivity in marking

▶

Assessment method	Advantages	Disadvantages
Written questions Direct (*continued*)	**Essays** (*continued*) Can be used formatively or summatively Appropriate as exam or a stand alone pieces of work	
	Short answer Versatile – ideal as introductory, plenary, homework or exam questions Used to reinforce learning Ideal when information needs to be remembered as opposed to recognised* Assesses comprehension* Quick to mark Can be used formatively or summatively Can be used as one word, simple sentence or extended answers	**Short answer** Answers can lack depth unless extended answers are requested
	Multiple choice Good way to check facts Low to high order cognitive test* Checks recognition and recall* Can test a lot of things as questions are short Answers are easy to mark Outcomes are reliable Questions can be 'banked' and selected to make different tests each time they are used High level of objectivity in marking Can be used formatively or summatively	**Multiple choice** Answers may be sorted to get a 50/50 guess scenario Difficult to prepare

Assessment method	Advantages	Disadvantages
Oral questions Direct	Can be used formatively or summatively Informal in style Supports theory in practical situations Responsive to needs Open questions probe knowledge	Sometimes difficult to devise questions May be posed as closed questions
Professional discussion Direct	Generally used supported by other assessment methods Allows for description, evaluation and reflection* Structured discussion allows for gaps to be covered	Expensive as it is 1:1 Can be too leading Can be disjointed; learners need preparation time to ensure logical flow of ideas Recording of discussion needs to be prepared (audio/writing)
Self-assessment Indirect	Generally used supported by other assessment methods Enables evaluation and reflection* Allows learners to develop responsibility for own learning Learning logs can record progress and aid reflection	Judgements made by self rather than an expert Difficult to be objective Limited to the extent of the profile document
Peer assessment Indirect	Generally used supported by other assessment methods Gathers ideas and emotions from similar people Informal feedback Aids reflection	Peers may not know the standards and so compare with what they do

Assessment method	Advantages	Disadvantages
Accreditation of Prior Learning (APL) Indirect	Generally used supported by other assessment methods Values previous learning, achievement and experience	Need to validate all claims May not cover current competence Difficult to prove Time-consuming to analyse Needs specialist staff
Group activities Direct	Motivational as tasks are shared Less intimidating Individual strengths can be played to maximise results Can be used formatively or summatively	Difficult to attribute results to an individual or particular skill Weaker learners can hide
Witness testimony Indirect	Able to collect information from work or other activities to support studies Generally used supported by other assessment methods	Reliability of witness can not be guaranteed
Products/ artefacts Direct	Items generated outside of the classroom can be used to support demonstration of competence Generally used supported by other assessment methods Links the importance of classroom and work-based assessment	The authenticity (ownership) of the product is not without doubt

*References are related to Bloom's Taxonomies of Learning (see Section 7.4).

13.2 Effective assessment

By the end of this section, you will be able to make decisions about your choices of assessment and identify what makes assessment **effective**.

If assessment is to be seen as a valuable tool and respected by learners, colleagues and other stakeholders, then it must be seen to do what it purports to do, i.e. it must be effective. Effectiveness means producing the intended or desired result. Therefore, the first thing you should establish is what you intend or want from the assessment.

- To demonstrate practical skill (psychomotor skills)
- To recall knowledge (cognitive skills)
- To value or appreciate an opinion (affective skills)

In this example, Bloom (1956, 1964, and Dave 1967) is used to identify the desired outcomes (see PEL section 7.4). Once you have established what you want, then you should select methods of assessment which will deliver the products of assessment you need in order to make the **judgement**.

To make decisions about effectiveness you should consider:

- the desired **outcome**
- the methods of assessment
- justify the choices you make (see Section 13.1)
- gather evidence – the products which demonstrate competence?

The products of assessment are:

- Documents – letters, printouts
- Photos
- Portfolios of evidence
- Essays, reports, presentation notes,
- Artefacts, artwork, finished items
- Models and diagrams
- Testimonials, references

- Personal statements, CVs
- Certificates
- Observation reports.

There are various ways to achieve confidence in your assessment and thus promote effectiveness. One of the easiest is to **triangulate** judgements: this means using more than one assessment method to confirm competence. For example, would you allow (believe) a student who presented a photograph or product and told you it was their work? It is more likely that you will check this out by asking some verbal questions to elicit information about how they did it. You may add to this by considering previous classwork activities they have done or by setting another practical task to confirm their ability. If the results of all of these assessment methods say the same thing then you can confirm competence. Each method is therefore contributing effectively to produce an assessment that is reliable and authentic.

Another easy method of delivering effective assessment strategies is that of variety. By testing learners in different ways, not only does it add interest, but it also appeals to different learning styles and in the same way as triangulation, it provides confirmation that decisions are accurate and consistent.

Communication aids effectiveness. By agreeing, sharing, negotiating, and discussing plans, methods and outcomes, the teacher (or assessor) will be able to justify and evaluate their assessments. It will also aid some 'joined-up thinking' – many requirements contained in standards are common across a range of units or modules. Communication about these common factors will lessen the assessment load on learners by consolidating tasks to cover more than one unit or module (a holistic approach). This can also apply to key and basic skills – why can't presentations be assessed for communication skills as well as content?

Finally, in trying to establish effectiveness, the assessor should consider the values, ethics and safety of the assessment. The values (**CADET** – see PPA Unit 1 Section 12.1) should not be compromised when aiming for effectiveness: the ethics concerning **confidentiality** and **integrity** in assessment are paramount and we should never forfeit standards of safety when creating or carrying out assessments.

ACTIVITY 1

How do you know everyone has learned the topic?
Quite simply, you don't unless you assess.

Give two examples of how you might assess each item in the list below.
State why you think your chosen examples are the right ones:

Discuss the effects of the Second World War on the economy of Britain.
Identify road signs for crossroads, t-junctions, speed restrictions etc.
Using a photocopier.
Baking a cake.
Reviewing and evaluating teaching methods.
Comparing and contrasting two issues.
Preparing for a job interview.
List the correct flag for a list of countries.

How will you know if your assessments are effective?

Qualifications for assessors

Awarding bodies will set the standards required of people who undertake assessments in relation to their qualifications. One of the most obvious is that of personal **competence**. Assessors are required to be competent in their subject themselves to at least a level higher than that which they assess. Government guidelines recommend that this is a minimum of Level 3 (A level on the NQF) and between 3 and 10 years' experience* in the field of expertise. Where there are no appropriate Level 3 qualifications available, lower levels are acceptable, supported by relevant industrial or commercial experience. Second, they look for competence in assessment. Depending on the type of qualification this may be a generic teaching qualification, which includes modules on assessment, or, in the case of NVQs, there is a requirement for a specialist assessment unit from the Learning and Development NVQ. You may hear these called D32, D33, D34 or the up-to-date versions, A1, A2, or V1.

Additional information

LLUK – regarding standards and regulations for teachers

ENTO – regarding Learning and Development NVQs

C&G – regarding qualifications for teachers and assessors

*Sector Skills Councils – for information regarding occupational competence

Glossary of terms

APL accreditation of prior learning

CADET consistent, accessible, detailed, earned, transparent

Competence the knowledge of or ability to do something

Confidentiality secrecy of information

Direct assessment evidence of the learner's work

Effective assessment to produce the intended or desired result or outcome

Indirect assessment evidence or opinion from others

Integrity having values and principles

Judgement a decision about an assessment

Outcome result or consequence of assessment

Triangulate measuring by different perspectives

 # SUMMARY

In this chapter, you have covered all of the theoretical aspects in relation to the second learning outcome of the third unit in your CTLLS qualification:

Methods of assessment, effective assessment.

Your Personal Development

You have investigated a wide range of assessment methods and looked at the advantages and disadvantages of each. This will enable you to make better choices about the assessment methods you plan to use and to justify your selection. You have further considered what makes assessment effective and how you will know when your assessments are producing the results you expect. Finally, you have looked at how the competence of assessors will aid effectiveness by adding confidence in assessment strategies.

You should be able to answer questions relating to choosing and justifying assessment tools to gain purposeful assessment outcomes. In your teaching practice you will demonstrate successful choices and increase the effectiveness of assessment and assessment systems.

CHAPTER 14
(PPA, UNIT 3)

Analysis of assessment

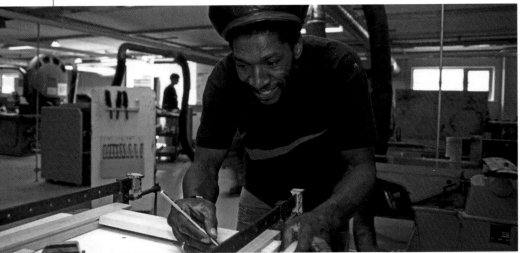

PHOTOFUSION PICTURE LIBRARY / ALAMY

LEARNING OBJECTIVES

In this chapter you will learn about:

- How to apply assessment to the needs of your learners and requirements of the curriculum
- The role of ILT in assessment
- The rules of ILT in assessment and associated legal responsibilities and ethical values
- The benefits of peer and self-assessment

14.1 Matching assessment to the needs of learners and the curriculum

By the end of this section, you will be able to develop the insight gained about inclusive practice in Part Two (see also Chapters 7 and 8), and apply that knowledge to assessment practice.

REVISION

In Part Two you established what inclusion meant and how to create inclusive teaching and learning sessions to meet the needs of all of your learners. You discovered that inclusive practice enhances motivation, and impacts on all aspects of teaching and learning, from planning through delivery and resourcing to supporting learning. In this chapter we will extend this process through to assessment.

Inclusion simply means 'available to all'. Inclusion begins when you first hear about your learners, even before you meet them, and we will discover that the routines you practice will not end until after your learners have left your care towards the next stages of their development, be that further education, training, higher education or employment.

A lot of the focus associated with inclusion centres on planning for differentiation. This starts in the classroom when you prepare outcomes to suit your learners whilst remembering that the curriculum should also be covered. It therefore follows that checking that those outcomes have been met will vary according to the type and depth of knowledge or skill learned. Hence it is easy to see that assessment must suit both individual needs and the curriculum.

EXAMPLES OF RELATIONSHIPS TO THEORY

Kolb's (1984) learning cycle states that assessment is a factor that is necessary to keep the cycle a circle. Something is done: a concrete experience which can be thought about (self-assessment). Try to understand it (questioning) and experiment with solutions (observation, peer assessment, more questions and an evaluation) which leads to…

Bloom's **taxonomies** (1956–1967) which can be used to differentiate the learning outcomes which will indicate the types of assessment methods. Low order cognitive skills suit multiple choice questions, high order cognitive skills and affective domain skills suit essays and short answer questions, psychomotor skills suit observations.

Differentiating formative assessment

It is far easier to adjust assessments for formative purposes than for summative assessment. This is because generally formative assessment is devised by the teacher and therefore it is controlled. Differentiation in this case is all about planning and preparation. If we know our learners we can enable them to access their assessment, however learners do not have to disclose their requirements. We should be watchful for their needs.

Some ideas:

- Nominated questioning at the end of the lesson to check progress
- Written question sheets with a mixture of short answer and multiple-choice questions
- Group activities resulting in collective decisions
- Tutorials or 1:1 progress reviews
- Self-assessment questionnaires
- Peer assessment following presentations
- Different command words used in homework or class activities
- Varied font type, size, paper colour
- Ask learners if they need assistance.

- *Varied* adds interest and meets all needs, known or unknown
- *Differentiated* is inclusive, relevant, motivational
- *Balanced* is never too much of one type, so meets varied needs.

Differentiating summative assessment

Differentiating for summative assessment is more difficult than for formative assessment. This is because you will probably need special permission from awarding bodies to deviate from the agreed type of assessment. Difficult, yes, because these things have to be agreed in writing prior to the events, but not impossible. Awarding bodies will always accommodate those with specific needs: however, they respond to needs, not wants!

You are advised to seek help from examinations administrators, support staff and external moderators (EM) or verifiers (EV). This is essential as you will need the following support in order to differentiate:

- From support tutors you will need professional statements declaring the need and specific allowances that should be made.
- From the examinations office you will need to confirm special arrangements and they will arrange/organise resources, accommodation and **invigilation**.
- From the EM/EV you will need their written consent, so that they are aware of what is occurring and therefore will expect different assessment products at their visit.

Under no circumstances should you modify a test date or time, or permit additional resources in an examination room without prior, written consent.

Variations to summative assessment are usually only applicable to those with a specific need or disability. The learner who always has to do the school run will have to amend their day to cope with an exam that starts at 09.00, whereas the learner who has difficulty in writing due to disability will be allowed extra time. In a formative assessment you may differentiate to cope with the *wants* of individuals, but in a summative assessment only *needs* are addressed.

If a learner has enrolled and completed their programme of study or course they must be able to access assessment. Some of the specialist arrangements include:

- Signers or lip readers
- Scribes (writers)
- Speakers/readers
- Viva (oral examination)
- Time – related to time allowed or date of test
- Location
- Specialist equipment and software.

These recommendations will be advised by support tutors or professionals, and are based on extensive assessment of need; typically these are those with physical or mental needs, hearing or sight impairment or dyslexia.

A teacher can support summative assessment by helping learners to prepare for their exams, tests, questions etc. This can include teaching study skills: note-taking, reading, researching, essay preparation, presenting work or referencing. You may talk through what will happen during observations or examinations, and perhaps use classroom role play or video/DVD to help learners prepare for their assessment.

ILT in assessment

ILT is used increasingly as a teaching tool; it therefore follows that it will be seen as an assessment tool also. For teachers and learners who enjoy this style (but remember this doesn't include everyone), it is merely a continuation of their learning when they are assessed in this way. Some of the ways in which ILT/ICT can support assessment are:

- word processing work,
- using presentation software, e.g. PowerPoint, for presentations,
- using interactive boards in question sessions,
- using the Internet for research,

- using forums for ideas and questions,
- using databases and spreadsheets to track progress,
- using email to submit and return work
- storing evidence in portfolios
- online screening or diagnostic assessment
- course material uploaded to virtual learning environments (VLEs)
- questioning using electronic voting systems.

The Qualifications and Curriculum Authority (**QCA**) has expressed a commitment to the development of **e-assessment**. It requires that awarding bodies develop opportunities for online assessment and on-demand assessment.

Advantages to e-assessment:

- Learners can take tests as they become confident/competent
- Immediate feedback and results
- Objective marking, especially when computer marked.
- Less requirement for paper records, results stored electronically
- More inclusive.

Disadvantages to e-assessment:

- Expensive technology and specialist software necessary
- Reliant on power – what if this is not available due to location or supply?
- Not everyone is comfortable with technological advances
- Difficult to assess values and attitudes, typically presented in essay format
- Overuse of 'cut and paste'.

Progress around ILT in assessment needs to be concerned with a **blended learning** approach. This will offer alternatives according to levels of confidence in using computerised technologies and provide changes in style (as opposed to death by computer technologies). E-assessment should be offered as an acceptable alternative rather than a required option.

14.2 The rules of assessment

By the end of this section, you will be able to define the rules associated with assessments to ensure valid, reliable and accurate assessments. You will also be aware of legal responsibilities and ethical values.

Assessment rules

Once you have sorted out the basics (PPA Unit 1 Section 12.1), you can get down to the actual assessment. There are a number of different ways of assessing, but all rely on the fact that you need something to measure against. These are usually written by awarding bodies but there are some courses where you may have to devise your own standards, for example non-qualification courses or recreational programmes. Some words of caution here: *never* substitute your own standards onto qualifications which are approved within the NQF, however well intentioned. These are National Standards and approved as such by bodies charged with the remit to create a standard across the country. By doing so you may disadvantage your learners, because you are creating your own qualification, which will not be recognised within your professional area.

The first task when planning assessment is to gain sight of the awarding body's specifications for your unit/module or qualification. In it you will find a series of paragraphs telling you what a learner will know/be able to do/demonstrate at the end of the unit or module. Again, there are variants here: some qualifications/units will tell you that you need to collect two of this, a report on that or an observation for the other, but more often it will be up to you to decide on the appropriate assessment task and the method, usually under the supervision of the moderator or verifier. There are some rules that will help you make informed choices. You should ensure that your assessments are:

- Valid/relevant: assesses what it is supposed to, according to the curriculum, in an appropriate manner

- Reliable: assesses in a consistent manner to the expected standards, regardless of who makes the judgement or when the judgement is made
- Authentic: is able to be attributed to the learner
- Current/recent: is up-to-date and recently written
- Sufficient: is enough to cover the content/performance criteria
- Power of discrimination: a balance of easy and difficult questions, so that learners are not disadvantaged
- Objective: judgements made are not personal opinion, which means that marking criteria need to be clear and not open to interpretation.

Some of the problems associated with assessment are concerned with the issues listed above. For example:

- Poor wording of questions and assignments leads learners in a wrong direction, causing their assessment to be completed inaccurately.
- Future criticism of competence, usually from future employers, because learners have not been tested sufficiently across the breadth of the syllabus.
- Ambiguous or inaccurate marking by staff who do not communicate well leads to different standards of competence of learners.
- Assessors inventing their own standards that can lead to varying degrees of competence.
- Poor research skills leading to inaccurate citation and/or **plagiarism**.

To overcome these issues you should follow the rules of assessment by:

- Always ensuring that your learners are prepared for their assessments
- Devising tasks that test what you have taught
- Telling learners how, when and where assessments will happen
- Offering study skills to support presentation of research in work
- Asking colleagues (or an internal verifier) to review the task before submitting it to learners (when devising assessments)
- Creating varied assessment tasks to give good coverage of material and opportunities for differentiation.

The rules of assessment associated with ethics are concerned with confidentiality and authenticity.

Confidentiality

This section is for guidance only; it does not constitute legal advice. Organisations will have their own codes of practice and teachers should always seek advice from colleagues or managers.

Most teachers automatically respect that information they have and keep about their learners is confidential, but this will be on two tiers. There are those issues which are confidential to the organisation and those issues that remain in confidence between the learner and the tutor.

There are laws and guidance to support this issue:

1   Data Protection Act (1998). Protects personal data which should only be used as stated, never disclosed (unless there are criminal implications), kept only for as long as is required and must be held securely. Individuals have the right to see the information you keep about them. However, we must remember that it might also be necessary to report things, even when mentioned in confidence – those issues around child abuse and illegal acts.

2   Freedom of Information (2000). The public's right to know. It states that individuals can request information held about them and about the organisation. Organisations must declare information about performance etc.

3   Human Rights. As far as education is concerned this is mainly associated with equality and welfare.

Authenticity

We must ensure that all work submitted for assessment is the work of the individual learner, equally, we must ensure that learners do not copy (plagiarise) the work of others. We should do this by addressing skills of referencing and advocating study methods and research strategies that do not leave a student vulnerable to accusations of plagiarism. Unfortunately, one of the downsides of the Internet is the apparent ease in which people can download information and cut and paste it into their work, or even acquire whole assignments.

How to spot plagiarism:

- Different writing style or writing level to that seen in classwork
- Variants in fonts and font size within text
- American spellings
- Different referencing to that which has been taught
- Word processed work when handwritten is usual
- Obscure references or sources of information
- Different opinions/context to those made in class or textbooks.

If you suspect something, you don't need fancy software tools to detect it. Just type the sentence, without the smaller words (e.g. of, and, the, etc.) or key words that seem obscure, into a search engine – like Google – and generally, it will appear verbatim in the list of 'hits' that appear as search findings.

In terms of authenticity, it doesn't hurt to get learners into the habit of signing and dating their work.

I confirm that this [assignment/essay etc.], is all my own work.

Signed: A. Learner

Today's date

This does not stop plagiarism, but it enters the learners into a contract concerning ethics.

14.3 Peer and self-assessment

By the end of this section, you will be able to describe some examples of relevant use of peer and self-assessment.

Both peer and self-assessment generally lead to reflective practice. Both are concerned with the ability to judge oneself and involve a critical analysis of the individual learner. It is useful when trying to develop a learner's evaluative and feedback skills. Peer assessment is based on learning from each other and is therefore a good way to share ideas and best practice.

The assessment strategy usually starts with some carefully posed questions, ideally devised by the learner although teachers can guide them to reach solutions and standards. The questions should be open and probing.

EXAMPLES OF RELATIONSHIPS TO THEORY

Kolb (1984). His learning cycle relies heavily on concepts of reflection – which involves self-assessment.

Schön (1983). Reflective practices in-action and on-action rely on self-assessment to influence changes in behaviour.

Boud (1995). Expressed his beliefs that learning and development will not occur without self-assessment and reflection.

Some ideas to include self- and peer assessment in teaching and learning:

● *Student presentations* – at the end of the presentation ask observers and presenters to assess themselves against some criteria – for example, content, communication, contribution and professionalism.

- *Micro-teach sessions* – as presentations, but ask observers to comment on whether the teaching appealed to their learning style and if they learned anything.
- *Tutorials* – specific questions such as which part of the course/assignment was the most difficult? How do your key skills lessons support your main qualification?
- *Profiles* – ask learners to describe their abilities against occupational or academic standards, or at the end of the course ask them to describe the key things they have learned and where their development now lies.

Glossary of terms

Blended learning a mixture of traditional and modern/computer learning technologies

E-assessment electronic versions of assessment

Invigilation supervision of examination candidates

Plagiarism to pass off somebody else's work as your own

QCA Qualifications and Curriculum Authority

 SUMMARY

In this chapter, you have covered all of the theoretical aspects in relation to the third learning outcome of the third unit in your CTLLS qualification:

Matching assessment to needs of learners and curriculum, the rules of assessment, peer and self-assessment.

Your Personal Development

You have considered inclusion through differentiated assessment at both formative and summative levels. You have reviewed ideas about how to differentiate assessment to suit needs and strategies to support special assessment needs in summative assessment. The role of ILT in assessment is analysed and suggestions made regarding appropriate use.

You have investigated the rules of assessment: validity, reliability, authenticity, currency, sufficiency, objectivity and the power to discriminate with reasons as to why problems occur if the rules are not followed. Confidentiality is also discussed with mention of related legislation.

Finally, you have reviewed peer and self-assessment and their importance is described with suggestions for relevant use.

You should be able to answer questions relating to:

● The importance of rules in assessment
● The purpose of inclusion
● Differentiated assessment
● Values of peer and self-assessment in learning.

CHAPTER 15 (PPA, UNIT 4)

Feedback and questioning in assessment

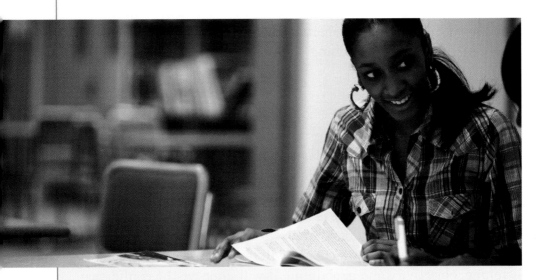

LEARNING OBJECTIVES

In this chapter you will learn about:

- Feedback skills
- Giving constructive feedback
- Making judgements in assessment
- Different types of questioning techniques

15.1 Feedback in assessment

By the end of this section, you will be able to identify the value of **feedback**, especially relating to assessment and progression, the methods of feedback, and be able to describe the skills required.

Feedback is the conversation between teacher/assessor and learner. It aims to celebrate strengths, give constructive advice on weaknesses and identify areas for further development. It is essential in the assessment process, and its main purpose is to let learners know how well (or not) they are doing. (See also Section 4.3.)

Feedback skills

Giving feedback is not easy; it is particularly difficult at the opposite ends of the feedback spectrum. If observed practice or an assessed piece is particularly good, it is difficult to identify development suggestions, or, conversely, it is difficult to feedback to learners without destroying confidence when their assessment is not up to standard. Giving effective feedback will test your own skills in listening, objectivity and explaining. It will improve the confidence of your learners and develop their potential, but it takes time to get it right. The hint here, although you will be encouraged to give immediate feedback, is that in the early days you may wish to consider what you want to say before diving in – so give yourself a few minutes to think and plan what you are going to say.

Feedback should:

- Be delivered promptly after the assessment, preferably immediately, especially after observation or verbal questioning sessions
- Be a two-way process – you can always ask the learner to say how they think it went and get an idea of their understanding, checking their ideas for development
- Be motivational – feedback increases confidence and self-esteem and therefore potential attainment

- Be specific – feedback should only be about the assessment; it should be unbiased, without opinion, unnecessary digression or imposing your own standards
- Offer choices and solutions – this develops potential
- Only comment on things that can be changed – e.g. behaviours or values, not appearance or inner character
- Positive – use strategies that will encourage a learner to develop
- Be constructive – use a balance of positive and negative comments.

Constructive feedback

Constructive feedback is the title given to a form of feedback which is helpful and supportive. It is motivational in that it neither gives false descriptions of a learner's ability nor does it destroy their self-esteem, but aims to develop and fine-tune skills. Whether produced verbally or in writing, this effective style of feedback follows a distinct pattern of:

1 A positive opener
2 A developmental statement
3 Motivational close.

also known as . . .

'the feedback sandwich'

By starting with a positive statement, you will reassure and relax the recipient of the feedback. Always identify something good, even if it is only the fact that they turned up on time! The comments you make should always link to the standards being assessed. The feedback should always be about the individual and you should never compare their performance with any one else or anything other than the standards expected.

Developmental statements are the point at which you should make comments about things which need to be improved. It is good to get contributions from the recipient of the feedback. Using open questions will aid this process and together you will formulate your future plans.

Some questions you might wish to consider are:

- How do you think that the customer felt when you…?
- What would you do if…?
- What alternatives are there to…?
- Why did that happen?
- At what point in the process would you think about…?

If there is going to be a 'but' the person giving the feedback should build up confidence (i.e. discuss the positive aspects of the work) before delivering the shock. The word 'but' should also be used cautiously.

> 'It was alright but it wasn't very welcoming' is not particularly helpful. It seems to suggest a negative outcome. An alternative suggestion might be: 'I liked the way that you welcomed the customer and believe it would be improved if you'd stood to greet them.' This is of the same flavour but not as hard as a 'but' statement. In the second statement the 'but' is delivered as an 'and'. Therefore, is not as critical and more developmental.

Ending the feedback in a motivational way will incite the learner to take on board recommendations and leave them feeling positive about their performance, even if they are not ecstatic about the outcome. Ideally in a feedback session, you should try to get the recipient to identify their own way forward. This ownership of the actions needed to improve will result in a high level of motivation. It is at this point that you can develop reflective skills in your learners.

Assessment decisions

Following an assessment and the resultant feedback, you will have to make a **judgement**. The decision will be a summary of what you saw that was good, the standard achieved and how much further development is needed. There will usually be parts of the assessment that are satisfactory, but there may be others that were not so good – and this may be reflected in the grade or pass mark. In **NVQ**s, all

performance criteria (pcs) must be met, which is why an assessment may consist of more than one method of assessment to cope with the things that don't naturally occur. Depending upon the type of qualification, purpose of assessment and level of formality in the assessment, the decision will either be:

- **Pass or Fail** – the assessment either meets or doesn't meet the standard required.
- **A graded result** – **pass**, merit [credit], distinction which describes how well a learner has achieved, but your feedback needs to explain the development between levels.
- **Marks** – out of 10, 20, 100 etc., usually expressed as percentage.

The teacher should be quite clear in stating the outcome of the assessment. Saying the words 'you've passed' is very often the thing that is forgotten at the expense of creating good feedback. Also, sometimes the feedback is so positive that a learner can misunderstand the outcome, maybe thinking that they've passed or achieved a higher grade than they actually have.

The 'F' word

The word **fail** is rarely used. This is because it is highly demotivational. Rarely is everything so bad in an assessment that the teacher cannot comment positively on some aspect. If an assessment is not at the required standard, i.e. *fails*, you should consider alternative expressions such as 'needs further training' or 'not yet competent' or simply 'refer'.

In discussing feedback, it is worth noting the research of Professor John Hattie of Auckland University (1999 and 2003). He investigated the effects of feedback on achievement and the ability of teachers to influence learning.

Having dissected the factors associated with teaching and learning and categorised them into responsibilities, he discovered, not surprisingly, that the teacher has a significant influence on learning. This furthered his earlier research which identified the extent to which feedback impacts on achievement, all of which supports the current beliefs in assessment *for* learning rather than the assessment *of* learning. This concept is discussed further in Section 16.1. In summary, effective feedback is more effective in developing learner progress than merely providing grades. This is generally because if a learner is told 'that's a pass' or 'it's a grade b' they are more likely to accept that outcome without seeking development or improvement. When given feedback, most learners will attempt to develop future work. In combination they are able to meet both learners' values and aspirations.

Additional reading

Additional reading on this research is widely available on the Internet using Hattie, feedback and assessment as key words in a search engine.

15.2 Questioning in assessment

By the end of this section, you will be able to compare and contrast a variety of different questioning techniques. You will be able to consider the strengths and weaknesses of each and make informed decisions about selection of **questions**.

REVISION

In Part One, Section 5.1, you looked at questioning as one of the methods of assessment and discovered what the main purposes were. In Section 13.1 the methods of assessment were analysed in more depth to identify advantages and disadvantages of their use. In this section, we focus on questioning and look in more detail at some aspects of questioning techniques and their benefits.

One of the most successful and versatile assessment methods is that of questioning. The variety of methods within the category of questioning is large and the way it can be used to differentiate, motivate and develop learners is very broad. Equally, it is the assessment method that is most criticised and open to inefficient and ineffective use.

1 Essay type	
Description	A structured, semi-structured or unstructured piece of writing on a topic. The level of structure is determined by the question posed. May also be called **extended questions**.
Main uses	Depth of subject knowledge is tested. Tests values and opinions and argument. Academic/research investigative pieces. Creative, evaluative or descriptive writing. Unsuitable as oral questioning.
Designing questions	Very easy, questions can range from unstructured, when learners decide upon their own topics as in dissertations, to semi-structured, when broad topic titles are given, to structured when learners answer a series of questions making up the topic title. Categorised as supply type of questions.
Making judgements	Difficult to mark – detailed assessment criteria required to allocate set marks for specific component of essay (e.g. 10 marks for…, 50 marks for…, etc.). Difficult to mark objectively so results may lack consistency. Generally marked as a percentage or grade.
Assessment rules	Formative or summative applications. May cover only a small aspect of the curriculum so impacts on validity and sufficiency. Open to plagiarism and cheating thus questioning authenticity.
Differentiation	Assesses understanding and cognitive skills. Assesses literacy skills (and numeracy when data collection requirements are included). Can be intimidating for learners, as essay writing is a skill in itself. Level of high order skills makes them highly suitable for learners at Level 3 and above.

▶

2 Short answer type

Description	Specific questions on a single or multiple topics, requiring a few paragraphs of text as an answer.
Main uses	Very versatile style of questions, which can be oral or written, requiring one-word, sentence or extended answers.
	Tests cognitive skills and either depth of knowledge or breadth of knowledge – dependent on questions asked.
	Good homework questions as they do not take too long to complete.
	Requires learners to remember information.
	Ideal as extended oral questions.
	Often called 'open' questions.
	Very effective when used orally in a nominated questioning style, so that questions are linked to learner ability.
Designing questions	Fairly easy to design using words such as How? Why? When? Where? What?
	Create open questions, requiring responses covering fact, opinion.
	Can design should/could/would options in questions.
	Categorised as supply type of questions.
	Can be one word or sentence/paragraph length responses.
Making judgements	Marking grids are required as answers will vary.
	Objectivity increased due to more focused responses.
	Weight of questions is usually reflected in number of marks available for each question.
Assessment rules	Formative or summative applications.
	Covers a wider range of topics in the curriculum and improves sufficiency in coverage.
	Widens opportunities to collect valid, reliable and **qualitative** responses.
	When questions are asked verbally it is absolutely authentic – unless the question is posed in advance and answered at a later time.

Differentiation	Less frightening than essay type questions.
	Develops essay writing skills, therefore ideal for learners progressing to or aspiring to higher academic levels.
	Degree of difficulty can be varied to support different needs of learners.
	Less analysis and argument needed, questions usually relate to fact or opinion, which makes them more suitable for Level 1 and 2 learners.
	Can be used to probe deeper into a subject to ascertain levels of understanding.
	Opportunity to collect ipsative/profiling information.

3 Multiple-choice type

Description	A question with (usually) four possible answers, which requires learners to identify the correct answer.
	Sometimes called **restricted response** or expressed as multiple-choice questions (**MCQs**).
Main uses	Requires learners to recognise information.
	Possible as oral questions if planned in advance.
	Very often used in summative tests.
Designing questions	Very difficult to prepare.
	Questions (the **stem**) have a correct answer (the key) and several (usually 3 or 4) incorrect answers (distractors). The **key** and distractors are collectively called 'options'.
	Learners call them multiple guess questions as once the obvious **distractors** are removed; it usually leaves two possible answers. C is the most common correct answer so the test needs to be tested so that correct answers are evenly distributed.
	Categorised as selection type questions.
Making judgements	Very easy to mark as only one answer will be correct.
	Computerised marking software can be used.
	Learners can participate in marking if given answer frames.
	Very objective way of testing.
	Opportunities to vary levels of questions to test range of ability – power of discrimination.

▶

Assessment rules	Questions can cover a large part of the curriculum. Large numbers of questions can be asked in a relatively short space of time. Can be used to gather **quantitative** data in larger research studies. Can be used formatively or summatively.
Differentiation	Questions can vary in level of difficulty. No test of writing skills, but good to develop reading and comprehension skills. Questions can be 'banked' and reused at a later date. Generally MCQs test recall rather than comprehension, however, more complex questions can be formed to test higher order skills.

4 Alternative answer type

Description	Either yes/no, true/false answers to specific questions resulting in very restricted responses.
Main uses	Requires learners to recognise information by giving limited answers. Very little depth of knowledge required. Tendency to guess, therefore low order cognitive skills are tested. Used in questionnaires to gather data. Often called 'closed' questions.
Designing questions	Simple to answer and prepare. In more complex questionnaires, avoid an odd number of responses as this allows people to remain undecided (sitting on the fence), which may not be helpful in eliciting data. Categorised as selection type questions.
Making judgements	Easy to mark, learners can participate in marking. Objective method of marking, but limited reliability due to guesswork.

Assessment rules	Doesn't test reliably due to chance of guessing answers correctly. Due to lack of reliability, they are more suitable to formative assessment.
Differentiation	Does not test writing skills. 50 per cent chance of correct answer. Use of Likert scale can bring in more responses (strongly agree, agree, disagree, strongly disagree).

5 Matching answer type

Description	Two lists of data or facts are written which have to be matched.
Main uses	Used to match, for example: events and dates; terms and explanations; facts and figures; etc. Can be used with individuals or groups. Unsuitable as oral questions.
Designing questions	Average ease to design, but messy to answer; answers tend to be lines drawn from one correct answer to the corresponding fact in other list, so may need to prepare answer sheets. Categorised as selection type questions.
Making judgements	Easy to mark, although answer sheets may be difficult to read. If one question is wrong it may limit opportunities to get all other answers correct. Very objective in scoring/result.
Assessment rules	Valid and objective method of testing factual data. Difficult to include the power to discriminate because of limited answer frameworks. Ideal formative assessment for low order skills.

▶

Differentiation	Suits fun activities and opener/closure activities.
	Very few literacy skills assessed.
	Can test whether learning outcomes are met.
	Covers wide curriculum or can link separately delivered topics to create learning links.

6 Completion type

Description	Text or diagrammatic sheets in which key words are omitted. Sometimes called gapped handouts.
Main uses	Can be used for recall tests at beginning and end of lessons or to create interaction during class time.
	Can be used as oral questions if planned in advance.
	Useful to create aides-memoires for learners.
Designing questions	Any document can be adapted to become a completion-type test.
	Cloze technique (missing out letters in regular patterns) can be used to determine reading ages and comprehension levels.
	Categorised as supply type questions.
Making judgements	Objective as there should only be one correct solution.
	Marking is usually correct responses out of maximum.
Assessment rules	Valid, in that tests are usually about current topics being taught in the curriculum.
	Formative strategy to check classwork progress.
Differentiation	Can be used with or without answer options to differentiate between abilities.
	Can test spelling and comprehension of technical terms.

General hints and tips about questioning

- Make sure that learners know how to answer the questions – special answer sheet, black ballpoint pen or pencil, style (essay, report or bullet points), word count.

- Make questions short and precise.
- Avoid negatives in questions – 'which of the following is not...' and multiple correct questions – with questions like 'which is the main reason for...' If these *must* be used then highlight the command word using **bold**, *italics* or <u>underline</u> formatting.
- Arrange questions logically and avoid repetition in subject type.
- If suggesting a word count, it is usually acceptable to add a '+ or – 10 per cent' rule, before marks are deducted for too few or too many words.
- The more unstructured the question the more creative and diverse the answer because of the freedom of ideas allowed.
- Reduce misinterpretation of questions by avoiding words like 'some', 'a few', 'a range'. How many *is* a few?

Glossary of terms

Constructive a term used to imply helpful feedback

Distractor incorrect answer choices in MCQs

Extended question a question that involves a long answer

Fail an assessment decision; not at pass standard

Feedback verbal or written comments about the assessment intended to bring about improvement

Judgement a decision about an assessment

Key the correct answer in a MCQ

MCQ multiple choice question

NVQ National Vocational Qualification

Pass assessment decision relating to satisfactory performance

Performance criteria standards of required competence

Qualitative data relating to opinions or thoughts

Quantitative data relating to statistics and number

Question a query inviting a response

Restricted response limited choices in answers

Stem the term given to a question in a MCQ

SUMMARY

In this chapter, you have covered all of the theoretical aspects in relation to the fourth learning outcome of the third unit in your CTLLS qualification:

Feedback in assessment, questioning in assessment.

Your Personal Development

In this chapter you have analysed the meaning and purpose of assessment in the context of questioning and feedback. You can recognise key terms relating to feedback and questioning. You have identified strategies to offer and deliver feedback and reflected on the possible outcomes of assessment.

You have reviewed several types of questioning techniques and can distinguish between the main types of questioning, considering their value to both teacher and learner in achieving valid and reliable data about progress.

You should be able to answer questions relating to the importance of feedback and justifying choices about appropriate assessment methods, whilst ensuring that they are fit for purpose.

CHAPTER 16
(PPA, UNIT 5)

Recording progress and achievement

PHOTOFUSION PICTURE LIBRARY / ALAMY

LEARNING OBJECTIVES

In this chapter you will learn about:

....

- The main aims of carrying out assessment
- Assessment for learning
- Procedures for carrying out assessment
- Quality assurance
- Methods of recording assessment
- Averages in assessment
- How to report progress

16.1 The purpose of assessment

By the end of this section, you will be able to describe the purpose of assessment in terms of measuring achievement and progress and developing potential. You will start to make decisions about the trend from assessment of learning to assessment for learning and how it will impact on your classroom delivery.

Purposes of assessment

Assessment is a key function in teaching and learning; it informs the reasons for teaching and collects information regarding the results of that teaching; this makes assessment integral to the process of learning. In their research, Black and Wiliam (1998) suggest that assessment together with constructive feedback will bring about raised levels of achievement. This has reformed the way assessment is perceived in the classroom, bringing about a subtle change from 'assessment *of* learning' to 'assessment *for* learning'. (ARG 2002, GTC 2007)

Much is written about assessment; in many of the key texts that you will read, assessment is defined as:

> [to] judge a learner's performance against identified criteria.
>
> Fawbert 2003, p. 247

> The process of obtaining information about how much the student knows.
>
> Reece and Walker 2006, p. 35

> Assessment equates to testing: if a learner is being assessed, then he or she is being tested.
>
> Tummons 2007, p. 4

There are three stages of assessment, which associate with its purpose:

1 Obtaining information
2 Forming judgements
3 Making decisions.

The first part, obtaining information, refers to the various methods of collecting the information, but more importantly, the teacher should ask 'why do we collect information?' (see Section 13.1).

You can gather information that relates to:

● learners' progress
● levels of motivation
● perceived and actual levels of attainment
● the effectiveness of teaching methods and practices
● diagnosing the needs of learners
● identification of the support needs of learners
● the confirmation of acquired learning outcomes
● start and end points of learning
● the amount and level of feedback needed to progress learning
● previous learning, experience or qualifications.

This collection of information enables you to make a judgement (assessment) about ability, competence or levels of knowledge and understanding. You can also use these outcomes to ascertain the effectiveness of your teaching. Assessment should be the tool to celebrate achievement and identify development. In reality it is all too often used as a negative tool to criticise poor achievement or failing standards and, therefore, it is very often seen in a threatening way, because we all fear failure.

Inside the Black Box

Prof. Paul Black and Dr. Dylan Wiliam (1998)

Assessment For Learning: Beyond the Black Box (1999), University of Cambridge, School of Education

A four-year study, commissioned by the Assessment Reform Group (funded by the Nuffield Foundation) to review the research available on classroom assessment. Their finding was that informal assessment in the classroom, with constructive feedback, raises achievement. .

Subsequent research suggested that increasing the amount of assessment does not enhance learning, rather it is using assessment effectively that raises achievement and potential. It recommended strategic and political changes to implement the change from assessment of learning, designed for grading and reporting processes, to assessment for learning, designed for development and progress.

Budge (2005), citing Black and Wiliam (1998), summarises the research and writes:

What works:

- regular classroom testing and the use of results to adjust teaching and learning rather than competitive grading;
- enhanced feedback between teacher and pupil which may be oral or written;
- the active involvement of all pupils;
- careful attention to pupil's motivation and help in building their self-belief;
- self- or peer-assessment by pupils, discussion in groups and dialogue between teacher and pupils.

. . . and what doesn't

- tests that encourage **rote** and superficial learning;
- over-emphasis on the giving of marks and grades at the expense of useful advice to learners;
- competitive teaching approaches that de-motivate some pupils;
- feedback, testing and record-keeping that serve a managerial function rather than a learning one.

David Budge, TES, Tasting the assessment soup. 18th February 2005.

The Association for Achievement and Improvement through Assessment (AAIA), sets out ten principles, devised by the Assessment Reform Group (ARG), as:

Assessment:

1 is part of effective planning
2 focuses on how students learn
3 is central to classroom practices
4 is a key professional skill
5 is sensitive and constructive
6 fosters motivation
7 promotes understanding of goals and criteria
8 helps learners know how to improve
9 develops the capacity for self-assessment
10 recognises all educational achievement.

www.aaia.org.uk/pdf/AFL_10principlesARG.pdf (accessed 30.09.07)

These principles advocate the assessment *for* learning instead of assessment *of* learning. The Learning and Skills Council (LSC) still requires measurements in terms of **success**, i.e., collecting data about outcomes (assessment of learning). This requires teachers to prove their performance in terms of targets, arguing that learner's performance, whilst born through **nurture** and tutoring (assessment for learning), is a contributory factor to the final result. Current research and trends seem to argue that it should be the leading role and are therefore pushing for significant policy changes (ARG 2002).

The links between outcome and purpose of assessment and the timeliness of assessment may not be absolutely clear. The following table attempts to make that link explicit.

	Pre-enrolment	Initial assessment	Diagnostic assessment	Formative assessment	Summative assessment
Increasing the motivation of learners	✓			✓	
Diagnosis of functional skills needs			✓		
Establishing understanding of topic				✓	✓
Demonstrating ability			✓	✓	✓
Identifying support needs	✓	✓	✓		
Assessment of unit or module outcomes					✓
Statement of competence					✓
Previous attainment	✓	✓			
Forward planning				✓	
Effectiveness of teaching and learning				✓	

16.2 Assessment procedures

By the end of this section, you will be able to specify procedures relevant in the planning, implementation, feedback and judgement stages of assessment, giving examples of appropriate documents and strategies to support the procedures. You will be able to explain the quality assurance practices that provide reliability in assessment.

Procedures are defined as 'the official way of doing things'. These routines are usually specified or informed by legislation or in this case by codes of practice. There are procedures associated with the planning, implementation, feedback and judgements of assessment.

NVQ qualifications have specific codes of practice relating to the delivery, assessment and quality assurance of programmes and the qualifications of assessors and verifiers. Guidance exists to ensure that learners, teachers, trainers and assessors, delivery and assessment institutions and awarding bodies are clear about strategy, method and role and that practices are able to stand up to scrutiny by inspectorate and audit teams.

Awarding bodies will also provide information on quality assurance (QA) processes. In particular, see:

NVQ Code of Practice
Ensuring Quality
Guidance on Internal Verification

Planning

Assessment needs to be planned. In the same way that teaching is planned in order to meet need, produce variety and structure, so assessment should be organised similarly. Some of the reasons for this include:

- Learning outcomes need regular assessment to ensure learners are on target to achieve their goals;
- Assessments in the workplace need to be arranged with supervisors, to minimise disruption to the business;
- Recreational courses will have learners working on their own projects, so the teacher needs to liaise closely to ensure learners goals are recognised, realistic and monitored;
- Special arrangements may need to be made – access to specialist equipment and resources;
- Complex programmes of study need to have all assessments plotted to ensure even distribution across the programme.

Planning, especially for one-to-one assessments, needs to be recorded and agreed. The candidate should have clear guidelines about what they are expected to do and what the outcomes are likely to be. In some, particularly vocational courses, assessment strategies require a number of successful formative assessments of practical skills, before a summative assessment of practical skill or knowledge tests. A suggestion is:

SUMMATIVE ASSESSMENT PLAN	
Name:	Date of proposed assessment:
Planned activity:	
Expected outcomes/criteria/evidence:	
Plan signed/dated by assessor:	Plan agreed, signed/dated by candidate:
Feedback following assessment:	Actions for development:
Outcome: Pass ☐ Needs further training ☐	Assessor signature: Candidate signature: Date:

In planning for more academic subjects, the teacher should consider the total number of assessments (which may consist of a number of tasks) and plot these into a calendar to distribute them across the programme of study. This involves liaising with other teachers on the team, whilst working within awarding body deadline dates. A suggestion is:

Unit	September	October	November	December	January	February	March	April	May	June	July
1		✕									
2				✕							
3						✕					
4							✕				
5									✕		
6											✕

In modular or unitised programmes, for example National Diplomas, then assessment will take the format of an assignment which includes a number of tasks, which relate to criteria and the demonstration of key skills. In this instance, an assessment plan may follow this style:

Unit title:			
Task	Interim due date	Links to criteria	Links to key skills
Task one *Description of what a learner must do or present for assessment*		*e.g. P1, P3, M1*	*Communication, Applications of Number, ICT and wider key skills links*
Task two *Description of what a learner must do or present for assessment*		*e.g. P2, M2, D1*	*Communication, Applications of Number, ICT and wider key skills links*
Task three, etc *Description of what a learner must do or present for assessment*		*e.g. P4, P5, M3*	*Communication, Applications of Number, ICT and wider key skills links*

To achieve a pass, the learner must:

This section will specify the P criteria using command words such as describe, identify, etc.

To achieve a merit, the learner must:

This section will specify the M criteria using command words such as analyse, etc.

To achieve a distinction, the learner must:

This section will specify the D criteria using command words such as evaluate etc.

The completed assignment must be handed in by:

Signatures: *Teacher and Quality Assurance Coordinator*

Implementing

....

The processes involved when implementing (doing) the assessment are related to ensuring that the rules of evidence are being met (Section 14.2). You should consider what type of assessment it is (Section 13.1), whether or not it is formative or summative (Section 12.1), and what you need to achieve in terms of outcomes and the time/location available.

Some of the things you may need to consider during formative and summative assessments are:

● Is the learner sufficiently prepared for the assessment?
● Do you have access to **registration** numbers; have you confirmed the eligibility to enter the assessment process?
● Do you and the learners have access to sufficient, adequate resources for the assessment?
● Does the arrangement of furniture facilitate equality and honesty?
● Has there been an accurate briefing of expectations and statement of proposed outcomes – shared planning?
● Is there a quiet area for oral questioning (if necessary)?
● Are you able to identify individual progress within the group?
● How will the assessment be recorded?
● Does the assessment need third party intervention (an invigilator) to ensure impartiality?
● Can you guarantee accuracy in timing of assessment – start and end times, a visible clock, adherence to specified durations?
● Have you checked the authenticity of candidates – are they who they say they are?
● Have you considered how the results of the assessment are to be conveyed?
● Do you need a feedback session afterwards?

Judgements

....

The procedures relating to judgements are associated with marking schemes, grading **criteria** and hand-in dates. These must always be clearly stated before the assessment. It might be a good idea to double check these during the planning processes.

A *marking scheme* may look like this:

ESSAY TITLE: Describe the importance of communication in a specific retail environment	
Definition of communication	One mark
Definition 'specific' retail environment	One mark
Theories associated with communication	Two marks
Links between communication and retail environment	Four marks
Stated factors of importance	Four marks
Coherence of expression	Two marks
Accuracy of spelling and grammar	Two marks
Structure of essay	Two marks
Bibliography, referencing and accuracy of citation	Two marks
Total marks available	20

In this example it is quite clear from the weighting of the marks (60 per cent) where the emphasis of the work should be. Yet marks can be lost, for example if the skills associated with essay writing (40 per cent) are not met. There may also be a stated requirement to achieve a pass standard – for example 10 out of 20.

Grading criteria relate to the quality and depth of the work. For example you will see grids written into many of qualification guides that specify what learners have to do to achieve a pass, merit and distinction grades. The information contained within the **grading** grids enables the teacher to challenge learners to aspire to a level greater than that which may be predicted or expected. It helps the learners to clarify what is expected of them in their assessment and hopefully stretch themselves.

For example:

To achieve a pass grade, learners must achieve *all* pass criteria. To achieve a merit grade, the learners must achieve all of the pass criteria and all of the merit criteria. To achieve a distinction grade, the learner must achieve all of the pass and merit criteria and all of the distinction criteria.

The processes involved in stating and achieving hand-in dates are going to be very specific to each qualification and/or organisation. Some will notionally suggest dates by which work should be submitted, probably using the individual learning plan to negotiate these; other qualifications may specify an absolute, non-compliance means a sanction, type of situation. You and your learners should be fully conversant with which applies and what, if any, sanctions are administered if pertinent.

Quality assurance

Quality assurance (QA) increases the levels of confidence in the value of assessment and the decisions made during assessment; they are mechanisms or policies for ensuring reliable, effective assessment, i.e. guarantees of quality. The purpose of QA is to assure the integrity of product nationally, to set entry and exit standards that are equal so that all stakeholders know, regardless of where the qualification was achieved, the standards are equal. This is one of the main differences between qualifications and unvalidated company training.

Qualifications have to be seen to be of a specific standard, whereas company training is designed to meet the unique requirements of a particular organisation. Both assure quality of provision, but company training certificates are less transferable between other sectors because the training is being designed around individual company practices.

The basic duties of assessors and moderator/verifiers have been clearly stated in the PTLLS (Section 5.2), but when it comes to quality assurance, you may find other personnel or functions involved in assessment.

For example, there is an increasing requirement to use independent assessors. This is to support the accuracy and reliability of assessment decisions. As many assessors are also involved in the delivery of training, it is difficult to assure objectivity when an assessor and learner have built up a successful learning and training rapport. By building another tier into the assessment, the quality of the assessment decisions are made more robust. Independent assessment usually means that a particular component must be assessed by someone not previously involved in the training, learning or assessment process. It is not validation of an assessment decision as this remains the role of the verifier or moderator.

Advantages:

- Assessors are protected from accusations of unreliability by using a third party to make certain assessment decisions
- Learners are guaranteed unbiased judgements.

Disadvantages:

- Another tier of assessment means additional costs.

Language of quality assurance

Standardisation (Section 5.2) relates to the consistency and agreement of expected standards or content. It can occur before assessment to set unified expectations or afterwards to agree the standard of marking.

Moderation refers to checking the marks and grades awarded by the assessment team.

Verification relates to checking that assessment processes are reliable.

Second (and *third*) *marking* refers to a process similar to standardisation, when one piece of work is independently marked by another person to (hopefully) get the same result.

Approval is the process involved with seeking permission to run particular programmes, under the guidance of an awarding body.

Awarding bodies, who **certificate** the programmes, are required to meet stringent audits by the Qualifications and Curriculum Authority (QCA) to ensure their quality assurance practices are sound.

16.3 Recording assessment

By the end of this section, you will be able to describe the need for record keeping at individual and organisational level.

REVISION

In Section 5.3, you saw examples of record keeping at an individual level for the purpose of tracking progress. You learned that records are an essential part of the assessment process by providing evidence of achievement and competence. In this section we extend that to the wider purpose of assessment and achievement records for organisational purposes.

The part of the job associated with record keeping often seems bureaucratic and repetitive. It sometimes takes longer to prove you did the job than it took to do the job in the first place. These feelings are quite common and you should not feel guilty about having them, although to move on you need to see the value in the process, so here goes . . .

Paperwork: The necessary evil or the answer to your prayers?

The need to record assessments or in fact any other aspect of the role is essential to you, your learners, your colleagues and your managers. Completing the necessary paperwork on time and distributing it to those who need it is essential for efficient and effective working practices.

Record keeping is best done in smaller chunks and not all left to the end of a programme, this ensures a distribution of the workload and timely completion of records which ultimately saves time. Records help you to remember what has occurred and act as a guide to others in case you are not available. A filing system suits methodical workers but not spontaneous types and so it is something that may need personal development time to fine tune. Records need to be kept in a logical sequence; **chronological**, alphabetical, by name, by programme or any combination of those. They may be stored as a paper record or saved electronically.

Who needs them and why:

Who	Why
Learners	To provide records to evidence achievement, progress and support needs. They will need support in storing their information.
Teacher	To replicate progress records of learners (in case of loss), inform reports to others, inform reflective personal and professional practice. To know who has done what and when. To vary assessment methods, to raise awareness of the overall assessment strategy of a learner.
Colleagues	To support team members in their absence, to share in team meetings and self-assess the effectiveness of their programmes. They need records to be assembled logically and accessible.
Managers	To monitor performance; plan for responsive provision, make strategic and financial decisions.
Quality unit	To generate comparative analysis across the organisation and compare performance with benchmarks.
Parents	To inform about the progress of their child on the programme. Learners may not communicate well with their parents and so this is the only link. Don't rely on learners giving reports to their parents, especially if they are anticipating less complimentary reports.

▶

Who	Why
Schools	To create a link between vocational and academic studies and develop a standardised approach to a learner's development.
Employers	To inform about the progress of their employee on the programme. As the financial sponsor, they require accurate and reliable progress information. To inform their business processes.
Awarding bodies	To register and certificate achievement, to action and record external quality monitoring processes, to inform responsive development.
Auditors	To check funding claims are legitimate and business processes are legal and above question. To scrutinize accountability and responsibility.
Inspectorate	To quality assure performance at organisation level against national standards, to justify appropriate use of public funds.

What are the consequences of failure to keep records?

- The learner's progress is haphazard and unstructured;
- Mistakes and trends are not noticed so they continue to impact on practice, possibly in a downward spiral;
- There is a lack of accountability with no-one taking the lead on responsibility to learners and other stake holders;
- Learners don't gain their qualifications, or if they learn the required elements they will not be accredited through a recognised body;
- Public confidence is reduced, which results in lower enrolments, which leads to fewer classes, fewer jobs, and eventually the demise of the organisation.

Hints and tips for record keeping

- Keep copies for third parties.
- Write in an appropriate style for the reader – the learner, parent, awarding body etc.
- Keep notes about informal processes – development needs and actions, late work, resubmission dates, problems, etc.
- Documentation should give an overview rather than record every 'if, but and maybe'.
- Documents should be fit for purpose.
- Keep records relating to the process and product of assessment.
- Records may be self-devised or devised by the organisation – ask what is in use before going your own way.

Minimum core numeracy – averages in assessment

You may be asked to prepare statistical information to record assessment, achievement or progress. You may wish to analyse the results of your own assessments for similar reasons. One way of doing this is to identify norms or standards, either to identify trends or compare data with other sets of data. To do this it is advantageous to present data in percentages or using averages. As part of your personal numeracy development, you need to be clear about the expressions mean, median, mode and range and how these can help you analyse results (see Section 17.1).

The *mean* is the average score; it is the easiest of the averages to calculate. It is done by totalling the scores and dividing by the number of learners.

Learner	Score
Jake	19
Sam	18
Phil	12
Sian	15
Sarah	17
Chloe	19
Adam	20
Rafiq	18
Mo	14

In this example:

The scores total $152 \div 9 = 16.8$. This means that the average score is just under 17 out of 20. This can be represented as a percentage – the average score is 85 per cent.

The *median* is the exact middle of the data set. Using our example above, first you should write them in ascending or descending order:

12, 14, 15, 17, 18, 18, 19, 19, 20. The median is 18 because there are 4 figures below and 4 figures above the middle value.

The *mode* is the number that appears most often. In our example there are two modes: 18 and 19.

The *range* of scores is calculated by taking the lowest score from the highest score. In this example 20 is the highest score and the lowest is 12.

$20 - 12 = 8$. The range therefore is 8.

16.4 Reporting progress

By the end of this section, you will be able to describe how and why progress is reported, to whom and about whom.

Much of this was covered in the previous chapter, but whereas that was concerned with record keeping, this part is about sharing those records with others in order to initiate a development. This is the move discussed earlier: record keeping is associated with assessment *of* learning, progress reporting is concerned with assessment *for* learning. As we have already seen, the benefits to the learner when the focus of assessment is changed from measurement to development impacts significantly on the learner's achievement.

Why does progress need to be reported?

Quite simply, because common sense (and current research) says it is the best way to develop potential. If the teacher tells the learner how they are doing, they can engage in a discussion to move forward, rectify mistakes and build on their strengths. It is highly motivational for the learner to be told how well they are progressing. Equally, with constructive feedback, it is equally valuable to know what isn't going so well, and, perhaps through motivational interviewing, you will come up with strategies to overcome this.

Parents are also interested to know how their child is performing in the classroom. It is increasingly important that the learning ethos is shared between home and the learning organisation. If homework is being set, it is good to know that parents are helping to ensure it is done.

Employers are interested because they have identified training needs in their employees and have contracted with learning organisations to realise those goals. They need to know that their employees are getting value for money and that they are attending and contributing to learning.

How and when is progress reported?

- One-to-one reviews – regularly throughout the programme
- Feedback – with all marked work
- Reports – usually once or twice a year
- Employer forums – usually annually
- Parents' evening – usually annually

The timing of reporting is only a suggestion; it will be determined by cost and availability of resources and staff. It is hoped that informal chats will be almost weekly and progress will be reviewed through feedback every time a piece of work is marked.

Who reports progress and about whom?

The teacher reports to the learner and may also report to either the parent or employer, dependent upon the age of the learner.

 ACTIVITY 1

Why do these learners need to know how they are progressing?

Case Study 1

From a younger learner's perspective...

Being aged between 14 and 19 is very exciting; the social life is getting better and relationships are being made and broken in a regular cycle; getting paid for work or through a grant or bursary is great – oh yes – there is that classroom stuff but so long as it is interesting and we get plenty of breaks and it doesn't get boring it is not too bad! However, along come teachers and parents who want us teenagers to gain a qualification and then talk about us as though we care, life is for now, not the future. There's plenty of time for that.

Case Study 2

From a mature learner's perspective...

I am doing this because I want to, I need to change jobs/get a qualification/earn more money/update my skills and I want the teacher's undivided attention to enable that to happen. I am motivated and want challenge, but I also want to come away from class with loads of notes, ideas and things to do. I want reassurances that I can do the things I have to, because it's been quite a while since I was last in study.

Recommended reading

The following documents and downloads relating to assessment procedures and quality assurance processes can be provided by the relevant awarding body.

NVQ Code of Practice
Ensuring Quality
Guidance on Internal Verification

Glossary of terms

Approval permission to deliver qualifications on behalf of an awarding body

Certificate a recognised outcome of a programme of study

Chronological in date order

Criteria the standard of competence

Grading the degree of competence, pass, merit, distinction

Inspectorate e.g. Adult Learning Inspectorate, OfSTED

Nurture development of characteristics, beliefs or attitudes

QA quality assurance – an official system to establish the quality of something such as an assessment

Registration an official list of entrants on a qualification

Rote teaching by repetition, e.g. learning multiplication tables

Success recognition of achievement

SUMMARY

In this chapter, you have covered all of the theoretical aspects in relation to the fifth learning outcome of the third unit in your CTLLS qualification:

The purpose of assessment, assessment procedures, recording assessment, reporting progress.

Your Personal Development

You have discovered the difference between assessment *of* learning and assessment *for* learning and are able to describe the subtle difference between the two concepts. You can recognise and describe terms associated with development of learning through assessment. You can state the difference between assessment and progression, by listing the principles that underpin development and improvement.

You have investigated procedures of assessment and can explain them, giving examples of relevant documentation to be used during record keeping. You have developed an awareness of the need for marking grids, and how to use grading criteria in order to challenge and motivate learners as well as preparing for assessment.

In terms of quality assurance you are now able to express the purpose of QA in assessment and describe some of the terminology.

Regarding recording and reporting progress, you are able to justify why these processes are essential to business practices and developing a learner's potential. To develop your ability to provide data, you have looked at how averages are calculated and the different types of presenting 'average' statistics.

Finally, your learning is consolidated by engaging in a case study activity to explore why particular groups, albeit stereotypical formats, need to engage in progress development activities.

CHAPTER 17
(PPA, UNIT 6)

Evaluating effectiveness

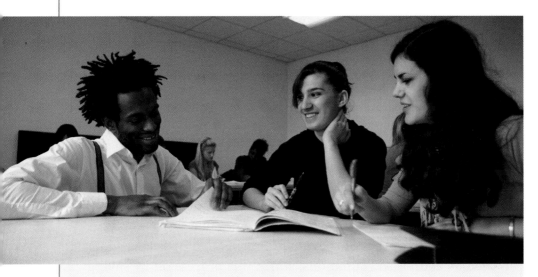

LEARNING OBJECTIVE

In this chapter you will learn about:

- Using assessment outcomes as a means of personal development
- Evaluation and reflection
- What assessment outcomes mean
- Dealing with emotions

17.1 Using assessment outcomes to develop yourself

By the end of this section, you will be able to identify how you can use assessment outcomes to develop the way you assess in the future, analyse the effectiveness of your teaching strategies and inform your personal development plan.

The expression **assessment**, which means 'to measure achievement', and **evaluation**, which means 'to measure effectiveness' are synonymous. This means they are interchangeable, but in academic language there is a distinct difference. For the teacher, assessment is gathering the information, and evaluation is making sense of that information. The results of assessment will obviously tell us how well our learners are progressing in their programme or how much information they have understood; it may tell us how well they can transfer knowledge or skills into different situations. It is essential that we look at assessment outcomes and try to analyse what they are telling us. This evaluation will open up issues which can then be addressed. Tummons, starts this process off by saying:

> Evaluation of the assessment is about judging the extent to which the assessment does what it is supposed to do.
>
> Tummons 2007, p. 87

A reflective practitioner will take this one stage further and comment about what those results mean to them and endeavour to improve their own performance. For example:

Extract from reflective diary

I set some short answer questions to do as part of the summary of the lesson. There were five questions collectively covering the learning outcomes I set at the beginning of the session, with a question about some 'nice to know' information that I covered immediately after break. I put the 'nice to know' question in to challenge the learners and I'm really pleased that they all answered it very well. In fact they all did very well in the test, mostly getting 4 out of 5. When I looked in more detail I found out that a lot of them (6 learners out of 17) generally went wrong on the same question.

I looked at my teaching notes later and checked that I had covered the topic; it was done by talking it through in some detail. I told the group to take notes and checked that they were writing, so I really can't understand why the question was poorly answered. In fact, I distinctly remember that it was just before break and that straight after break I covered the 'nice to know' bit which they did well in.

If you were reflecting on this event, what conclusions would you make?

Evaluation

In this situation the teacher has not made the link between the teaching style used, the time within the lesson that the topic was covered and the outcome of the test question. Perhaps there is also a link between those that got the question wrong and their learning style; the topic was ideal for auditory and kinaesthetic learners, but not good for visual learners. Add to this that it was just before break and things like tiredness and low attention spans may have an impact on the learners' ability to retain information. The topic may have been one of those parts of the subject that is quite complicated and so has to be explained in detail to be understood. The teacher may have believed that the information was important so had to be delivered by verbal exposition, but that can be boring, because it is a passive activity.

Reflection

What would you do next time if you were the teacher?

What can assessment tell us?

Progress. A test can reveal how well, or not, a learner is progressing. This information can be used in tutorials to offer additional help in the topic, perhaps by directing attention to self-study packs or by advice to attend support workshops. It could be that the learner needs additional training in the skill before attempting another practical test. Do you need to arrange additional sessions, more practice or support?

Effectiveness of teaching. As in the reflective practice exercise above, if it was clear that a large number of learners had not grasped a topic that topic should be revisited. It also reinforces the need to ensure that the questions or observations cover as much of the topic or curriculum as possible. If you don't ask the question, you won't know the answer! Do you need to change the way you teach a particular topic?

Effectiveness of assessment. Were all of the questions valid and reliable (see Section 14.2). Did the questions produce the expected answers? Were you able to mark them objectively? Was there a good coverage of topics/**syllabus**? These questions will establish how good your questions were in testing knowledge. If you were observing performance, you need to think about how useful this activity is in generating evidence for what is being assessed. Do you need to redesign certain aspects of the assessment? Look at the self-assessment checklist below and use the right-hand column to comment upon whether or not the assessments you use follow the rules.

ACTIVITY 1

Checklist to evaluate your assessment techniques.

Think of an assessment activity you have done recently. It could be something you've done at the end of the class to check learning, a module assignment, a unit task or programme end test.

Answer the questions fully. The more detailed the answer, the better your analysis will be.

Validity
How do the questions or tasks relate to material covered in class or in syllabus requirements?

State how the assessments are balanced to reflect the (importance/significance of the) topics.

Is the language or expression clear, unambiguous and understood?

How do learners know what is expected of them?

Reliability
Describe the purpose of the marking guide or sample answer sheet.

Describe how consistency in marking is to be achieved.

Describe the format of the assessment. Is this the most effective way of gathering evidence (proof of competence)?

Sufficiency
How does the assessment cover aspects of the syllabus:

- In its entirety?
- Over a number of assessments?

Authenticity
How do you guarantee that it is the learners own work?

Relevance
Describe how the assessments fit into the overall programme.

Describe how they are related to industry/commercial standards.

▶

Recording

State how the outcomes of the assessment are reported and recorded:

- To other tutors
- To learners
- To stakeholders.

Review how all aspects of the assessment were effective:

- Were there hard bits?
- Were the tasks successfully achieved?
- Were there tasks suited to all learners?
- Do the results show an even distribution of correct responses/competence?

What do you think were the key strengths of the assessment?

What do you think were the key weaknesses in the assessment?

Administering the tests. Sometimes the answers can reveal how well we carried out the assessment. Things like too little time to complete fully, classroom activity could not guarantee that everyone completed it independently, homework activity was not completed by everyone, proximity of learners meant that copying occurred, similar question/s not being answered or answered incorrectly. Do you need to review the timing or resources?

Statistics and outcomes. What do the results show? You can look at average scores to identify how easy or difficult the test was, if there are similarities or trends between correctly and incorrectly answered questions. What does it tell you about the way you wrote the test, delivered the topic or distributed easy and hard questions?

The evaluation is 'How well have you taught?' If you consider that imparting knowledge is a key role and the measure is the recall, application or **mastery** of knowledge and skills, then you have to ask yourself, 'If the measure is not achieved, do I assume that the teaching is poor?' Not necessarily: it tends to mean that you have not taught in a way the learner can learn. In summary, teaching in a differentiated way is known to support the needs of everyone in your class, and therefore, assessment results will confirm the effectiveness of your differentiation.

Assessment and emotions

Assessment brings about many different feelings. The teacher can alleviate these emotions and thus help learners to do their best in assessments.

ACTIVITY 2

Reflection

Think about the last time you were assessed. What were the emotions you experienced? How did your teacher prepare you for the assessment?

Consider:

- O/A Levels, GCSE exams
- Driving test
- Job interview
- University or college tests – dissertation, exams, assignments, NVQ observations
- Classwork and homework activities

Describe your emotions in two lists:

1   Positive emotions – for example: excitement, relief, ambition
2   Negative emotions – for example: fear, anxiety, nerves

How could the teacher overcome the negative emotions?

How has the assessment developed since you did it?

In this activity you will find that the positive aspects of assessment are fewer than the negative aspects. Some of the things that can be done to help learners prepare for assessment include:

- Explaining what will happen
- Visits to assessment centres or rooms
- Practice tests
- Feedback to support strengths
- Practice form filling
- Imitate style of assessment

- A **SWOT** – strengths, weaknesses, opportunities, threats – analysis to show collective emotions
- Motivational interviewing.

Evaluating and reflecting on the assessments you use in the classroom and at the end of the programme will facilitate a positive move forward in your own development.

Glossary of terms

Assessment to make a judgement about something, measurement of achievement

Evaluation to form an idea about something, to measure its effectiveness

Mastery comprehensive ability

Reflection a considered opinion expressed in speech or writing; thoughts or considerations, developing ideas and thoughts

SWOT analysis of strengths, weaknesses, opportunities and threats

Syllabus the structure of a qualification

 ## SUMMARY

In this chapter, you have covered all of the theoretical aspects in relation to the sixth learning outcome of the third unit in your CTLLS qualification:

Using assessment outcomes to develop yourself.

Your Personal Development

You have compared the terms assessment and evaluation and how they apply to your development. You have used your skills

◀

learned to date to engage in an activity/case study which requires you to link assessment outcomes with teaching performance.

You have completed a self-assessment to investigate a specific assessment method you have used. You have then analysed the information to identify key strengths and weaknesses in that assessment.

In a final activity you have explored the emotions that surround assessment and how you might overcome negative feelings.

You should be able to use ideas and checklists to identify your own strengths and areas of development, with the aim of improving your assessment techniques.

Appendices

Appendix A Optional units

Your Certificate in Teaching in the Lifelong Learning Sector (CTLLS) includes one further unit which is selected from a range of options. It needs to have a value of six credits to gain the full award.

Full lists of the options, which are frequently amended, are available on the LLUK website – http://www.lifelonglearninguk.org.

Your provider may not offer every option on the list as traditionally taught provisions, but may be receptive to either accrediting previous learning or achievement or offer alternative learning methods, for example online or distance learning packages.

Optional units currently available are:

Title	Level 3	Level 4	CATS
Conflict management	✓		6
Developing employability skills		✓	6
Equality and diversity	✓	✓	6
Evaluating learning programmes		✓	3
Preparing for the coaching role	✓	✓	3
Preparing for the mentoring role	✓	✓	3
Preparing to use e-learning and e-assessment in the lifelong learning sector		✓	9

▶

Title	Level 3	Level 4	CATS
Principles and practice of instructional techniques		✓	6
Specialist delivery techniques and activities		✓	6
The coaching and mentoring role	✓	✓	6

You should consult specialist texts to support your studies in these topics.

Appendix B Abbreviations

AAIA	Association for Achievement and Improvement through Learning
ACL	Adult and Community Learning
ADHD	attention deficit hyperactivity disorder
AI	awarding institution
ALI	Adult Learning Inspectorate
APEL	Accreditation of Prior Experience Learning
APL	Accreditation of Prior Learning
ARG	Assessment Reform Group
ATLS	Associate Teacher Learning and Skills
AVCE	Advanced Vocational Certificate in Education
BSA	Basic Skills Agency
BSL	British Sign Language
BTEC	Business and Technology Education Council
CADET	consistent, accessible, detailed, earned, transparent
CATS	Credit Accumulation and Transfer Scheme
CPD	continuous professional development
CTAD	Cambridge Training and Development
CTLLS	Certificate in Teaching in the Lifelong Learning Sector
CV	curriculum vitae
DfES	Department for Education and Skills
DTLLS	Diploma in Teaching in the Lifelong Learning Sector
EFL	English as a foreign language
EM	external moderator
EMA	Educational Maintenance Allowance
ESOL	English for Speakers of Other Languages
EV	external verifier

FE	further education
FEHQ	Framework for Higher Education Qualifications
FEnto	Further Education National Training Organisation
GCSE	General Certificate in Secondary Education
GLH	guided learning hours
GNVQ	General National Vocational Qualifications
HE	higher education
HND	Higher National Diploma
IA	initial assessment
ICT	information and communications technology
IfL	Institute for Learning
ILP	individual learning plan
ILT	information learning technology
ITT	initial teacher training
IV	internal verification
LCD	liquid crystal display
LLUK	Lifelong Learning UK (Sector Skills Council)
LSC	Learning and Skills Council
MCQ	multiple choice question
NCFE	Northern Council for Further Education
NQF	National Qualifications Framework
NQT	newly qualified teacher
NVQ	National Vocational Qualifications
OCN	Open Colleges Network
OHP	overhead projector
OHT	overhead tansparency
OTL	Observations of Teaching and Learning
PAT	portable appliance testing
PTLLS	Award in Preparing to Teach in the Lifelong Learning Sector
QCA	Qualifications and Curriculum Authority
QTLS	Qualified Teacher Learning and Skills
SEN	special educational needs

SENDA	Special Educational Needs and Disabilities Act (2001)
SSC	Sector Skills Council
SWOT	strengths, weaknesses, opportunities, threats
URL	universal resource locator
VLE	virtual learning evironment
WBL	work-based learning
WBT	work-based training
YTS	Youth Training Scheme

Appendix C Study skills

This section has nothing to do with your qualification; it is about *how* you learn.

The same philosophy can be adapted for your learners: there is more to teaching than teaching the subject matter. We assume that by the time our learners reach us in the post-compulsory sector, they have learned how to learn. *This is an assumption.*

Learners enter colleges and training providers with their various previous experiences of learning. We aim to develop autonomous learners who are able to achieve their qualifications and reach their full potential. They will, if you help them by teaching them how to do this. You are no different. To your tutor you are a learner!

Therefore, by the end of this section you will be able to:

- List the skills required in order to develop study skills
- Describe the safety issues relating to studying
- State the ethical values which underpin study
- Identify the most appropriate locations for personal study
- Explain the skills of note-taking
- Explain the skills of efficient reading
- Summarise the most effective strategies for time management
- List the key components of writing essays
- State the most common sources of information
- Use the Internet effectively
- Use a search engine
- Describe how to reference your sources using Harvard referencing system
- State the meaning of some common Latin words

- Describe a way to declare authenticity
- Specify the meaning of plagiarism
- Explain the meaning of the main command words in assessment
- List some alternative words for 'said'.

What are study skills?

These are the skills which help you to learn your subject. It is not a passive activity; you need to help your tutor to develop the skills by talking to them, attending tutorials and reflecting on feedback. Study skills include note-taking, efficient reading and research and accurate citation in well-structured essays. *How do you learn?*

Everyone is different. Some learners like to learn by seeing things; they are called *visual* learners. Some learners will learn by listening to things; they are called *auditory* learners. The last category is those learners that like to do things; they are called *kinaesthetic* learners. All of these relate to our senses: hearing, seeing, touching. How you learn and study will depend on your senses.

Safety issues

Ensure that the area in which you work has got a desk and chair that is comfortable and adjustable. If using a computer, be careful not to look at the screen for too long without taking a break.

Ethics and values

There are really two considerations here. One is the fact that should you decide to use a tape recorder in the class you should notify and seek permission from your peers and the tutor. The teacher training learning environment is one in which people need to be comfortable to speak openly about a range of issues and students may be a little self-conscious if the discussion is recorded.

The second is to do with citation. It is not acceptable to pass off other people's views, opinions and writings as your own. You can cite them, but must always acknowledge the original source. Every organisation will advise on the relevant method of doing this. Similarly, if you are using primary research, for example questionnaires in your essay, you should always ensure that there can be no link back to the originator and protect their anonymity.

Where to study

- Somewhere with few distractions and interruptions.
- Somewhere quiet. If background noise (music) is necessary, then keep the volume low. Avoid the temptation to sing along with your favourite artist.
- Somewhere with suitable furnishings: a desk big enough to have a computer, a place to write, and a place to keep your reference books or notes.
- An area to keep your study things separate from other uses of the space.
- Suitably ventilated, comfortable and light.

Note-taking skills

Thinking is quicker than speaking, so use this time to think about what your teacher is saying. This time allows you to understand what is being said.

Speaking is quicker than writing, so be selective when listening to your teacher and only write key things.

You may make your notes in a linear format (subheadings and written text), plain text (loads of writing in a prose style), or diagrams (for example spider diagrams or pictures).

Some examples of different types are:

- Listen for key words. Develop your ability to use key words by asking the teacher to stress them or write them on the board.
- Don't try and write everything down, it is not supposed to be dictation!
- Are you sitting where you can hear and see everything?
- If you are continuing a topic from a previous session, then re-read your notes before attending the next session. This acts as a

reminder, helps the transition from the known to the unknown and reminds you to ask about things you didn't grasp first time or have not retained.

- Always have sufficient resources. Be prepared. Pencils need sharpening and pens run out of ink!

- Perhaps a tape recorder would help if you have difficulty in listening and writing at the same time, but check permissions before switching on.

- Use a highlighter pen or coloured pencils/crayons to identify important facts.

- Use abbreviations to help you write quickly in class, but be consistent or you'll forget which abbreviations you've used. Some examples:

    (a) assmt = assessment;

    (b) fdbk = feedback;

    (c) t&l = teaching and learning;

    (d) sow = scheme of work;

    (e) LP = lesson/session plan;

    (f) diff'n = differentiation.

- Number handouts and put the corresponding number in your notes to remind you about additional information.

- Check a citation source if you plan to use printed material in lessons or study.

- Organise your notes. For example, use either different pages for different topics, or arrange notes in chronological order, or arrange them according to your assignment topics, or separate class and research notes.

- Leave white space around your notes so that you have room to add things later.

- Write legibly. Notes are for your use only, so don't bother too much about 'best writing' or spelling, as long as you can read them later. New vocabulary should be spelled correctly – with a definition.

- Rewrite notes to help deepen the knowledge.

Reading skills

Reading is the method of finding out information; you will do this when researching topics or trying to develop understanding. Depending upon why you are reading, you will read in one of three ways:

Skim This is a brief look at something, possibly looking at the introduction, the chapter outline and summaries before deciding whether or not the subject matter is relevant to you.

Scan This is a more detailed look at a particular topic or relevant section. You can use indexes to find appropriate readings. It will enable you to broadly describe the content, without any specific detail.

Digest This is when you read thoroughly. Every word will be considered until you fully understand the meaning. You will be able to describe in detail the author's points and may know some by heart. It is a very slow way of reading so needs to be both focused and necessary.

You should follow reading with writing. Make notes on key points and remember to fully reference the book title etc., for future use. There is nothing worse (and this is learned from bitter experience) than trying to use a brilliant quote but not being able to remember which book it was in, or remembering the book but having to re-read it to find the page reference.

Time management skills

I haven't got the time!

I know. It is difficult balancing all of the things that have to be done, so here are some ideas to help:

1   Identify what has to be done and by when. There are only 24 hours in a day, so decide when you will do your study. Writing an assignment at two in the morning the day before it is due is not

evidence of well-planned study time. Especially when you email it to your tutor and expect feedback and amendments before tonight's class!

2   Fit study time into your life: realistically

- Work
- School run
- Watching TV
- Me time
- Prep for lessons
- Domestic responsibilities.

Try keeping a diary for seven days, just to check what you actually do in a week. If you like a practical or technological way of doing this then you will find many questionnaires on the Internet which help you to plan your time: however, never underestimate how long things take to do.

- Plan your study needs. Start from when work has to be handed in and work backwards. Set yourself 'by now I should have done…' targets.
- Be in control.
- Persuade the family to respect your study time.
- Try to get quality time. Half an hour of good time is better than two hours of faffing about!
- Always meet the deadline – better a referral than a fail. If you hand something in your tutor will give you focused feedback which may give you a clearer direction. If you don't hand in anything, you may struggle and enter the spiral of more work, less time etc.
- Be strict with yourself. Are you researching something on the net or surfing? Do you *really* need to look at your emails now?

Essay writing

The hardest part of an essay is the start. There is nothing more daunting than staring at a blank sheet of paper, so always be clear about what you are going to write about. Plan the essay, and run it past your tutor or mentor for advice. Make notes about what you feel it is important to include. Keep going back to it to check that you are still on track and not waffling.

You may find writing an essay plan easier than just starting to write. You may also like to show it to your tutor in tutorial to check that you are on the right lines. This is a typical example:

ESSAY PLAN
Essay title:
Introduction *For example:* *The essay will review/analyse [topic] and summarise key issues relating to …*
Main themes to be included are: ✳   ✳   ✳ ✳   ✳   ✳ ✳   ✳   ✳
Information sources will be: ✳ ✳ ✳
Expected summary or outcomes of essay:

Every essay needs structure, that is, a *beginning*, a *middle* and an *end*.

1   At the start of your essay, tell the reader what they can expect to read about; this is usually directly linked to the assessment criteria. If you have to put the essay into context, now is the time to do it. By the end of your introduction, the reader should have a clear understanding of what to expect and what you aim to discuss.

2   The middle is about the content. It is about what you said you were going to write about in the introduction. Make sure your points follow a logical order and if you are using quotations ensure that they are relevant and don't disjoint the essay. Your tutor may advise you to write this in the third person, or they may prefer you to talk about your own experiences and link this to the theory. Check this out.

3   Finally your essay needs an ending. If you wish to evaluate and reflect on your future development, write this before you summarise your essay; do not introduce anything new in the section. In this part you need to tell the reader what they have just read, so it may be helpful to go back to the start and check what you said you were going to do, and ask yourself if this is what you did.

Make a draft of the essay:

● Does it flow?

● Spellcheck your work – most computers have a program to do this, but please check that the language is set as UK English and not US English.

● Proofread your work – remember that 'fro'/'for' and 'from/form' are bona fide words. They are a common typing error, but their misuse will not be picked up using a software spellcheck.

● Check presentation at this point. Watch for headings at the bottom of pages or tables that go over two pages. I know that this type of thing isn't in the criteria, but you are working as academic professionals so your work should be at that standard.

● Save frequently and make back-up copies.

● Do not use abbreviations in a formal essay.

● Use double line spacing as this gives you and your tutor plenty of space for comments.

Make a note of references as you find them and write the reference list or bibliography as you use the quotes. That way you won't forget any.

If you get stuck, leave a space and carry on writing about something that you are not stuck on. Then ask you tutor for guidance on the difficult bit. When you are in a writing mood, keep going ...

To get brownie points for your essay:

- Check that it is logical and coherent
- Ensure it is well structured
- Relate theory to practice
- Proofread and spellcheck
- Check that it makes sense.

Information sources

You will find helpful information for your study in:

- textbooks,
- journals,
- magazines,
- study centre intranet/VLEs,
- the Internet,
- newspapers,
- dictionaries,
- encyclopaedias,
- thesaurus.

Remember that your class notes are also there to be used, as is your tutor.

Using the Internet

The World Wide Web is a mass of information. Some of it is useful, some of it is not. Because anybody can write stuff and put it on the

Web, it might not always be accurate, so if you are using the Internet for a project or assignment, stick to the more reliable sources.

When you find something good, download it to your computer and save it, rather than wasting paper printing everything off. You can then read it and get the really good bits to include in your work. *Do not* just cut and paste it. This does not demonstrate your understanding. To comply with copyright, you may take a personal copy of information from a website, but must not make multiple copies for your class. You can give learners lists of useful URL (universal resource locator) addresses. If you do want to quote from the Internet, you can, but you must write the source in your bibliography in the same way as you would reference a book. For example:

www.igotitfromtheweb.co.uk (accessed on 09/09/2007)

Using search engines

This is a huge database of things on the Internet. The more commonly used search engines are Google, Ask and Yahoo. You should use a search engine to help you locate information. Write in key words; forget the small words or common words as they will give you too many 'hits'. Unless you want info from abroad, click the tab for 'UK only' search, as this will also help in finding information and research relevant to this country.

Avoid words that are very common, such as 'research about learning', because that will give you too many listings (hits).

Usually the best information is found in the first 10 listings, anything after that tends towards obscurity.

If you've got thousands of hits, go back and refine your search.

Be careful choosing the words you input to the search engine, both in terms of how common the word is and also in terms of alternative meanings.

You can use a search engine to do a quick plagiarism check by typing in a sentence from a piece of work, or an obscure reference. The link is usually in the first few websites.

Harvard referencing

Harvard referencing is a style of citation. Its purpose is to acknowledge the original ownership of the thought. Failure to use a citation style and passing off other people's work as your own is plagiarism. Plagiarised work is likely to be failed and may result in exclusion from the programme.

In an essay you are likely to use either direct quotes or paraphrasing.

Direct quotes are when you write the author's word exactly as they were presented in the document, and they will be in quotation marks ('...'). You should type exactly, so if it is an American work you may well see 'z' instead of 's' in words, or color not colour. *Do not alter it;* if you cite correctly the reader will know it is an American work and you will not be penalised for such errors. Long quotes, say of more than four lines, should be in their own space on the page and indented on both sides. You do not need quotation marks in this instance because it is obviously a quote. If the rest of your work is in double line spacing, then these long quotes would be in single line spacing. The purpose of quotation marks, indenting and different line spacing is to make them stand out. What you are saying is 'hey! here is a quote, and I'm not trying to hide it.' Any quotation should be introduced with the author's surname and the year of publication and page in brackets.

Paraphrasing is when you are expressing the idea, but putting it into your own words, maybe condensing the idea. This must still be cited using Harvard referencing; just because you've put it into your own words does not make it your thought.

For example:

Wilson (2008: 47) said: '...'

Wilson (2008: 46–9) states: '...' This is used when a quote goes over two or more pages or if you are paraphrasing a section.

The reference list at the end of the work is a list of all of your sources used in the text. A bibliography is a list of everything you have read, some of which you haven't used. It is more common to present a reference list. There should be a clear link between the names and dates in the text and the names and dates in the reference list. Books are listed in alphabetical order by author and presented:

Author surname and Initial/s (year) Title of the book. Location of Publisher: Publisher's name.

The title of the book is written as presented on the book cover So It May Have Capital Letters In Funny Places. You would either <u>underline</u>, **embolden** or *italicise* the title to make it stand out.

It will look like this:
Wilson, L. (2008) *Practical Teaching: A guide to CTLLS*. London: Cengage Learning.

For a magazine or newspaper, you should write the journalist's name, article title, paper title, date and page of article. It will look like this:

Smith, B. 'How to write an essay', *Popular Magazine*. 12/03/2007, pp. 23–5.

For class notes or handouts, it is similar to magazine articles, so the information you need is: the teacher's or group's name, class notes and lesson title, date. It will look like this:
Brown, P. Class notes: Module 4. 30/09/07, or
Group A. Class notes: Module 4. 30/09/07

Citing from the Internet

You should follow the same rules. If you can identify the author from the site then use it as you would a book. Alternatively you can use anon (anonymous) or the organisation's name. In the reference list at the end you should make the link to author or organisation. The URL becomes the 'book title' and you should add (accessed on [date]) instead of publisher details.

JONES, M. www.igotitfromtheweb.co (accessed on 09/09/2007)

For fuller details of how to reference, ask your tutor for their guidance document, or type the key word 'Harvard' into a search engine on the Internet.

Latin words

et al. – and others, usually a number of contributors to a text

ibid. – in the same source

loc. cit. – in the passage or place cited

op cit. – in the work already cited

de facto – in reality, according to practice – in actual fact

in loco parentis – in the place of a parent

ipso facto – by that very fact or act

q.v. – referring to text in a work – which see

sic – literally used as spelled or given.

Authenticity

You will probably be asked by your tutor to make a statement at the end of your work to confirm that it is your own work. This statement may look like:

> I confirm that the work submitted is my own work, and that no part of this work has been submitted to another organisation or towards assessment for another qualification.
>
> *Linda Wilson*
>
> October 2007
> Word Count: 3,500

Plagiarism

Plagiarism is when a writer uses somebody else's work without saying so, or expresses someone else's opinions as their own. Even if you reference work, you are only allowed to use a small amount of that text (copyright and licensing laws govern this). This is a problem given the amount of information on the Internet, which is easily pasted into your own essays. Educational organisations do not tolerate plagiarism. You can prevent being accused of plagiarism if you *reference* your sources. Referencing is used to acknowledge the rightful owner (the author, the learner or the teacher).

Command words

These are the words that you will see in assignments; they instruct you to carry out a particular action. You will also use similar words in your lesson plans in order to identify outcomes. See also section 3.1 – lesson plans and outcomes.

Analyse	To examine in detail; to discover meaning
Complete	To make whole or perfect to ending
Demonstrate	To show or prove by reasoning or practical skill
Deliver	To carry out; to produce or perform
Describe	To give an account of
Evaluate	To assess the value or worth of something
Explain	To make something clear by giving a detailed account of relevant facts, circumstances
Identify	To determine or list availability or identity of something
Investigate	To examine thoroughly and systematically in order to discover the truth

Justify	To prove validity
Obtain	To get or acquire something
Outline	To state the main features or general idea of something
Plan	To devise a purpose
Prepare	To make ready for an event, to construct or equip
Present	To show or exhibit something
Produce	To bring into existence, to make something
Reflect	To look back upon something and effect changes
Research	To carry out investigations into a subject or problem
Review	To look at or examine (again), to look back on
State	To express something clearly in speech or writing
Summarise	To express concisely the main outcomes
Use	To put into action

Different ways to say 'said'

When you are writing and referencing in your essays, you will often open the sentence with 'author said', you may vary this with 'stated' but may wish to include other variants:

Advocate, agree, allege, argue, articulate, assert, believe, certify, claim, comment, confirm, contend, contest, debate, declare, defend, define, dictate, disagree, enunciate, explain, express, imply, indicate, insist, maintain, make a case, mention, observe, profess, recommend, refer, reflect, remark, report, stipulate, subscribe, suggest, tell us, think, voice.

Summary

I hope that you will find this section useful as you complete the many tasks required of you in order to gain your qualification. Please remember that the most valuable study aids available to you are your tutor and your mentor.

Appendix D Teaching observations

This section is to reassure you about the purpose, process and possible outcomes of your teaching observation. They may be called:

- Teaching Observations
- Lesson Observations
- Teaching Practice Observations
- Session Observations
- Observations of Teaching and Learning (OTL)

Observations are your opportunity to showcase your expertise. They are very daunting, and it doesn't matter how long you have been in teaching, it remains traumatic to be observed. Observers know this and take this into consideration.

Teaching, traditionally, is a 'behind closed doors' activity, so it is not surprising that in order to find out how effective teaching and learning is, it must involve opening those doors.

Part of your teacher training programme will include observations of your teaching. Most probably these observations will be carried out by your tutor/assessor, i.e. the person responsible for making assessment decisions to prove your competence and so gain your award. However, you should also prepare for observations by others. Your mentor will provide particular guidance because he or she is likely to be from the same subject area that you teach in and therefore can advise on content, handling a particular group and level. You may also be observed as part of the organisation's self-assessment process: this will be by a trained observer who is looking to make judgements about the quality of the learners' experiences.

	CTLLS	DTLLS
Total number of teaching hours to be undertaken during the programme	30	150
Total number of observations during the programme	3	8

Who may watch you teach and why?

- The teacher training team – to assess your abilities against teaching competences
- The teaching (or lesson) observation team – to make judgements about the organisation's performance
- A mentor – to advise and guide your development
- A peer – to share ideas
- Ofsted inspector – to make judgements about the quality of the education or training provider
- Internal verifier/moderator – to validate the accuracy of your assessment decisions
- A manager – to monitor your performance and gather information from yourself and your students about programme delivery.

How to prepare for a lesson observation

Prepare your lesson as usual, although it will probably be a little more thoroughly done for an observed session.

An observer will spend between 40 minutes and an hour-and-a-half in your class. The average time spent observing is an hour. If your teaching session is timetabled for an hour, then your observer will see the entire lesson, but if it is longer, then they will use your lesson plan to make decisions about the part of the lesson that isn't observed. They may see any part of the lesson, although different people may want to focus on different aspects or alternatively, if there are a large number of observations to do, it will be when your session can be fitted in to the observer's workload.

Your mentor will probably come in by invitation and focus on an aspect of the session that you have already spoken about. The teacher training team will probably like to see the beginning or the end of the session, because these are the most difficult parts and they will be able to advise you more developmentally. Their visit will be expected. The lesson observation team or Ofsted inspection team will come in unannounced, although you will know that there is a significant likelihood of a visit.

Your observer will not participate in the lesson. They may, if the structure of your lesson permits, interview some learners. Questions they may ask learners include:

- 'Can you explain to me what you are doing today?' The observer is trying to find out if your learners know what they are trying to achieve, and may compare their answers with your stated learning outcomes.

- 'Do you usually do (specify an activity)?' The observer is trying to find out if what they are seeing in the lesson is typical and if you vary the methods in your lessons. They will compare this to the scheme of work.

- 'Are you working on any assessments/assignments at the moment?' The observer is trying to find out how learners are progressing, if they are getting timely feedback, or if there is any kind of assessment plan. They may compare this with paper evidence you have supplied.

They are trying to make judgements about the learners' experiences on the course and the impact your teaching has on the learners' experiences and will need to validate their judgements by cross-referencing evidence.

What documents to have available for the observer

When you are being observed, it makes sense to prepare a pack of documents for your observer. They need to make decisions about your teaching and some of their questions can be answered quite easily by providing certain things. For example: they need to find out if you are prepared for your class, so a copy of your lesson plan provides sufficient evidence to prove that you are.

Lesson (session) plan to demonstrate you are prepared and that your lesson has a clear beginning, middle and an end, using a range of teaching and learning methods, differentiated strategies and assessment plans.

A *scheme of work* to put this lesson into context with what has happened previously and what is planned for the future.

A *class profile* to explain about the group, its characteristics, and unique circumstances. This is particularly important if you are aware of particular issues that impact on the session. For example: x is unlikely to participate in this session because…or there are x authorised absences this week. You may provide the tutor file if you are the group's personal tutor. You are trying to provide the observer with information about what has led you to deliver the session in the way that you have. You may also wish to provide additional information to support current trends – for example, how you meet the Every Child Matters strategy or how you ensure your lessons meet equality and diversity agendas.

Assessment file with details of assessment plans, tracking and progress sheets, examples of marked work, or feedback given to learners.

Register to show attendance and punctuality over a period of time.

Handouts and teacher's notes copies of everything used in the session and notes about links to websites or books used. You may include a teaching or teacher's file to show consistency and variety.

What happens after the observation?

The observer may not stay until the end of the session. Usually they will try to leave at an appropriate time; for example, during some group work or at a break time so as to cause the least disruption to the flow, but it is not always possible. Don't worry if the observer gets up and leaves the room. They will try and say goodbye, but they will not deliberately interrupt the lesson, so may just get up and go, with a brief nod.

What happens next depends on who observed you. Observations that are carried out for development purposes will have a detailed feedback session immediately afterwards. These will usually be pre-arranged, especially if your lesson is planned to continue after the observation. The observer may give you cursory feedback, with an opportunity to arrange a more detailed session later.

The lesson observation team, and particularly the Ofsted inspectors, may give brief strengths and weaknesses as feedback, but it will be minimal. This is because the purpose of their observations is judgemental, not developmental. It will seem uncomfortable not to receive detailed feedback but it is quite common, so don't feel threatened.

Ten key points to survive your observation

1 Be prepared and keep your lesson plan to hand.
2 Lay out your desk with the resources you will use in the class, it saves time fumbling around for that board pen later!
3 Sit the observer out of your eye line, but where they can see what is going on.
4 Slow down, take deep breaths and try to overcome your nerves.
5 Give your observer plenty to read; whilst they are reading they are not watching!
6 If you are nervous, don't hold a piece of paper in front of you, it wobbles as you tremble.
7 Don't hide behind the desk, move around the room to check what's going on or just to remove a barrier.
8 Have lots of activities that engage your learners, group work, gapped handouts, discussion groups and practical activities. The observer is looking for active learners.
9 Start the lesson promptly. Have an opener activity whilst you take the register and settle the group.
10 End the lesson with a means of assessing learning – quiz or nominated questions.

Observation outcomes

Depending on the nature of the observation, you may or may not have a judgement offered to you.

Your mentor may not give you any kind of grade; they are using the observation to initiate reflective practice.

The teacher training observer has to decide whether your teaching meets the criteria (laid down by LLUK) or not. The decision will therefore be 'pass' or 'refer'.

The lesson observation team and Ofsted inspectors will grade you as either:

Grade one – outstanding

Grade two – good

Grade three – satisfactory

Grade four – inadequate.

Ofsted inspectors will not reveal the grade, nor will some lesson observation teams; it depends on the policy of the organisation. In either instance, you should be able to ascertain your grade by the judgements offered in the strengths and weaknesses feedback. Listen for the cue words: good, very good, exemplary, satisfactory, poor, etc.

Appeals against judgements

Hopefully you will not need to read this part, but if you do think that your observer has been unprofessional or has made an inaccurate judgement, read on.

The first course of action should be to discuss this with the observer; it will probably be that you want to justify your actions. Would a class profile have negated the need for this? Hopefully, your observer will meet you to discuss the outcome and the reasons why they made the decision.

If you cannot reach an amicable outcome, then you should report the matter to your line manager. Be prepared that one of the ways to mediate might be another observation.

Appendix E Teaching qualifications

In summary, from September 2007.

New staff

All new employees will work towards Qualified Teacher – Learning and Skills (QTLS) within five years of appointment, using the new qualification structure. This period gives them plenty of time to acquire a qualification, develop personal functional skills and widen, through cpd, academic and pedagogic skills. Private trainers or visiting speakers are exempt. (*The Further Education Teachers' Qualifications (England) Regulations 2007*)

Existing staff

Existing staff – employed since 2001 – will have or be in the final stages of working towards a Level 4 qualification (e.g. C&G 7407 stage 1, stage 2, Cert Ed/PGCE). Staff employed before 2001 may have other qualifications, such as C&G 7306/7 or TCOS, which are Level 3 qualifications, but are encouraged to update them to Level 4. (*The Further Education Teachers' Qualifications (England) Regulations 2001 – Statute 1209*)

All staff

All staff must register with the Institute for Learning and undertake regular continuing professional development. (*The Further Education Teachers' Continuing Professional Development and Registration (England) Regulations 2007*)

The Qualification structure for new entrants and unqualified teaching staff

The level of qualification for Associate Teacher Learning and Skills (ATLS) or Qualified Teacher Learning and Skills (QTLS) is determined by the role the teacher undertakes. Every teacher will be expected to complete the Award in Preparing to Teach in the Lifelong Learning Sector (PTLLS – C&G 7303). The Certificate in Teaching in the Lifelong Learning Sector (CTLLS – C&G 7304) is for those who are working as Associate Teachers. The Diploma in Teaching in the Lifelong Learning Sector (DTLLS – C&G 7305 – In university awards this is equivalent to Certificate in Education) is for those working in a full teacher role.

Table to compare new qualifications

Qualification	Number of guided learning hours of contact	Credit value	Number of teaching practice hours	Number of observed teaching hours
PTLLS Intro Award Level 3 or 4	30 glh	6 credits	30 mins micro-teach	30 mins
CTLLS Assoc Role Level 3 or 4	120 glh	24 credits (of which 6 from PTLLS)	30 hours	3 hours
DTLLS Cert Ed Full Role Level 4 Year 1 and Level 5 in Year 2	360 glh	120 credits (of which 15 from CTLLS)	150 hours	8 hours

PTLLS 6 CATS	CTLLS APL = 9 CATS	DIPLOMA (YR 1) 45 CATS	DIPLOMA (YR 2) 60 CATS	120 Credits
PTLLS 6 CATS	CTLLS 18 CATS			24 Credits
PTLLS 6 CATS				6 Credits

Descriptors for teaching roles

Associate teacher role (irrespective of hours worked)

Will teach predominantly in one of the following ways:

- From pack/pre-prepared materials and therefore has fewer responsibilities in design of curriculum and materials
- On a one-to-one basis
- A programme confined to a particular level/subject/type of learner (i.e. does not develop or deliver a full range across a curriculum area)
- Short courses.

Assessor/trainers, instructors, adult and community learning (ACL), work-based learning (WBL) and uniformed services will fall into this category

Full teacher role (irrespective of hours worked)

Will take on the full professional responsibility by:

- Using materials they have designed and evaluated
- Working across a range of levels, subjects and learner types
- Working across or contributing to a range of programmes of varying lengths
- Engaging in the wider role of teaching, e.g. tutoring, advice and guidance etc.

Unit titles and content

PTLLS   Award in Preparing to Teach in the Lifelong Learning Sector

6 credits, offered at Level 3 and Level 4

5 learning outcomes

Threshold qualification required by all teachers

CTLLS

Preparing to Teach in the Lifelong Learning Sector (as above)

Planning and Enabling Learning (Level 3 or Level 4 – 9 credits – 6 outcomes)

Principles and Practice of Assessment (Level 3/4 – 3 credits – 6 outcomes)

Option Unit * (6 credits)

DTLLS

Preparing to Teach in the Lifelong Learning Sector (as above but Level 4)

Planning and Enabling Learning (Level 4 – 9 credits – 6 outcomes)

Enabling Learning and Assessment (Level 4 – 15 credits – 6 outcomes)

Theories and Principles for Planning and Enabling Learning (Level 4 – 15 credits – 4 outcomes)

Option Unit * (15 credits)

YEAR TWO

Continuing Personal and Professional Development (Level 5 – 15 credits – 4 outcomes)

Curriculum Development for Inclusive Practice (Level 5 – 15 credits – 5 outcomes)

Wider Professional Practice (Level 5 – 15 credits – 5 outcomes)

Option Unit * (15 credits)

Note:

Option Units (*) are varied and subject to development. For up-to-date information please refer to Lifelong Learning (UK).

Appendix F Professional standards of competence

Teachers in the lifelong learning sector value:

AS1   All learners, their progress and development, their learning goals and aspirations and the experience they bring to their learning

AS2   Learning, its potential to benefit people emotionally, intellectually, socially, and economically, and its contribution to community sustainability

AS3   Equality, diversity and inclusion in relation to learners, the workforce, and the community

AS4   Reflection and evaluation of their own practice and their continuing professional development as teachers

AS5   Collaboration with other individuals, groups and/or organisations with a legitimate interest in the progress and development of learners.

Domain A   Professional values and practice

They are committed to:

AS6   The application of agreed codes of practice and the maintenance of a safe environment

AS7   Improving the quality of their practice.

Domain B   Learning and teaching

They are committed to:

BS1   Maintaining an inclusive, equitable and motivating learning environment

BS2   Applying and developing their own professional skills to enable learners to achieve their goals

BS3   Communicating effectively and appropriately with learners to enhance learning

BS4   Collaboration with colleagues to support the needs of learners

BS5   Using a range of learning resources to support learning.

Domain C   Specialist learning and teaching

They are committed to:

CS1   Understanding and keeping up-to-date with current knowledge in respect of their own specialist area

CS2   Enthusing and motivating learners in their own specialist area

CS3   Fulfilling the statutory responsibilities associated with their own specialist area of teaching

CS4   Developing good practice in teaching their own specialist area.

Domain D   Planning for learning

They are committed to:

DS1   Planning to promote equality, support diversity and meet the aims and learning needs of learners

DS2   Learner participation in the planning of learning

DS3   Evaluation of their own effectiveness in planning learning.

Domain E   Assessment for learning

They are committed to:

ES1   Designing and using assessment as a tool for learning and progression

ES2   Assessing the work of learners in a fair and equitable manner

ES3   Learner involvement and shared responsibility in the assessment process

ES4   Using feedback as a tool for learning and progression

ES5   Working within the systems and quality requirements of the organisation in relation to assessment and monitoring of learner progress.

Domain F   Access and progression

They are committed to:

FS1   Encouraging learners to seek initial and further learning
       opportunities and use services within the organisation
FS2   Providing support for learners within the boundaries of the
       teacher role
FS3   Maintaining own professional knowledge in order to provide
       information on opportunities for progression in own specialist
       area
FS4   A multi-agency approach to supporting development and
       progression opportunities for learners.

Each domain then has a series of statements about specific professional
knowledge and understanding and professional practice.

Source: http://www.lifelonglearninguk.org

Glossary

Academic relating to education, school or scholarships

Achievement meeting learning goals

Achievement data the number of students who achieved their qualification, usually expressed as a percentage of those who completed

Acronym an abbreviation or series of initial letters which together make another word

ADHD attention deficit hyperactivity disorder

Affective domain concerned with emotions and values

Aim a broad statement of intent

Analysis a detailed examination

Andragogy how adults learn

APEL/APL accreditation of prior learning

Approval permission to deliver qualifications on behalf of an awarding body

Assessment to make a judgement about something, a measurement of achievement

Attainment reaching the goal or qualification aim

Authenticity to establish who wrote/ owns the subject

Autonomous learner one who requires minimal guidance from the teacher

Autonomy independence in the ability to learn

Awarding body an organisation which devises qualifications and awards certificates

Benchmark a standard or point of reference to compare performance

Blended learning a mixture of traditional and modern/computer learning technologies

Body language using conscious or unconscious gesture to express feelings

BTEC Business and Technology Education Council; a qualification title part of Edexcel; an awarding body

Buzz group activities small groups interact with the teacher to gather answers

C&G City and Guilds; an awarding body

CADET consistent, accessible, detailed, earned, transparent

Certificate a recognised outcome of a programme of study

Chronological in date order

Cognitive concerned with thinking skills

Communication a means of sending and receiving information to share or exchange ideas

Competence the knowledge of or ability to do something

Concept an idea

Confidentiality secrecy of information

Constructive a term used to imply helpful feedback

Context the setting in which learning occurs

CPD continuous professional development

Criteria the standard of competence

Critical analysis a detailed examination resulting in an opinion or argument

Critical incidents events that have a significant effect

Curriculum a programme of study

Deep learning learning which is memorised and fully understood

Demography a study of population trends

Diagnostic assessment assessment used to identify capability or skill level

Differentiation catering for the needs of all learners to reduce barriers to learning

Direct assessment evidence of the learner's work

Direct feedback/communication
clear and unambiguous link

Disaffected learners no longer satisfied
with the learning environment

Disengaged uninvolved with learning

Distractor incorrect answer choices in
MCQs

Diversity valuing and celebrating the
differences in people

Domain an area or section of learning;
a classification

Dyscalculia associated with difficulties
in making sense of numbers and
calculations

Dysfunctional unable to deal with
normal social behaviours

Dyslexia associated with a difficulty in
reading and interpreting words and
symbols

E-assessment electronic versions of
assessment

Effective assessment to produce the
intended or desired result or outcome

Efficient productive working without
waste

Ego self-importance or personal identity

EMA Educational Maintenance
Allowance – a grant paid to learners to
support their further education

Embedded fixed firmly in the
vocational context

Empowered given responsibility for
something

Engage to participate or become
involved in

Equality the state of being equal or the
same

Equality of opportunity legislation
and focus on gender, age, culture etc.

Evaluation to form an idea about
something, to measure its effectiveness

Extended question a question that
involves a long answer

Extrinsic motivation motivation
derived from outside the person

Facilitator one who supports or
stimulates learning

Fail an assessment decision; not at pass
standard

Feedback verbal or written comments
about the assessment intended to
bring about improvement

FEnto Further Education National
Training Organisation

Font a type or style of lettering in a
printed document

Formative continuous assessment

Formula a mathematical rule

Functional skills basic skills of literacy
and numeracy

Gifted and talented learners highly
skilled or adept

Goal an aim or desired result

Grade a level or degree of
competence

Grading the degree of competence,
pass, merit, distinction

High order most thorough level of
learning

HND Higher National Diploma

Holistic the big picture; the whole
curriculum

Hub the centre

Ice-breaker an activity used to
introduce learners to each other

ICT information communication
technology

ILP individual learning plan

ILT information learning technology

Inclusion finding opportunities to
integrate all learners

Indirect assessment evidence or
opinion from others

Indirect feedback/communication a
link via a secondary method

Induction a formal introduction to a
programme/role

Initial assessment an assessment tool
to identify and establish potential or
aspirations or discover facts

Inspectorate e.g. ALI, OfSTED

Integrity having values and
principles

Interact to have an effect on

Intervention an interruption

Intrinsic motivation motivation from
within the person; natural desire

Invigilation supervision of examination
candidates

Ipsative self-assessment against
standards of competence

IT information technology

IV internal verification

Jargon language, words or expressions of a specialist occupation

Jigsaw group activities small groups discuss different themes within a topic which are collated by the teacher at the end of the activity

Journal a diary

Judgement a decision about an assessment

Justified text even distribution of words across the page within fixed margins

Justify explain and prove something

Key the correct answer in a MCQ

Language written or spoken communication

Learning to gain knowledge or a skill; what the learners do during the session

Learning goals what a learner sets out to do

Learning needs things which will help a learner to achieve their goal

Learning outcome the result of a learning session

Learning styles analysis of how learners learn

Lesson plan a written structure for a session

Level 3 A position within the NQF indicating the value of a qualification

Literacy the ability to read and write

LLUK Lifelong Learning (UK) Sector Skills Council

Low order a superficial level of learning

Mastery comprehensive ability

MCQ multiple choice question

Minimum core standards of competence in language, literacy, numeracy and ICT

Motivation enthusiasm or interest

NCFE Northern Council for Further Education; an awarding body

Negotiation agreement and compromise towards outcome

NQF National Qualifications Framework

NQT newly qualified teacher

Numeracy the ability to use numbers

Nurture the development of characteristics, beliefs or attitudes

NVQ National Vocational Qualification

Objective a specific statement of intended outcome

OHP overhead projector

OHT overhead transparency

On-programme a term to describe a period of learning

Opener an activity at the beginning of a session

Outcome result or consequence of assessment

Participation to take part in

Pass assessment decision relating to satisfactory performance

Pastoral concerned with the well-being of learners

Performance criteria standards of required competence

Philosopher someone who studies theories, attitudes or beliefs

Plagiarism to pass off somebody else's work as your own

Policy course of action by an organisation

Profile how information about a thing or person is recorded

Programme of study a structured list of sessions

Psychomotor concerned with physical, practical and co-ordination skills

QA quality assurance – an official system to establish the quality of something such as an assessment

QCA Qualifications and Curriculum Authority

Qualification a skill that makes someone suitable for a job

Qualitative data relating to opinions or thoughts

Quantitative data relating to statistics and number

Question a query inviting a response

Rapport a common understanding

Recreational learning a skill for pleasure

Referencing a source of information

Reflection a considered opinion expressed in speech or writing; thoughts or considerations, developing ideas and thoughts

Reflective practice thoughtful practice to develop skills

Registration an official list of entrants on a qualification

Reliability a strategy to ensure that assessment decisions are consistent

Research an investigation

Restricted response limited choices in answers

Retention the number of students who complete their programme

Rote teaching by repetition, e.g. learning multiplication tables

Sanction a penalty for disobeying rules

Scheme of work a document listing sessions within a programme

Screen shot a visual image from a software program reproduced into a document to support understanding

Self-assessment (1) an organisation's ability to monitor and quality assure its provision

Self-assessment (2) a method of confirming own ability

SEN special educational needs

Session a period of learning

Shallow learning learning which is retained for a short period

Snowball (pyramid) group activities pairs discuss then form gradually larger groups to gain a consensus of opinion on a topic or subject

Spider diagram a visual form of note-taking to collect thoughts

Standard an agreed level of competence

Stem the term given to a question in a MCQ

Success recognition of achievement

Success rate the number of students who complete and achieve their qualification, usually expressed as a percentage of those who commenced

Sufficiency to check that there is enough evidence to cover the criteria

Summative final or summary assessment

SWOT analysis of strengths, weaknesses, opportunities and threats

Syllabus the structure of a qualification

Target an objective or focused path towards a specified outcome

Taxonomy a classification

Teaching to impart knowledge or a skill; what the teacher does in the session

Tracking a method of recording progress

Triangulate measuring by different perspectives

VAK visual, auditory and kinaesthetic learners different ways learners like to learn

Validity a strategy to ensure that judgements are made against criteria

VLE virtual learning environment – a modern teaching and learning style using computer technologies

Vocational skills related to employment

VRQ Vocationally related qualifications

WBL work–based learning – learning that takes place predominantly in the workplace

Reference and bibliography

Armitage, A. *et al.* (2003) *Teaching and Training in Post-Compulsory Education,* 2nd ed. Maidenhead: Open University Press, McGraw Hill.

Assessment Reform Group (1999) *Assessment For Learning: Beyond the Black Box,* University of Cambridge, School of Education.

Bandura, A. (1994) 'Self-efficacy' in V.S. Ramachaudran (ed.) (1998) *Encyclopedia of Human Behaviour* (Vol 4, pp. 71–81), New York: Academic Press.

Basic Skills Agency (2006) *Identifying and Meeting Needs,* London: DfES.

Berne, E. *Transactional Analysis* on Business Balls website: http://www.businessballs.com/transact.htm (accessed 12/05/2007).

Black, P. and D. Wiliam (1998) *Inside the Black Box,* Kings College London.

Bloom, B.S. (ed.) (1956) *Taxonomy of Educational Objectives, Handbook 1: Cognitive Domain,* London: Longman.

Bloom, B.S., D. Krathwohl and B. Masica (1964) *Taxonomy of Educational Objectives, Handbook 2: Affective Domain,* London: Longman.

Boud, D. (1995) *Enhancing Learning Through Self-Assessment,* London: Kogan Page.

Budge, D. *Tasting the Assessment Soup,* Times Educational Supplement, 18 February 2005.

Cohen, L., L. Manion & K. Morrison (2004) *A Guide to Teaching Practice,* Abingdon: Routledge.

Cooper, R. (1996) 'Identifying real differences in thinking and learning styles', *National Journal of Vocational Assessment: Assessment Matters,* Issue 2, Spring: 3–5

Cowley, S. (2003) *Getting the Buggers to Behave,* 2nd ed. London: Continuum International Publishing Group Ltd.

Department for Education and Employment (1999) *A Fresh Start – Improving Literacy and Numeracy* (The Report of the working group chaired by Sir Claus Moser), London: DfEE.

Department for Education and Skills (2001) *Adult Literacy: Core Curriculum including spoken communication,* London: DfES.

Department for Education and Skills (2001) *Adult Numeracy: Core Curriculum,* London: DfES.

Devany, A. (2007) *Equality and Diversity* (unpublished), St George's Centre, Birmingham.

Ecclestone, K. (1996) *How to assess the Vocational Curriculum,* London: Kogan Page in Gray, D., C. Griffin and T. Nasta (2005) *Training to Teach in Further and Adult Education,* 2nd ed. Cheltenham: Stanley Thornes.

Fawbert, F. (2003) *Teaching in Post-Compulsory Education: Learning, Skills and Standards,* London: Continuum.

Further Education Funding Council (1996) *Learning works: The Kennedy Report.*

FEnto. (2004) *Including Language, Literacy and Numeracy Learning in all Post-16 Education: Guidance on curriculum and methodology for generic initial teacher education programmes,* March 2004, Further Education National Training Organisation/National Research and Development Centre for adult literacy and numeracy.

Gardner, H. (1983) *Frames of Mind, The Theory of Multiple Intelligences,* New York: Basic Books.

Gray, D., C. Griffin and T. Nasta (2005) *Training to Teach in Further and Adult Education,* 2nd ed. Cheltenham: Stanley Thornes.

Honey, P. and A. Mumford (1982/1992) *The Manual of Learning Styles,* Maidenhead: Peter Honey Publications.

Kandola, R.S. and J. Fullerton (1994) *Managing the Mosaic: Diversity in Action (Developing Strategies),* Chartered Institute of Personnel and Development.

Kolb, D. (1984) *Experiential Learning: Experience as a Source of Learning and Development.* New York: Prentice Hall.

Kyriacou, C. (2007) *Essential Teaching Skills,* 3rd ed. Cheltenham: Nelson Thornes.

LLUK (2004) *Addressing literacy, language, numeracy and ICT needs in education and training: defining the minimum core of teachers' knowledge, understanding and personal skills. A guide for teacher education programmes,* July 2004, Lifelong Learning UK/FEnto.

LLUK (2007) *Addressing literacy, language, numeracy and ICT needs in education and training: defining the minimum core of teachers' knowledge, understanding and personal skills. A guide for teacher education programmes,* June 2007, The Sector Skills Council for Lifelong Learning.

Pearsall, J. (ed.) (2001) *Oxford English Dictionary* 10th ed. Oxford: Oxford University Press.

Peter, L.J. (1969) *Why things go wrong.*

Petty, G. (2004) *Teaching Today: A Practical Guide,* 3rd ed. Cheltenham: Nelson Thornes.

Reece, I. and S. Walker (2006) *Teaching, training and learning: A practical guide,* 6th ed. Sunderland: Business Education Publishers.

Schön, D. (1983) *The Reflective Practitioner,* San Francisco: Jossey-Bass.

Scottish Funding Council (2006) *Overcoming barriers; enabling learning. Planning, designing and delivering the full time FE curriculum in Scotland's Colleges,* HM Inspectors for Education and Scottish Funding Council (October 2006) http://www.sfc.ac.uk (accessed on 12/05/2007).

Tummons, J. (2007a) *Becoming a professional Tutor in the Lifelong Learning Sector,* Exeter: Learning Matters (1).

Tummons, J. (2007b) *Assessing in the Lifelong Learning Sector,* 2nd ed. Exeter: Learning Matters (2).

Turner, C.H. (1990) *Corporate Culture: From vicious to virtuous circles,* Random House Business Books.

Walklin. L. (2000) *Teaching and Learning in Further and Adult Education,* Cheltenham: Nelson Thornes.

Wallace, S. (2007) *Teaching, Tutoring and Training in the Lifelong Learning Sector,* 3rd ed. Exeter: Learning Matters.

Websites:

Business Balls
http://www.businessballs.com (accessed 12/05/2007).

Open University
http://www.open.ac.uk/inclusiveteaching/pages/inclusive-teaching/barriers-to-learning.php (accessed on 30/12/2006).
http://www.open.ac.uk/inclusiveteaching/pages/inclusive-teaching/learning-environment.php (accessed 12/05/2007).

Assessment Reform Group
http://arg.educ.cam.uk/publications.html (accessed 29/09/2007).

Qualifications and Initial Teacher Training
www.lifelonglearninguk.org.

Index